D1757058

CULTURE AFTER HUMANISM

Culture after Humanism asks what happens to the authority of traditional Western modes of thought in the wake of postcolonial theory. Drawing on examples from music, architecture, literature, philosophy and art, Iain Chambers investigates moments of tension – interruptions which transform our perception of the world and test the limits of language, art and technology.

In a series of interlinked discussions, ranging in focus from Susan Sontag's novel *The Volcano Lover* to the philosophy of Martin Heidegger, and from Jimi Hendrix to Baroque architecture and music, Chambers weaves together a critique of Western humanism, exploring issues of colonisation and migration, language and identity. *Culture after Humanism* offers a new approach to cultural history, a 'post-humanist' perspective which challenges our sense of a world in which the subject is sovereign, language the transparent medium of its agency, and truth the product of reason.

Iain Chambers is a professor in the faculty of Arts at the Istituto Universitario Orientale in Naples. He is the author of *Migrancy, Culture, Identity* (Routledge 1994), *Popular Culture: the metropolitan experience* (Routledge 1996) and co-editor of *The Postcolonial Question* (Routledge 1996).

90 0598244 1

COMEDIA
Series Editor: David Morley

Comedia titles available from Routledge:

CULTURE AFTER HUMANISM

HUMANISM

History, Culture, Subjectivity

Iain Chambers

London and New York

First published 2001
by Routledge
11 New Fetter Lane, London EC4P 4EE

Simultaneously published in the USA and Canada
by Routledge
29 West 35th Street, New York, NY 10001

Routledge is an imprint of the Taylor & Francis Group

© 2001 Iain Chambers

Typeset in Garamond by Florence Production Ltd,
Stoodleigh, Devon
Printed and bound in Great Britain by
University Press, Cambridge

British Library Cataloguing in Publication Data
A catalogue record for this book is available from
the British Library

Library of Congress Cataloging in Publication Data
A catalog record for this book has been requested

ISBN 0–415–24755–1 (hbk)
ISBN 0–415–24756-X (pbk)

In memory of my father,
Lionel Wilfred Chambers (1912–1995),
who first introduced me to the magic of music and
maps, to the insistence of history, and to a vulnerability
attendant upon being inhabited by distance.

To risk the Earth, dare to explore its forbidden or misunderstood impulses. Establish in so doing our own dwelling place. The history of all peoples is the ultimate point of our imaginative unconscious.

> Edouard Glissant, *Caribbean Discourse: Selected Essays*

Bringing into play the danger of a new flowering devoid of protection. Unsheltered. Outside any abode. Unveiled?

> Luce Irigaray, 'He Risks Who Risks Life Itself'

After the slow climb over Kaiser Pass, in an overloaded car with overheated brakes, we descended towards the camp site. It was on the second day, towards evening that we met the poet. Tall, tanned and pony-tailed, he stopped us on the trail wishing to know where we came from. Santa Cruz, aah, home of that great poet Adrienne Rich. The names – Robert Duncan, Gary Snyder . . . – fell on the alpine pasture. Italy. . . Fellini, the poet of cinema, segues into an anecdote invoking Anita Ekberg's arrival at the Beverly Hills Hilton in 1952 that brought the lobby to a standstill.

He is 70 and lives all summer up here in the Sierras, guiding tourists among the peaks on horseback early in the morning. Later that night, passing along the path by his tent, we hear the measured intonations of poetry coming from a cassette player. Underneath the trees, sacks swinging from their branches safe from the bears, words in the high mountain air: the replay . . . the repetition . . . the relay.

> Iain Chambers, Mono Hots Springs, California, 1994

CONTENTS

ACKNOWLEDGEMENTS

Much of the material in the following chapters began its gestation in the preparation for talks, conferences, papers and lectures. So, I would like to thank the following for their invitations and hospitality: Ien Ang at the University of Western Sydney, for extending considerations on the stranger; Iain Borden at the Bartlett School, University College, London, for the prospect of buildings, space and historical places, and the same goes for Stephen Cairns at the University of Melbourne; Anthony Chennells at the University of Zimbabwe, Harare, for the whole experience; Rey Chow at the University of California, Irvine, for offering the space to teach, reflect and research; David B. Clarke at the University of Leeds for forcing me to confront the relationship between sight and sound; James Clifford and Chris Connery at the Center for Cultural Studies at the University of Calfornia, Santa Cruz, for the stimulus of a Pacific take on things; Tim Cresswell in Wales for the geographical bricolage in a bucolic weekend at Gregynog; the Dipartimento di Sociologia dell'Università 'La Sapienza' in Rome and the Dipartimento di Sociologia dell'Università 'Federico II' in Naples for the stimulus to return to the poetics of sound; Dick Hebdige at the California Institute for the Arts, Valencia, for, once again, proposing an experimental ambient; Tony Kaes for the invitation to participate in a research cluster at the Humanities Research Institute at the University of California, Irvine, and for inviting me to speak at both the Los Angeles County Museum and the University of California, Berkeley; Hamid Naficy for the invitation to think of home, homeland and exile at Rice University, Houston; Carlo Pagetti and the Associazione Italiana di Anglistica for providing the occasion to deliver a lecture in Milan that allowed me to consider some of the other sides of occidental modernity.

Returning to a domestic scene, I want to thank the students with whom I have participated in courses, seminars, research groups and conferences at the Istituto Universitario Orientale; they have been closest to experiencing the development and deviations of this book. The final acknowledgement, as does the first, goes to Lidia Curti for her support, energy, enthusiasm, and for pulling me through and beyond the superficial film of immediate events into the unsuspected possibilities of the elsewhere.

Many of the arguments and perspectives in this book have already experienced the passage from talks to print. They have all, however, been substantially rewritten and extended in response to the architecture of this book. The section on positionality and postcoloniality in Chapter 1 first appeared in *Postcolonial Studies*, 2(1), 1999, while further parts of the chapter have appeared in English in *Anglistica*, 3(2), 1999, and in German in Jörg Huber (ed.) *Darstellung: Korresponenz*, Vienna and New York, Springer-Verlag, 2000. The discussion of Jimi Hendrix in Chapter 4 first appeared in Italian in Iain Chambers and Paul Gilroy, *Hendrix, hip hop e l'interruzione del pensiero*, Genoa, Costa & Nolan, 1996; other parts of Chapter 4 have also been rehearsed in David B. Clarke (ed.) *The Cinematic City*, London and New York, Routledge, 1997. Chapters 3 and 6 originally appeared in *New Formations*, 24, Winter 1994, and *Communal/Plural*, 6(1), 1998, respectively, while parts of Chapter 5 have appeared in Iain Borden, Joe Kerr, Jane Rendell and Alicia Pivaro (eds) *The Unknown City*, London, MIT Press, 2001. A different version of Chapter 7, entitled 'A Torn Map, a Fold in Time, an Interruption', is due to appear in Gabriele Schwab (ed.) *Forces of Globalization*, New York, Columbia University Press, 2001.

INTRODUCTION

Dunhuang, with its small crisp apples, wild grapes, scented plums and oasis melons, is a dusty desert town on the old Silk Road in western China. Seemingly a peripheral settlement, where China fades into central Asia and rural floodplains give way to sand dunes, where the Great Wall peters out in lonely fortresses abandoned to the wind, Dunhuang is one of the historical crossroads of the world. Here Buddhism and Islam, kebabs and dumplings, are brought together in what both Paul Gilroy and James Clifford would describe as a 'travelling culture' that reveals an intersection of diversities; all pragmatically moulded and lived in the shifting humus of historical appropriation. If the direct flight of China Northwest Airlines from Ürümqi to Jeddah, from Chinese Turkestan to Saudi Arabia, offers an immediate link across a shared Islamic world it is also in this region, in the spiritual journey out of India, across the Tibetan plateau, and then on into China and the Japanese archipelago, that Buddhism has left a significant testimony. Commencing in the third century after Christ, and spanning more than a thousand years of continuous development, the caves at Magao, south of Dunhuang, are surely one of the largest art galleries of Buddhist murals and sculptures in the world. (It was also a deposit for thousands of Buddhist manuscripts in Sanskrit, Tibetan and Chinese, most of them being pirated away to London and Paris at the beginning of the twentieth century.) Here in the diversified tonalities of colour, figuration and physiognomy of Buddha, his disciples, illustrations from his life and teachings, it is possible to trace how the initial 'Western' forms from the Indian sub-continent came to be modified and 'Sinified'.

This mongrel past and hybrid incubation betrays an altogether wilder and uncertain version of 'China', its people, language and culture, than that promoted officially. There is something else here, something more, that interrogates a sense of the past, and hence of the present and the future. This particular history 'lesson' is not, of course, peculiar to China;

it interrogates all state forms of national identity and their promotion of cultural modernity. However, in the 'tiger's leap' into the past proposed by Walter Benjamin, there also lies the revelation of another future: one that exceeds both the control of the present and the institutionalisation of the past.[1] Such an observation serves to accompany a traveller's obsession for 'the whiff of a snow leopard at 14,000 feet' (Bruce Chatwin) with a further narrative that crosses, complicates and connects the tourist track to a more unstable, and potentially more open, understanding of modernity.[2]

Rendering someone else's modernity problematic, plural and porous is also to render one's own modernity less secure. If the epoch of modernity can be characterised as the epoch of occidental humanism, of a world centred on the continual confirmation of the observing subject, then it might surely also be legitimate to consider what occurs to the authority of critical languages, historiography and the Western disposition of knowledge and power in the light of the questioning and dispersal of that particular historical arrangement. This is the principal argument that will be pursued in the following pages. Just how novel this procedure might be is initially questionable. For this is a story that has already been told; modernity has always picked a quarrel with itself, and its facile predication of 'progress' has always been accompanied by a series of histories speaking of, and from, elsewhere. It is in this light that the postmodern, as Jean-François Lyotard insisted, marks not the end of modernity but a *different* relationship to it. More immediately, and more incisively, postcolonial studies have extended a firm invitation to occidental culture to review not only its manners, but also its modalities, of thought. But there also remains something more at stake here than the transgression or even radical review of inherited understandings; there is something that persistently interrupts the drive for coherence and renders successive political adjustment and cultural accommodation altogether more arduous, if not impossible. In disentangling the web of modernity, not only is its design challenged but also its loose ends return to propose a diverse pattern of time and its subsequent inhabitation.

In considering these questions the following chapters are clearly indebted to Martin Heidegger's insistence that the recovery of a sense of being in the world is irreducible to the sum total of individual beings. Being in the world does not add up, it never arrives at the complete picture, the conclusive verdict. There is always something more that exceeds the frame we desire to impose. At this point, an inherited sense of the world in which the human subject is considered sovereign, language the transparent medium of its agency, and truth the representation of its rationalism, comes under radical review. Again, what happens to history, culture, subjectivity and critical analysis once the languages that constitute these formations and practices are understood to precede and exceed individual volition and communal control? The site of this questioning might provocatively be referred to as posthumanism. Such a prospect does not inaugurate an anti-human universe, or announce the end of the subject, but rather, in seeking to displace the hegemonic ratio, proposes a *differing* subject, and a diverse ethics of understanding. Paradoxically, to critique the abstract universalism of Western humanism is to release the human into the cultural and historical immediacy of a differentiated and always incomplete humanity.

If all of this is to bend attention to the power of culture and to proclaim a political question, it is also to evoke a politics that reaches beyond instrumental solutions to invest the very reason of language and narration. Here the political slides imperceptibly into the ambiguous potential of language, into the journey of its poetical extensions. Pursuing this perspective, and registering the inseparable nature of the ethical and the aesthetical, has provided the scaffolding of this book. At this point, a proposed configuration that acquires shape *after* humanism touches an altogether deeper chord when an inherited universalism comes to be located in a precise historical and cultural landscape.

In Immanuel Kant's *Critique of Judgement* (1790) and the noted discussion of the beautiful and the sublime, the philosopher maintains the necessity of critical distance and of the disinterested gaze in the appropriation of beauty and the subordination of the sublime to the universal consensus of reason. Although aesthetic judgement, unlike theoretical judgement, is unable to establish its validity on a priori concepts, in its insistence on the *universality* of the disinterested taste of the human community it participates in the realm of universal objectivity. With this rationalisation of sentiment, the basis of critical judgement and the continuing authority of the subject is assured. However, if reason is able only to exhibit inadequately what the sublime suggests, then the provocation of disquieting grandeur and infinite formlessness potentially alienates reason from itself. This leaves open a gap for the passage of the subsequent critique of the limits of a reason unable to receive a knowledge that exceeds and undermines its dominion. It was this indeterminacy, subsequently explored by German Romanticism and persistently exposed by Friedrich Nietzsche, that fuels the challenge to the systematic arrangement of knowledge in a self-referring, conceptual totality. What lies in this latter inheritance which, acknowledged or not, is also our inheritance, is ultimately the undoing of humanism as a critical disposition. For through this opening runs the release of

3

knowledge to follow other directives. Disciplinary distance is disturbed by unexpected proximities that transform the status of the aesthetic, of the poetical, and the languages that bear our potential.

This conducts me to seeing, hearing and experiencing in the art work a continual disturbance, a tear in the texture of the expected. A sense of displacement comes to be understood in the insistence of language that renders the order of the ordinary extra-ordinary, irreducible to a conclusive rationality, hence magical, even sacred, perhaps divine. For in exceeding ordained meaning, the work of art reveals not so much a distinctive 'message' as a sense that is ultimately a non-sense, a refusal to cohere that opens on to that void which resists rationalisation; on to that void where immediate meaning is in abeyance, suspended, silent.[3] In this fashion, the dissolution of the aesthetic and the severing of critical distance, is simultaneously the dissolution of the humanist paradigm that each has historically propagated.

Beyond the confines of aesthetic criticism a sense of beauty, that is neither systematic nor conclusive, emerges. This arises in the wake, both in the sense of a passage and a mourning, for what has occurred.[4] Such is a sense of the beautiful that is obviously post-Kantian, for it announces what cannot be contained. A rationalist pleasure is not confirmed. Rather a border, an intimation of the sublime, the shiver of the world, an encounter with the angelic and the extraordinary, is declared. We are taken beyond our selves into the eroticism of time and the subsequent sense of loss that proclaims an identity.

To take critical leave from the history of possessive subjectivism, and its self-confirming knowledge, need not mean to abandon 'use-value' and the 'human' to the fetishisation and alienation of modernity.[5] To propose a poetics of disquiet is not to propose a medium of communication, but is rather to sabotage that order and rudely review the premises of the subject, of historical agency and occidental humanism. In 1963, Louis Althusser wrote: 'So everything depends on the knowledge of the nature of humanism as an ideology.'[6] Considering anti-humanism in the light of the inheritance of Marx, Nietzsche, Freud and Heidegger, however, does not necessarily mean to opt for the bloodless logic of impassive structures and over-determined social relations, rather it returns critical force to the complexity of a world irreducible to a homogeneous vision or unique point of view.[7] At this point, the poetical that sings of the threshold and the non-represented invests the political; and it speaks without the immediate intention of informing or necessarily benefiting the subject. This is to return to understanding all the sensed cultural complexity of the textures, tensions and unresolved tendencies of historical formations.

To return to China for a moment, there lies in the millenarian practice of calligraphy the intriguing osmosis between writing and painting,
where signification slides beyond immediate semantics into an altogether
more ambiguous and freer sense. Unlike pragmatic understandings of
writing, calligraphy does not seek to communicate an absence, to represent 'reality'. The subscription to painted characters turns attention to
the medium itself. Calligraphy, in its diverse schools and styles, is not
merely a means of communication, standing in for something else, but
a means in itself: the art of writing – writing as art; a historical and
cultural signature that ends up revealing much more than any intentional message. Beyond the obvious cultural and political authority of
writing lies the intriguing nexus of a style of inscription that is also
the symptom of a train of thought: a textual practice, a sense and direction, that simultaneously serves and surpasses the signified.[8]

I would like to suggest that the style and language of this book also
seeks to evoke this possibility. Within a circumscribed time and place
the following pages pursue the political and poetical implications of the
languages in which we move and make our home. This is in order
to suggest that, notwithstanding the instrumental understandings that
hegemonise contemporary life, in its deepest implications and potentiality, reality both commences and concludes in the house of language.
It is there in our material, historical, cultural and psychic life that we
ultimately reside, recognise and reconsider our selves. It is in the light
of this mode of residence that the following chapters consider cultural,
geographical, architectural and historical studies with a view to their
potential reassessment and reconfiguration.

Notes

1 Walter Benjamin, 'Theses on the Philosophy of History', in Benjamin,
   Illuminations, trans. Harry Zohn, London, Fontana, 1973, p. 263.
2 Bruce Chatwin, 'Introduction', in Robert Byron, *The Road to Oxiana*, London,
   Picador, 1981, p. 15.
3 In a few incisive pages published in 1970, and tellingly entitled 'The Most
   Disturbing Thing', Giorgio Agamben rehearses this argument, pondering
   whether the time is ripe for the destruction of the aesthetic and the subsequent
   acknowledgement of the void that permits the work of art to emerge in its 'divine
   terror'; Giorgio Agamben, *L'uomo senza contenuto*, Milan, Rizzoli, 1970.
4 Christine Buci-Glucksmann, *L'Enjeu du beau: Musique et Passion*, Paris, Galilée,
   1992, p. 16.
5 Gianni Carchia, *La legittimazione dell'arte*, Naples, Guida, 1982, p. 61.
6 Louis Althusser, 'Marxism and Humanism', in Althusser, *For Marx*, Harmondsworth, Penguin, 1969, p. 231.

7 Also confirmed by the French philosopher himself in his later writings: see Gregory Elliot, 'Ghostlier Demarcations: On the Posthumous Edition of Althusser's Writings', *Radical Philosophy*, 90, July/August 1998.

8 This, no doubt, is to indulge in a minor orientalism. Writing and interpretation in imperial China was, above all, a regulated activity designed to ensure the central authority of the state. Yet, if graphic scripts 'were not simply transparent indicators of content', then styles of inscription betray something more than merely the authority of approved texts; see Christopher Leigh Connery, *The Empire of the Text: Writing and Authority in Early Imperial China*, Lanham, Md, Rowman & Littlefield, 1998.

1

A QUESTION OF HISTORY

> Knowledge, viewed as a transitive process, has no foundation
> – only a structure in time.
>
> Roy Bhaskar[1]

From a flagship

The Bay of Naples, 1799. In the early months of the year a revolution
had led to the seizure of power by the local liberal intelligentsia and
the abandonment of the city by the Bourbon monarchy. The new state
lasted a hectic five months before being crushed by the peasant army of
Cardinal Ruffo, aided and abetted by the naval presence of Horatio
Nelson and the British fleet. Many of the leaders were publicly executed
in Piazza del Mercato: decapitation for the aristocrats, hanging for the
bourgeoisie. Directly inspired by the French Revolution, the short-lived
Republic of 1799 is still today lived by many Neapolitans as an open
wound whose spilt blood stains the formation of the contemporary city.
In this vision of the past, '1799' represents a lost moment, and subsequent history the testimony of the brutal negation of its possibilities.
This historical, and historicist, explanation is considered to evoke a
singular event – the sole independent republic in modern Italian history
– that sets the history of Naples apart from the rest of the peninsula.
Beyond the confines of an often numbing idealisation, there nevertheless emerges an important proximity between 1799 and, say 1999, when
that specific history comes to be inscribed in a more extensive charting
of occidental modernity. Perhaps the manner in which to appreciate this
proximity lies not so much in once again investigating 1799 as a peer-
less historical affair, but rather in listening to the questions that emerge
from that particular moment; questions that query the eventual conception and representation of both then and now.

I could begin with a simple scene, borrowed from the work of the
American critic and writer Susan Sontag, *The Volcano Lover* (1992). There
is a British warship anchored in the Bay of Naples that offers a view of
the city from the sea. From the ship, orders are issued for the suppression of the fledgling republic. On board there is Nelson, Sir William

and Lady Hamilton. Sir William is a lover of Vesuvius, a founder of the new science of vulcanology and a member of the Royal Society. Nelson, Lady Hamilton's lover, is admiral of the fleet sent by London to sustain the Mediterranean front in the war against France. The previous year he had destroyed the French fleet in Egyptian waters at the battle of Aboukir. In the meantime republican France was on the verge of transforming itself into the Napoleonic state. The local Neapolitan revolution and subsequent republic were also part of this history.

This telescopic view encourages the insertion of the local history of Naples in a European, even global, perspective, and invites me to consider the events of 1799 under other eyes. Here, for example, Naples finds itself located in a genealogy of modern revolts and revolutions. This particular narrative commences in 1776 with the revolt of the British colonies in North America, which, in turn, lent inspiration to the most famous: the French Revolution of 1789. But the longest and most bloody was the revolt of the 'Black Jacobins' – the slaves of Saint-Domingue led by Toussaint L'Ouverture and directly influenced by the events in France. After thirteen years of combat against the British, Spanish and, above all, the French, the revolt resulted in the establishment of the first black republic of Haiti in 1804. In the year previous to the founding of the Neapolitan Republic, the Catholic–Protestant alliance of Wolfe Tone's 'United Irishmen' fought for Irish independence before being vanquished in blood. In the following twenty years all of Latin America was shaken by a series of revolts as the colonies violently seceded from the Spanish Crown. In the diversified contestation of authoritarian, centralised and non-representative powers (frequently in order to ensure local interests and oligarchies), it becomes possible in hindsight to identify the transit towards a modernity characterised by the uneven acquisition of mass politics, mass democracy and mass culture.[2]

To return to the Bay of Naples, to Nelson's ship. This warship, like all those of the British Navy, with 30 per cent of the crew composed of black sailors, had its decks painted red in order to hide the blood of those who fell in action. This ship, this fleet, represented the brutal pragmatism of an imperialism in which the Mediterranean, like the Caribbean, the Atlantic, the Indian Ocean and recently colonised Australia, were pieces of a global political economy. The question is whether this perspective represents only a view of Naples seen from a British warship and dictated by the Foreign Ministry in London, or whether this other point of view permits the emergence of a wider prospect? I would suggest, just as the presence of a Japanese project that presently dominates the architectural skyline of Naples, that the view that arrives from elsewhere offers, whatever the eventual verdict, an opening that interrupts the official consensus of a local picture. Transferring the history of the Neapolitan Republic on to a less provincial and more worldly map, the events represented by the five months of life of the republic are able to acquire a wider ethical resonance and enter a more extensive political and historical configuration.

Before a wider horizon, the presence of France in this particular history, beyond the symbolic force of 1789 and the physical presence and support of French troops in the early days of the republic's constitution, reveals a series of concerns and conditions as difficult to explain as the presence of the British fleet in the Bay of Naples a few months later. The hesitancy of the Paris Directory in recognising the Neapolitan Republic, like its equal reluctance to accept the demand for the abolition of slavery in the richest island of its colonial empire (Saint-Domingue), exposes a policy dictated more by the political and economical needs of the metropolitan centre than by requests for local liberties. In this perspective there emerges a Naples as both the object of more powerful European interests and a particular European city caught up in the complexities of wider, global concerns.

One of the principal chains, largely invisible to its inhabitants, that linked the specific locality of Naples to the rest of the world in this historical period was a colonial system sustained by the labour of black slaves imported from Africa into the Americas. The recognition of the centrality of that economy to the cultural and political formation of modernity draws attention to subaltern histories narrated from elsewhere; in this case, to the 'Black Atlantic', as Paul Gilroy's important study eloquently suggests.[3] Returning that discourse to our initial locality, and restricting it to gastronomy, coffee, chocolate, tomatoes, chillies, potatoes and sugar were all goods and tastes that developed in the wake of colonial expansion, sustained by the same political economy that provided the basis for the demand for new political rights. New World 'discoveries' also inaugurated the new world of post-feudal political demands that came to a head in events as the English Civil War, the French Revolution and the Neapolitan Republic. It is to this paradoxical development that Jaurès referred when insisting that slavery and the slave trade were the economic bases of the French Revolution: 'The fortunes created at Bordeaux, at Nantes, by the slave trade, gave to the bourgeoisie that pride which needed liberty and contributed to human emancipation.'[4] Occidental modernity, whether evidenced in Georgian London or Bourbon Naples, were part of that shared picture.

Using a fictitious account in order to approach the question of the Neapolitan Republic, and thereby extract further dimensions from the story, might seem a rather oblique appropriation (illegitimate, subversive?) of the historical archive. Still, beyond the rhetorical play of different points of view, such an approach is fundamentally connected to a sought-for reconfiguration of the contemporary sense of 'knowledge' and 'truth'. In the historical account, in the accounting of the past, I am here invited to consider, as Paul Ricoeur insists, that 'sense' does not arrive from nude 'facts' and isolated 'events', but is something that emerges within the temporality of the narrative, in the telling of time.[5] So, where and how does the distinction of the narration of '1799' proposed in the historical representation of Benedetto Croce and the careful research exposed in all its historical details in *The Volcano Lover* lie?[6] On what bases are such distinctions established? In narrating the world, from where are the protocols drawn? In the constellation of narratives that orbit around '1799', suspended in writing, in the language of representation, where does fiction conclude and 'reality' commence? Even if it were possible to return to the past and collate the 'facts', that reality would still have to be transmitted in the logics and languages of representation: public documents, private diaries, statistical data, the testimony of costume and the arts; elements that all require re-elaboration in order to become legible in a structure organised by writing. Here we are on the threshold of a debate in which the tropes of historiography, as Hayden White has consistently argued, become objects of analysis in their own right.[7]

To put the discipline of historiography in question implies a reconfiguration of its language, transferring it from the abstract regime of 'truth', guaranteed by the neutral 'scientificity' of 'facts', to a site in which language itself becomes the factor of temporal meaning. Historiography itself becomes history. At this point, and given the symbolic weight that 1799 has for the history and culture of present-day Naples, perhaps a more adequate manner to honour the sacrifice of those who died in its name lies not so much in a narrative of heroes and victims but rather in the elaboration of a mourning that opens up a living space in the languages that represent both that historical moment and our present selves. Considered in this light, the return to, and of, 1799 could be experienced as a disturbing question that interrogates our manner of using, understanding and constructing the past.

When a revolt and revolution becomes part of the official history of a city, of a culture, it is almost inevitably authorised in a narration of the past that contributes to the conservation of the hegemonic configuration of the present. In this use, and abuse, of history it is possible to read the betrayal of the historical constellation of 1799. Concentrated in a restricted historical–cultural specificity, the light that the Neapolitan Republic might throw on the present state of the city is actually obscured. In order to allow the emergence of another history of the Republic, a history of a European city involved in a complex global scenario, and thus a history with political, historical and ethical resonances close to the contemporary world, it becomes necessary to undo and rewrite the version that holds sway. This calls for a critique of the culture that constructed and conserved that particular history. At this point, prior to entering into any attempt at a socio-historical and cultural explanation of the particular formation of Neapolitan society, it is necessary to consider the institutional structure of 'scientific' and historiographical 'knowledge', which, as Michel Foucault insisted, is always a structure of power, through which the particular manner of representing '1799' is established and diffused.

The vulnerability of interpretation

In the case of Naples this is to confront an approach to history identified with the premises (the ideology?) of historicism. To rethink the time and place of Naples is to dislocate the historicism that has directed the culture and the history of this city, and to open up that 'history' to a distinction between the closed consolation of the already determined and the vulnerability of a history susceptible to other modalities of narration. If historicism narrates the continuity of the winners, secured in a homogenous understanding of time and knowledge, a critical, open and vulnerable history might, on the contrary, be conceived as a narration, an account, suspended between inclusion and exclusion, between representation and repression, in which the final word never arrives. This would be a history that lies beyond the grand design of historical destiny. It would equally be a history irreducible to empiricist representation and the discursive tyranny of a purportedly objective realism. This would not be a history of the past 'as it actually was', but a history of the present shot through with the interrogations of the past, a mutual confrontation and configuration in which both past and present become sites of temporal transit, cultural translation, and ethical inquiry. This would be to abandon the impossible task of a neutral or 'objective' account of the past for the altogether more imperative terms of taking responsibility for the accounting of time, bearing testimony to past generations in a language open to judgement in every instance.[8] This, clearly, has:

> nothing in common with the self-effacing posture of the historicist, who fondly imagines that he can abstract from the conditions of his existence and who himself, as a result, turns into a bloodless shade. For Benjamin, as for Nietzsche, such selfless objectivity

is in fact 'empathy' with the 'victor'. Historicism is thus far from disinterested; but the interests it represents are far from its own. The 'methodological' bracketing-out of the present, coupled with the contrary enthronement of the present as the sole presiding, sole surviving judge of the past – this constitutes the basic contradiction of historicism.[9]

If empiricism offers the incontestable authority of facts and artefacts, historicism proposes the assurance of a coherence that is impermeable to questioning, for it relies on a rhetoric that is oblivious to the ontological question of language and the unstable co-ordinates of narration. Where does the account commence; how, why and for whom? Where does it conclude? As Hans Kellner points out, 'the source of the assumption that the past is in some sense continuous is a literary one.'[10] If empiricism appeals to the non-mediated facticity of the world, historicism evokes the perennial structure of a unique temporality marching out of the past into the future. For both, historical truth lies not in the languages that provide us with our sense of inhabiting and making sense of the world but elsewhere, in the 'facts' and 'truth' revealed by reason. In particular, for historicism, intellectual coherence is guaranteed by the continuum in which history and reason mirror one another, resulting indivisible and unique. Here the historian is not so much one who returns to the past to revisit, represent and rewrite it, but is rather the custodian of the growing archive of human knowledge; an archive that remains stable in its form, fundamentally unalterable in its premises. This is a vision of the past destined to produce only 'victims': all is explained in the unfolding of the historical process itself. In a technical lexicon this is teleology, in more immediate terms it is 'destiny'. It is in this light, as Walter Benjamin announced in the 1930s, before the then triumphant storm of fascism, that historicism reveals an empathy with the version of the past proposed and imposed by the victors.[11]

That historical time may be both crossed, constructed and contested by, and in, language; that it can only be apprehended and interpreted in the framings of cultural transit that precede and exceed all appeals to the stability of meaning, poses an irrefutable challenge. Perhaps, instead of merely testifying to the official memory of the Neapolitan Republic as if it were now a closed event, buried in its defeat, it might be the case of seeking to extract from that historical and critical event the energies to crease, bend and fold the present in order to contest a destiny seemingly imposed by 'history'. This would mean to see in the events of 1799, in its specific details and complexities, not the arrest of a process that was expected to open up a direct passage leading the city to modernity and the realisation of 'progress', but an altogether more disturbing sign: Naples as an allegory of the precariousness of modernity. Here the city would be transferred from a site where a determined continuity is reaffirmed and celebrated in a folkloric identity to become a disturbing place where it constantly confronts itself in the unfinished business of worldly modernity.

This is to think of the world I inhabit as a product of time. To think of time, and of my being in the time dubbed modernity, is to consider the categories that render this earthly transit comprehensible. However, to consider such categories is also to register the mutable configuration of time; it is to appreciate the cultural construction of how time comes to be represented: the languages and limits of what we usually refer to as history. If all that passes away is destined for the domain of history it is equally the case that not all that passes comes to be registered as history. The history of *time* is also the *history* of time. Diverse conceptions of temporality, and diverse configurations of its social and semantic organisation, have come to be historically hegemonised in the ascendancy of occidental modernity by a linear temporality. Here the representation of the past is subordinated to the insistence of progress. Whether conceived directly in causal terms, or in the contradictory developments of dialectical movement, historical time is presumed to reveal a teleological purpose. But whose particular time and definition is this? Can time be treated as the homogeneous transmitter of our desires and actions? Does time respond only to the linear imperative, to an abstract public identity that never dies?[12] Such metaphysical speculations seem impossible to respond to until we remember the proposed premise that time, what we instinctively register in a heart beat, the lines of a face, and what is officially custodised in monuments, museums and institutional archives, is always received, transmitted and understood in the languages, that is, in the cultural and historical formation, in which we emerge and make sense of our lives.

Such a history that does not lie outside each of us, as though an independent object to be investigated and explained, but is a history in which each of us is in-corporated and, as it were, 'spoken' and articulated. We make history under conditions not of our own choosing, Karl Marx rightly reminds us. History itself emerges from the act of incorporation that we might better grasp as the act of interpretation. In a television interview in 1969, Martin Heidegger deliberately glossed Marx's famous insistence in the *Theses of Feuerbach* that philosophy has only interpreted the world when the question is to transform it by suggestively rendering proximate the apparent opposition between transformation and interpretation. The transformation of the world, he argued, presupposes a mutation in the *representation* of the world that is dependent upon *interpretation*.[13] To which Salman Rushdie's more recent words can be added: 'it is clear that redescribing a world is the necessary first step towards changing it.'[14] Marx's denouncement reveals a critical, philosophical announcement.

History is an interpretative act that presents itself in natural guise. Realism, as the privileged modality of historical narration, reinforces and extends this disposition until the limits of the historical discourse become the limits of the world. Out of the presumed division between imaginary and realistic accounts of the world emerge the modern disciplines of 'literature' and 'history'.[15] Both disciplines are nevertheless bound to an underlying matrix that limits the epistemological pretensions of 'history' to explain 'what happened'. Both proffer accounts of the world in the world. Both are sustained and verified in language, where language is not merely the technical support of linguistics and print culture but the ontological sustenance of making sense. That history is considered the bedrock of explanation and literature its imaginary embroidery, is itself a form of narration, a social articulation, that speaks of the history of a particular cultural formation.

History otherwise

Still, such a knowledge of the past, and the present, given its contemporary hegemony, and despite subaltern, counter-vailing, instances, cannot simply be cancelled. Its limits, what institutional 'history' itself represents and represses, can, however, be acknowledged and inscribed into further and contesting configurations of time. This would imply wresting modernity away from the tyranny of an omnipotent rationality and the universalism of a single, linear, point of view, in order to set its terms, languages, understandings and desires in a more open terrain, and there to move in a world irreducible to its identity.[16] In the mourning light of a positivist and self-assured modernity, there here emerges not the expression of grief for the lost figures of certitude but a necessary burying of the dead in order 'to reinvest the world and the self with symbolic significance'.[17] Such a mourning issues in a cultural and political constellation attentive to mortality and modesty, to limits. This is not to give up the dream, to abandon the utopic, but to transform it into a contemporary act, that is, into an ethics attendant upon the uncertain historical configuration in which it speaks and which permits it to speak.

But what, exactly, is this configuration? Where does it arise, and what does it respond to? To begin to answer that question is inevitably to acknowledge a differentiation of cultural and historical place that is increasingly dependent upon a largely unacknowledged global structure that has been evolving since the inception of occidental modernity five centuries ago. In the mutual complexities of the westernising of the world and the worlding of the West, each and every history bears witness to its particular worldly location, and the manner in which that has come to be represented and . . . repressed. So, in speaking from somewhere the voice that testifies to a particular past and present increasingly resonates in the channels of global amplification. This, however, is not merely to cast a particular history and location into the pluralist cacophony of disparate voices seeking to tell a story; it is, rather, to brush a sense of narrative, a testimony of time, of life, up against the structural powers that frame us in different and unequal fashion.

The United Nations Programme for Development, published in 1997, speaks of 18 per cent of the world's population (circa 800 million) enjoying 83 per cent of its income, while 82 per cent (circa 5 billion) have 17 per cent of its income at its disposal. The same publication suggests that extreme poverty could be eliminated by spending each year less than the patrimony of the seven richest people in the world. In the United States 1 per cent of the population owns 40 per cent of the wealth, another 20 per cent own 40 per cent, while the remaining 71 per cent is left with 20 per cent. It is foreseen that by 2010 in the state of California one child in four will suffer malnutrition.[18] The United States simultaneously houses 25 per cent of the world's incarcerated.[19] Such statistics speak of a profoundly undemocratic framing of the political resources and responsibilities of everyday life, most acutely signalled in the 'First' world in the United States where appeal to law and the unquestioned status of the Constitution − 'a plan of government drawn up by a group of merchants and slave owners at the dawn of the modern era' − invariably takes precedence over justice and democratic process.[20]

In Bulawayo, stepping between the cars, a casually smart black youth with a multi-coloured Star Tac™ Motorola cellular phone hooked to his belt crosses by the lights. Yet the south of the world, with its unstable mix of global signs and local realities, remains the south of the world. Investments, standards of living and life prospects remain so dramatically diverse that even the drone of statistics cannot mute the tragedy they embody. In Zimbabwe, average life expectancy has dropped by 30 years in the wake of the HIV epidemic. No US airline flies to any city in Africa, and that includes Cairo and Johannesburg. In a continent in which power appears to be sustained more by patronage than by profit or development, to speak of Africa as being in a neo-colonial relationship to the West has little sense in economic terms when its share in world trade was only 1.9 per cent in 1990 (it was 5.2 per cent in 1950), and returns on investments in the continent have dropped from 30.7 per cent in the 1960s to 2.5 per cent in the 1980s. The scene is one of almost total disinvestment, with external, private, commercial investment totalling only $504 million in 1992, 'or 1.6 per cent of the total investment in Africa, Asia and Central and South America as a whole.' The gross national product (GNP) of the whole of sub-Saharan Africa in 1992, at $270 billion, was less than that of the Netherlands. Sub-Sahara Africa includes South Africa. Put bluntly, 'the continent is slipping out of the Third World into its own bleak category of the nth world'.[21] This is the part of the world where the 60 per cent of the world's population who have never made a phone call in their lives is concentrated. There are, Zillah Eisenstein reminds us, more telephone lines in Manhattan than in all of sub-Saharan Africa.[22]

In the global calculus a continent – Africa – has simply gone missing. The World Bank predicts that one-third of all food required will have to be imported by 2000. Between 1961 and 1995, Africa's food production per person decreased by 11.6 per cent (by comparison Latin America's increased by 31.4 per cent and Asia's by 70.6 per cent). In this scenario the state is a 'neo-patrimonial' structure in which it is not development but staying in power that is the main issue:

> Staying in power is the main objective. The army must be kept happy, urban masses must be fed, conflicting interests of political coalitions must be balanced. To this end every aspect of the economy becomes an instrument of patronage. Quotas, tariffs, subsidies, import licences, the over-valued currency and so on become channels of enrichment, through rent-seeking activity. The privileges of the élite depend on the monopoly of power within a society, and not on the productivity of society as a whole, much less on any feelgood factor permeating the population at large. In the short term at least, a successful programme of economic development conflicts with that. The political and economic exigencies of personal rule follow their own logic. Mismanagement actually has a rationale with the neo-patrimonial system.[23]

This, too, is a central part of the complex historical inheritance and contemporary configuration of modernity. It is not a peripheral idiosyncrasy but a structural component of that history, that modernity.

Out of the past

How, in this light, might the past, the pasts, be narrated? Of course, the coherence of established accounts cannot be matched by an alternative coherence. After all, it is precisely the sense of coherence, leading to the conclusive nature of rational finitude, that is the problem: a finitude, like subject-centred perspective, that is ultimately infinite in its pretensions. Perhaps, the Baroque motif of the 'ruin' is more appropriate here. The established edifice of occidental historiography is not swept away, it persists and lives on, but it is now haunted by a series of interrogations, its structure fractured by unforeseen cultural movement and shaken by the accommodation of new, previously unacknowledged, historical inhabitants. The history that emerges from this building no longer offers the revelation of an abstract destiny, nor neatly corresponds to the articulation of verifiable socio-economic structures: it now houses a more unruly temporality produced by the social production of a location in time. All of this is to speak of a multiple modernity in which past and present are conjoined and mutually interrogated. For in such a con-temporary affiliation a sense of the present, and its associated 'progress', finds itself in debt to the questions that come to meet it from the past.

So, the past erupts into the present not only announcing the other, repressed, side of modernity but also seeding a more unruly disturbance. Modernity does not merely become more complex through the addition of the unacknowledged, it remains irretrievably undone by the questions it can no longer contain. The archaic, presumed to lie back there in the mist of time, appears in the midst of modernity bearing another sense, another direction. An absence, the 'lost' world of the past against which the present measures its 'progress', unexpectedly returns to haunt modernity. Rational certitude confronts a ghost that bears witness to the return of the apparently timeless economy of the 'archaic' and the 'primitive': 'a rumor of words that vanish no sooner than they are uttered, and which are therefore lost forever.'[24] For the potent traces of such lost languages, of diverse cultural configurations of time and place – prehistoric rock paintings in South Africa and Zimbabwe, pre-Colombian cities in the jungles and deserts of the Americas, song lines in the Australian bush, prayer flags in Asian mountain passes – can prise open the present to interrogate its all-inclusive manner of knowing. The tourist 'exotic' can unexpectedly testify to a deeper testament when an absence of immediate meaning can open up a rift in time.[25]

The disturbance of the idea of stable cultural formations located in the mythic time of 'primitive' societies comes to be countered by the evidence of austral Africa and north America (not to speak of the evidence of perpetual Pacific and Asian migrations): historical spaces traversed by migrations, movements and shifting territorial claims and confines, both before and after 'first contact' with Europeans. The pressure of the Iroquois Confederacy from the Eastern Seaboard to the Great Lakes stretched out into the eastern prairie as it pushed other nations, including the Sioux or Lakota further west. Eight hundred years ago a part of the Athabascan linguistic group migrated out of north-west Canada into the present south-west of the United States; in the process they became Navahos and Apaches. In southern Africa, there was the early-nineteenth-century movement of the Ndebele out of Natal into southern Zimbabwe (itself probably induced by coastal slavery in Mozambique), putting military and territorial pressure on the Shona and the San peoples of that area prior to the direct usurpation of that space by Anglo-Boer colonisation. The land as mythic point of origin, as the constant horizon of identity and the testimony of tradition, is, despite appearances, never timeless. It is cultivated by language and, if transformed by myth into a constant referent, is not immune to a new inscription, a new telling.[26] This is to insist on the historical nature of the 'archaic' introducing a temporality that disturbs the unilateral assumptions of occidental 'progress' and its historiography, but which, nevertheless, remains a temporality that registers historical being and cultural transformation in its own terms.

The maintenance of temporal and cultural distance, both by instrumental rationality and the transcendental certitudes of historicism, can be confounded not only by historical evidence but also by the contemporary traces of the archaic announced in the human transit traced on a rock face, in a hieroglyphic narrative whose mystery and magic resists the imperatives of teleology and instrumental transparency.[27] In the presence of another language, and associated forms of knowledge, there emerges an unsuspected dynamism that sunders the sharp distinction between the presumably natural and static universe of the 'primitive' and the perpetual cultural movement of the 'modern'. A logocentric linearity that insists on the passage from the pre-historic to the historical, from nature to culture, from orality to writing, dissolves into something less reassuring.[28] For if writing enters into the archaic, fracturing any illusion of recovering that world 'as it was', the archaic also re-emerges to become a contemporary instance of the writing that seeks to represent and circum-scribe it. A world as 'it was' is lost forever, what remains are the remnants of representation. Such traces, however, are not dead objects, waiting to be classified and explained in a universal logic, but living interrogations that ghost my understanding with other stories, with others. The archaic, as Pier Paolo Pasolini's cinema, for example, strives to suggest, is not simply and safely back there, before my time, but is also a disturbing presence that proposes a new configuration of my present.[29] Such scenes do not represent modernity's 'exotica' so much as its interrogation, its interruption: an invitation to reconceptualise and reconfigure modernity itself. In *Oedipus Rex* (1967) mythical Greece and contemporary North Africa are temporal, cultural, physical and psychic peripheries that Pasolini renders disturbingly proximate. The 'aboriginal', the 'native' and the 'primitive' suddenly become contemporary, part of the modernity that structurally excludes them.[30] This is to draw upon other orders of sense – archaic, mythical, unconscious, poetical – in order to re-write the world, to set stories to another rhythm and there seek to render the mundane magical.[31] To insist upon the archaic as a strategic narrative that interrogates the presumptions, rationalisations, repressions and negations of modernity is not to seek the recovery of a lost innocence, but is rather to propose a critical research on how to narrate, how to eroticise the real.

Against this possibility, the spatialisation of knowledge seeks to insure the distinction between centre and periphery, that is, the perspective between subject and object. This permits the realisation of a controlled plane over which the subsequent narrative can unfold in a continual reaffirmation of the narrator. Such distancing permits a recognition of the other always and only in terms of the subject:

> A part, of the world which appeared to be entirely other is brought back to the same by a displacement that throws alterity out of skew in order to turn it into an exteriority behind which an interiority, the unique definition of man, can be recognised.[32]

Resident narratives

In this context, writing, and its associated organisation of knowledge and understanding, comes to be re-located in the more extensive world of graphic inscriptions where the transparent logic of mimetic utility, the linear transmission of a clear and coherent 'message', is overtaken and subsumed in the traces, in the tracing, of heterogeneous worldly states. The desire for symmetry and the subsequent establishment of distance between the modern and the archaic, between the occidental observer and the 'objects' of his or her discipline and field of research, is unexpectedly brought into a shared vicinity. The archaic returns as an asymmetric presence to interrogate the apparent triumph of monotheism and the separation of the spiritual from the material world, of culture from nature, of rationalism from other forms of reason. It is precisely this space, the

19

space of non-identity, that draws us elsewhere. Like the horizontal slash, the terrestrial cut, across the monochrome intensity of a Mark Rothko canvas, in the beauty of nothing some 'thing' issues forth.

Such a perspective, no longer subject-centred, but inter-worldly might lead, in the words of the Indian artist Anish Kapoor, 'to bring to expression . . . and then move towards a poetic existence.'[33] It is Kapoor's idea of 'resident narrative', what lies in the material, what can be excavated from what is already given, deposited and disseminated, that can prove suggestive here. For material is what insists, and which awaits a form. It is what comes to meet and interrogate us. It is what, in being framed, invites us to consider the very process of framing which constitutes the perspective of sense, knowledge and affect, but which simultaneously, in drawing attention to the act of framing, accentuates and acknowledges the limits of those registers. We find ourselves conversing with what opens up the interval and the tension between terrestrial material and the particular world and languages that enframe and register that interval. What pushes us against the frame what, in becoming, renders the impossible possible: it is in that 'what' that the poetical acquires its potential. It is, to quote the title of one of Anish Kapoor's own works, a giant, blood-red, hollowed, disc suspended from the ceiling, to find oneself, 'at the edge of the world'.

To arrive at this point, and to investigate the possibilities of an altogether less assured sense of historical 'truth', breaches the existing borders of institutional representation, and threatens to cut the umbilical cord that traditionally ties the humanities to the continuum of a historicist and humanist rationale.

It is the injunction of history, transported beyond a historicist and empiricist understanding, that most precisely registers the temporal and ontological limits of the humanist enterprise. There is a conjunctural constellation, most obviously delineated in the terminology of postmodernity and postcoloniality, that sharply, even if often only superficially, announces this disengagement from the humanist formation. What needs to be retained in this passage elsewhere is not a sense of cancellation but rather one of re-elaboration: relations of power, discrimination, inequality, exploitation and repression in their class, colonial, gendered and racial manifestations persist in a diverse, but continuing, configuration of the world.

Attention to the interrogations sown by intercultural forms that circulate in the world, dealing in the traffic between histories, traditions, literatures and oralities, leads to an emphasis on the volatile location of historical and cultural translation. In this hazy border zone there looms the possibility of a frontier lore. Such a knowledge evokes a geopolitical

understanding of location, but also, and more immediately, a transformed relationship to existing disciplines and institutionalised figures
of understanding. Here a critical language that extracts its ethics from
the experiences, practices and proposals of the subaltern insinuates
itself. This does pretend to be the knowledge of the 'other' – it is not
an academic ventriloquism that speaks in the name of the subaltern,
thereby reconfirming existing hegemonies – but an 'other' knowledge
that irritates, disturbs and ultimately disrupts a preceding arrangement
of knowledge and power.[34] This is to return the occidental voice, accustomed to universal acknowledgement, to its repressed and deeply troubled
site in history.

Positions

At this point, is it possible to translate that 'return' into a more immediate syntax by considering, for example, who and what is a postcolonial
intellectual? In recognising and registering the impossibility of providing
a clear and obvious answer to that question, it is nevertheless possible to
consider the space, and subsequent places, in which such a question
emerges. This particular space is certainly institutional, but it is also significantly historical, geopolitical and ontological. I, personally, am interested in acknowledging in these co-ordinates a precise positionality that
inflects my subsequent response to the question posed by the 'postcolonial'. So the following comments attempt to speak not in the name
of that space or theoretical abstraction, but in terms of a particular
position in which the discourse nominated by the postcolonial is spoken
and performed.

In the details and detours of debate, the postcolonial – as a critical
voice, intellectual lexicon and institutional practice – is surely also the
sign, symptom, of a historical permutation. This is clearly not a homogeneous alteration, either in its presence or its effects. As a term that
deliberately seeks to reconfigure the body of previous knowledge and
understandings (for the 'post' is not merely a chronological signal, it is
also an epistemological one), the 'postcolonial' invokes a historical and
theoretical encounter in which all are invited to re-view and re-consider
their worldly and differentiated positions in the articulation and admin-
istration of historical judgement and cultural definitions. Here the
postcolonial presents itself as a theoretical and political space that permits
the excavation of the ground of occidental knowledge as both an arrangement of disciplines and a specific historical disposition of truth.

If the postcolonial is profoundly connected to critically revisiting
the precise histories and fall-out of colonialism, and in particular its

subaltern, repressed and subversive narration, it also implicitly proposes a fundamental critique of the institutions, languages and disciplines that historically organised, defined and explained the 'colonial'; that is, the knowledge, both scientific and humanist, wrapped up in the 'history' that occidental modernity told itself. It is that history that constructed my 'home', permitting me to speak; and it is commencing from that history that I seek to respond and acquire a responsibility.

As someone born, although Heidegger's insistence on the involuntary state of being 'thrown' is perhaps more suited for a nuanced historical sense of being, as someone born in the heartland of Blake's 'green and pleasant land', the postcolonial invokes for me a double movement. For it shifts seemingly peripheral concerns, moored in the irrevocable time of slavery, colonial conquest, imperialism and the rationalism of racism, to the constitution of the meridian while simultaneously relocating that centre on another, altogether less provincial, map. The question of the 'other' – ex-slave, minority, dispossessed, migrant – becomes the controversy of the historical formation of my 'self'. The past slips from the faint appeals of a silenced repository into an insistent interrogation of the present. Although this radical relocation can by no means guarantee an absence of intellectual narcissism – both white European and 'Third' world intellectuals profitably re-presenting themselves and their existent cultural capital under the illumination provided by this new critical light – it does, if insistently pursued, lead to irreversible consequences for historical and cultural understanding.

The postcolonial operates an incision on the existing corpus of knowledge, and most precisely in the humanities; it thereby also imposes an interruption in the seeming inevitability of historical 'progress'. The teleology of modernity's historical time, the linear unfolding of development and supercession from the primitive to the perfections of the future, is here interceded by a spiralling series of transversal returns that transmit the past into the present, the archaic into the avant-garde. In this unexpected punctuation, the historical narrative is not merely forced to amplify its acknowledgements, it is also asked to reconsider its design, drives and desires.

This is to disrupt the linearity of explanation and return modernity to the initial phase that inaugurated a world picture in the fifteenth century. To return to the violent European appropriation, colonisation, imperialisation and subsequent hybridisation of the rest of the world would be to invert prevalent critical tendencies that see in globalisation merely the latest (and inevitable) manifestation of the former's economic history. This is to argue that globalisation not only is about the reach and power of trans-national corporations and capital, but also, and most

significantly, is about the more extensive ontological mapping that transforms the world into Western identity and interest in every branch of
historical activity. It is this particular historical design that is betrayed
in the assumed universalism of its humanism and technologies of the
self. In this prospect, the postcolonial space is perhaps better understood
as an over-determined site in which both the once coloniser and colonised
have been physically and psychically colonised. Here, perhaps, 'history'
itself has to be disbanded in order to exceed the frame each has inherited and thereby recover room to move.[35]

History is not merely partial, it is also partisan. To recognise and
register time and location, the voice, the body, conscious and unconscious intent, is surely to be more, not less, historical. To narrate the
past in this more flexible disposition may involve reading less 'history'
and listening to more music, turning to novels rather than statistics, in
order to de-centre the 'realist' understandings (and their epistemological foundations in the presumed transparency of language and reason)
that many histories evoke. Here the spiral of language – as testimony,
evocation and literature – interrupts the linearity that devours time in
the name of progress. Here history returns not as 'fact', but as survival.
Such a recurrence opens on to the tension between history and narrative, between writing and orality, or, as Michel de Certeau pointed out,
between the objective and the imaginary, between positivism and poetics.
It is the transgression of this frontier that underscores the limits of
objective and objectifying structures. Here there emerges the counter
force of 'eclectic atlases' in which what flees the objectifying gaze and
its classificatory structure of seeing become productive sites of understanding.[36] Beyond the abstract authority of the rationalising eye/I exist
details that differentiate and reveal individual and collective biographies
of worldly being and becoming.

In insisting on the limits of historical representation I am not simply
seeking to draw attention to a potential plurality and diversity of 'points
of view', but am intent on establishing the more radical ontological
terms of the unseen and unseeable, of what persists in a particular time
and place outside the realm of institutional recognition and representation: of what persists as a cut-off point, a limit, an unknown dimension
and potential interrogation. It is out of such margins that the postcolonial emerges as a question that interpellates both the one-time
coloniser and the colonised. As a critical disturbance that reverberates
through different places it provides a simultaneous sense of connection
and distinction. While suggesting links between worlds previously
separated in intellectual, historical, political and physical distance, the
postcolonial proposition simultaneously renders proximate the intractable

and incommensurable; what was previously repressed, exorcised from the equation, or more simply ignored.

Certainly the concept of the postcolonial has been coined to the advantage of the West. Its genesis, institutional currency and seeming benefit most certainly lies there as many of its critics sourly point out. But, in the idea of benefit there is both the significance of direct profit, and also the more ambiguous gain that emerges from an understanding that does not necessarily conclude with the acquisition of self-confirmation. Where such a self-confirmation begins to vacillate and the underlying premises of selfhood are rendered a little less secure is precisely where the tenacity of alterity can no longer be displaced or avoided.

In a relationship to otherness and alterity, invariably projected and produced by the subject who distinguishes him or herself from an other, I inadvertently also stumble across the disturbing body of the cyborg: the technological hardware and software that frequently alienates us from ourselves. Such a technological aside actually opens up an avenue into the historical formation of knowledge and culture, here organised around the practices of 'science', that also leads into the overall dislocation of the occidental *épisteme* in the same force field that the postcolonial releases. For both the colonised and the cyborg are deeply disturbing symptoms of the metaphysics of modernity. What exactly is the relationship, not to speak of the proximity, between the once, sometimes still, colonised body and the cyborg? Each is a body that has been construed and managed by powers that have rendered it an object of study and research, but also, and simultaneously, an object of control, exploitation and discipline. Both seemingly emerge from nothing: the colonised body out of a history and place that is negated, the cyborg out of the inanimate, the non-human. However, such bodies have also acquired the powers to reply, and to reply in the languages that previously subordinated and negated them. The object reveals itself as a historical subject. My languages return in the body of the other, rendering my sense of identity disturbing, vulnerable, open to inquiries that arrive from elsewhere. I am obliged to reply. Further, to nominate the relationship between the colonised body and the body completely constructed and colonised by technology – the cyborg – is also to introduce the idea of the sublime, of that which attracts me and simultaneously threatens me: in this particular case the racial and technological sublime; as such, I am conversing with a desired, but negated, part of my own identity.

This disquieting encounter with alterity, both in the form of the historical and cultural non-European body, and in the form of the non-natural body, the machine and its associated technologies, has always shadowed the development of occidental modernity and ideas of itself.

Historically, and not only in the West, the construction of the 'I' – as sexed, ethnic, historical, cultural and nationalised individual – has occurred through the presence, both real and imagined, of an other, invariably configured in the alien vestments of monstrosity. The weakening of this relationship, the refusal of the other to mirror me and my obsessions, leads to a crisis in the preceding sense of my self. The proximity of the other to me achieved through the economical and political forces of modernity and the technological suppression of distance (from the sailing ship to the aeroplane to digital technology and robotics) opens up to critique and criticism that preceding cultural arrangement, and its secure sense of racial, sexual, geopolitical and instrumental distance and the subsequent assurance of a detached identity.

But I also want to suggest something that snaps, or breaks away from, the simple dualism and division between centre and periphery, between hegemony and subalternity, between myself and the other. Considerations of the ethnic, historical and cultural differences that compose and interrogate the present day world occur in a context that is forever changing. It is a context in which the presumptions of the seemingly anthropological stability of ethnic and racial identity, of gender identity, of the identity of the human itself, are seen and experienced in an altogether less certain fashion. Here, as Frantz Fanon insisted, – 'I am not a prisoner of history. I should not seek there for the meaning of my destiny', – it is a question of diluting, even disclaiming, these anchors of identity in the critical passage beyond the borders of both the hegemonic structures of occidental power/knowledge and the automatic affirmation of historical struggles against them.[37] Here identity becomes a point of departure for a voyage without guarantees, and not a port of arrival.[38]

To venture beyond the absolutism of identity – we all know who we are, don't we? – is to cross a series of frontiers, most obviously that of the Enlightenment and European humanism, and to enter an ethnography in which the 'man' of knowledge, the scientist, the subject, becomes the object of a discourse, of a history, of a world, of an ontological space that is interrogated and interrogating. This implies the abandonment of a fixed sense of the self that, in its presumed universality, exposes a unilateral point of view. Such a humanism, as Rey Chow notes, historically and ontologically has its racial and geopolitical specificity, and, as some have insisted, was fully realised in the rationalisation of terror and the programmed genocide of the other.[39] Perhaps we need to proceed by criticising both such absolutisms and their counterparts? What happens to the presumed autonomy of an absolute 'otherness', when it finds itself having to confront 'the end of the innocent notion of the essential black subject' already announced in 1988 by Stuart Hall?[40]

Here the idea of race, of identity, even of the human and the body as the foundation of truth, are confronted to permit an exit from the strait-jacket of a particular historical 'time' into another way of being in time.

Returning to the consideration of the powers written on the body – on the body constructed according to racial, sexual, scientific and techno- logical laws and logics – invokes an invitation to rethink such mechan- isms not as abstract structures, but as cultural formations, as historical configurations, as social and psychic inscriptions. Today the historical constellation that reveals such a situation is seemingly framed by the dif- ferentiated processes of globalisation. But globalisation, the tendency to treat history, culture and, above all, political economy, as a world system began with modernity itself. The possibility of reducing the world to a single and unique point of view, and from there to manage its economy, its politics, its history and culture, was, if not initiated, certainly most successfully installed by occidental modernity. The *Quattrocento* pers- pective of the Renaissance in which every object is distributed in space and directed by the gaze of the observer-subject, artist or scientist, is what inaugurates such a world picture. And it is here that today I encounter the inevitable dis-location and de-centring of such powers and languages in the instance that the 'objects' of my gaze reply. When my constructions, the extensions of my world reveal themselves to be inde- pendent and express their histories, their desires, their logics, in my lan- guage, then I am drawn beyond the frame (and powers) of that earlier world picture. Here, at the borders of Western humanism I am invited to consider my 'home' no longer as a fixed structure, with my roots guar- anteed by the epistemic premises that are grounded in logical allegiances and institutions of national tradition, but as a contingent passage, a way that literally carries me elsewhere. At this point, to be post-humanist does not mean to renounce the human; on the contrary, it announces some- thing that is more human precisely through its attempt to exit from the abstract confines and controls of a universal subject who believes that all commences and concludes with such a self.

To accept the idea of post-humanism means to register limits; limits that are inscribed in the locality of the body, of the history, the power and the knowledge, that speaks. It is here, within these precise histor- ical confines, that I find myself conversing in the vicinity of the other who refuses to be the 'other' for me; that is, refuses to remain at a distance, as an object dependent on my desires and powers.

Donna Haraway has suggested that it is in the extremes of the cyborg, in this cipher without history, that I am most starkly solicited to con- template this possibility.[41] In the combination and contamination of the human and the machine, in the simultaneous extension of my self and my desired separation from the instrumental device, in the mixture of organic and inorganic, my subjective, mental and physical autonomy is put in question. I am invited to enter that passage between danger and saving power, to cite Heidegger's noted definition of technology, in order to think and proceed in a different manner.

So what is the sense of this historical and global moment when the objects of my gaze, of my language, ask for more ... recognition, response, justice, freedom, and throw me into a state in which I am called upon to reflect on limits, on my limits, on the limits of a vision that believed itself capable of grasping and understanding all? And then, how can I acquire a sense and direction from this interruption that offers me a perspective beyond myself? This type of enquiry can serve, above all, to undo the traditional knot that has invariably bound together blood and soil in discussions of identity. The announcement of the other scatters the presumed homogeneity of my individual and collective identity. If the alienated body of the colonised and the cyborg has been integral to the realisation of my world, my modernity – and this is most certainly the case – then I need to acknowledge heterogeneity as an integral part of that history, of that cultural formation and the making of my own identity.

In this manner, as Julia Kristeva rightly suggests, the stranger transforms me into a stranger, rendering my history, my language, the formation of my self, unfamiliar, disquieting.[42] In this interruption, in this split and interval – often painful and difficult to accept, especially by those who have always lived history as the mirror of their selves – I find myself travelling without the possibility of closing the gap, forced to live my history as an ethical opening. This might mean not merely to 'use' and 'exploit' the postcolonial instance for institutional and individual benefit, but to accept it as an invitation to rethink the very premises of the 'historical', and thereby the cultural, political, psychic and poetical consequences that follow from disturbing, excavating and cultivating the ground that bears me.

Modernity's sublime

In this challenge to a rationalist truth and universal subject lies the challenge to occidental modernity. Yet prior to contemporary talk of postmodernity and postcoloniality, this particular challenge is already deeply seeded within occidental art and literature itself, most precisely in the eighteenth-century attempts to confine the sentimental and emotional excess proposed by the sublime. Kant's *Critique of Judgement* of 1790 examines the relationship between the imagination and reason, and concludes with the subordination of the former to the latter. In a rationalist refinement of Edmund Burke's more physiological account of 1759, *A Philosophical Enquiry into the Origin of our Ideas of the Sublime and the Beautiful*, the sublime is considered purely a product of the mind, a mental construct; pleasure lies in grasping its magnitude rather than in dealing with a particular object as is the case with the beautiful. For this reason Nature and its objects cannot be sublime. They can only be beautiful. The sublime is a sensation. It resides in the mind, and it represents the inadequacy of the imagination to grasp the magnitude of what it contemplates. The imagination is surpassed by reason. In *The Feminine Sublime* Barbara Freeman critically comments: 'Reason's function is to comprehend a totality that the imagination cannot itself represent, and thereby to disclose a superiority over nature that the mind could not otherwise achieve'.[43] The beautiful and the sublime are not permitted to challenge or diminish the power of reason, but only to reaffirm its reach into every corner of the universe. The subject extends his sway, untouched by the doubts, questions and ambiguities that are registered only to be 'resolved' in the rational unity of the purpose and progress of a totality of generations stretching towards infinity. All – even the 'wildest and most ruleless disarray and devastation' – remains within the fold of reason:

> For what is sublime, in the proper meaning of the term, cannot be contained in any sensible form but concerns only ideas of reason, which though they cannot be exhibited adequately, are aroused and called to mind by this very inadequacy, which can be exhibited in sensibility.[44]

As Barbara Freeman goes on to point out, Mary Shelley's *Frankenstein* is the realisation, or acting out, of this Kantian scenario. Kant, like Victor Frankenstein, believes that reason can reveal and bring all within the compass of the thinking subject. All can be represented and rendered transparent to reason. Knowledge is not what is encountered, but what is conquered, acquired and claimed. Victor Frankenstein 'provides a portrait of Kant, or mirror of metaphysical desire.'[45] For Kant the sublime must always operate within limits determined by reason and its moral authority, otherwise it becomes, as he puts it, 'monstrous'. Monstrosity is what disturbs the project of reason, transgressing its theoretical borders and usurping its rational imperatives. To echo Judith Butler's *Bodies that Matter* (1993), the sublime is what most directly registers 'the movement of boundary itself'.

Confronted by the purity of reason, bodies, physical flesh, blood and bone, differentiated by sex, gender, race, age and mortality, bear witness to the terrifying confusion of borders, a disquieting imprecision, and the potential undermining of male coherence by unruly feminine excess. There a body without confines, where the internal and the external, the fixed and the fluid, are confused, transfigured, is most telling announced in the gestation of the maternal body: from a woman to a monster is but a short step. In the abyss of the indefinite, where the horror of the abject subverts codified control, rationality is brought dramatically to account for what it seeks to repress and distance. The misogyny and racism of reason is forced to acknowledge its universal pretences. As Freeman suggestively concludes, at this point the sublime and monstrosity, alterity and hybridity, become figures of theory rather than what theory seeks to exclude and deny.[46]

J. M. W. Turner's picture *Slavers Throwing Overboard the Dead and Dying: Typhoon Coming On* (also known as *The Slave Ship*) was first publicly shown in London in 1840. A sailing ship is tossed on the wild waters of an oncoming storm. Between the waves fish and screeching gulls can be glimpsed. In the bottom right-hand corner, a manacled black leg is about to slip beneath the surface forever. This painting by Turner brings to the heart of an aesthetic discourse a complex manifestation of the dreadful sublime, condensed in a historical and social signal: slavery, an institution that had been abolished only seven years earlier in the British Empire, and was still active elsewhere around the Atlantic. Here the object of reason, the disinterested gaze contemplating beauty, is rendered doubly disquieting. For there is both the disquiet of the sublime, of excessive sentiments and irrational passion, and the disquiet of facing the repressed: the repression of slavery whose indirect profits from sugar, cotton and coffee plantations financed the productive world and society that sustained the exhibition, the art gallery and the eventual purchase of Turner's painting.

This is not to condemn the picture, but rather to grasp its ambiguity – Turner's reasons for painting this scene were clearly not to support slavery – and to grasp in that ambiguity different ways of interpreting and responding to the work and, with it, to occidental modernity.

The picture's first owner was the art critic John Ruskin. It was a gift from his father. In his book *Modern Painters* Ruskin discusses the painting entirely in terms of how water should be painted, suggesting it to be 'the noblest sea' ever painted by Turner and by man. The fact that 'the guilty ship' is a slave ship throwing slaves overboard is relegated to a footnote. Of course, the painting can be discussed in terms of painting water, but the elision here, whereby slavery slips out of the picture, is perhaps also revealing. Twenty years later, Ruskin sold the painting. It was said that he found the subject matter too painful to contemplate. What he had found too painful to contemplate was not, however, allowed to interfere with his aesthetic judgement.[47]

What I'm briefly suggesting here, following the black British critic Paul Gilroy's commentary on this affair, is that it might be, on the contrary, very revealing to interrupt an aesthetic judgement with an ethical one, or even to mix and conjoin the two. This would be to arrive at the Wittgensteinian maxim that ethics and aesthetics are the same thing. But, and this is what Gilroy suggests (and what German Romanticism in its critique of the Kantian subordination of the sublime to reason, also held out), if we were to mix the two, this would open a door not only on to a new view of the painting, but also of modernity itself.

To put slavery back into the frame, to take those discarded black bodies and return them to the picture, is not only to confront the limits of a reason and an aesthetics unwilling to contemplate the other side of the representation. To return those bodies to the picture is also to mark the limits of such a reason, and its political and cultural accounts, and to suggest that there are further stories, further modernities, to be narrated.

So, the question of art, the beautiful and the sublime, reveals more than a regional debate confined to the area of aesthetics and the authority of the Enlightenment. This is to return the art of modernity to its inaugural claims. From the outset modern Western art was considered to offer a window on the world, to reflect what the eye observes so that 'things seen appear upon this plane surface as if it were made of transparent glass' (Leon Battista Alberti).[48] Such a logic of representation legislated the supremacy of optics and the centrality of the eye. It is the technology of perspective that assures the eye that space is uniquely determined 'by three co-ordinates perpendicular to each other and extending in infinitum from a given "point of origin"'.[49] Perspective, a point of origin, a regulated and homogenous geometry of space, locates the eye of the viewer at the centre of the frame, controlling and defining what is to be seen, catalogued, described, explained. The grid of theory, the frame of vision, the self-centred order of sight, protects the observer from exposure to what she cannot see, contemplate or represent. It is this individual and absolute power over space that renders it uniform and fully transparent to the beholder. It is the systematic elaboration of the principles of perspective that the Renaissance painter, architect and town planner embodies in the history of art. The knowledge, and aesthetics, that arise from this unique and self-centred point of view are, of course, deeply embedded in the formation and subsequent execution of modernity itself. Thus, the biography of the artist emblematically becomes interchangeable with the biography of the universal genius that is occidental modernity.[50]

Perspective installs the rationalisation of space, its colonisation, permitting the viewer to pull back from the brink of infinite disperson. As with the Kantian sublime, the threat of dispersal and abjection, the 'vanishing point' in the picture, is relocated within the realm of rational appropriation: the continuum that opens up between the eye of the subject and infinity is rendered discrete, susceptible to measurement, calculation and convergence.[51] This is an art which centres the viewer. It is her or his vision that activates the perspective that guarantees her or his position as the point of origin for what is represented. Although drawn along lines of sight towards the infinite, the viewing gaze neither falters nor disappears. Held in the frame, and suspended in the calculated geometry of the visual field, the subject confirms the picture in the shared instance that the picture reconfirms the pivotal position of the subject.

In this persistent centrality of the eye/I, the distance between the simple Renaissance apparatuses employed to delineate perspective and the present day digital video camera, both rendering reality immediate, as though without technical intervention ('an orchid in the land of technology', Walter Benjamin), is far briefer than the five centuries that separate them suggests. It is the on-going displacement of this 'world picture', and its subject-centred humanism, it is the historical, political and poetical implications of this displacement, that suggests something profounder than simply the chronological passage of a historical epoch.

Critical thought, writing, art and debate since the 1940s has increasingly forced a fundamental re-evaluation of occidental modernity in the light of the global migrations, historical displacements and cultural translations that have emerged as being central to modernity *from its very inception five centuries ago*. So, if the West has in many ways become the modern world, with its political economy, languages, techniques and technology supplying and sustaining a global frame, that space has also become the differentiated place, the 'home', for other histories, cultures and identities. In worlding the world the presumptions of the West to own and direct the language and institutions that carry its name have been irretrievably transposed.

This emphasis on dislocation, migration and re-appropriation is not proposed in order to recuperate the migration of others for my benefit, and to claim that we are all 'migrants' now. It is, rather, to register a response, a responsibility, within the languages at my disposal for the necessary interruption and reassessment of my voice, history and culture in a world in which the historical transit and cultural translation of migration have become inseparable from definitions of modernity. Here both a poetical and a political configuration of the world come to be reworked or worlded differently. The self-confirming vision provided by the critical distance of subjective perspective, and the universalism of the bird's-eye view from on high, is now supplemented and subverted by an oblique gaze coming out of a particular history and locality, invariably from 'below', that leads to the former's displacement and potential dispersal.

What comes into view, what comes to be registered and heard, once this movement is recognised?

Historical locations

The unilateral rigidity of the observer–observed/subject–object relationship that we have inherited from humanism gives way to a diverse language: one that is less violent in its insistence and more open in its signification. Direct intentionality and unilateral agency give way to a less conditioned encounter, to receptivity, and the adoption of listening. The other is not positioned in order to be deciphered and explained as the object of my discourse and knowledge, but is received as the reverberation, the resonance, of what escapes the intentions of my representation.[52]

Here the subject, the 'I', is provoked and invoked by the other to the degree that she or he is brought to the threshold of also becoming an object in the shared belonging of the interpreter to the object of interpretation – what Gadamer famously calls the 'fusion of horizons'. But what emerges here, and what breaches the conclusive circle of Gadamer's own hermeneutic aestheticism, is not so much the replacement of a Kantian 'critical distance' with an organic sublimation of subject and object in the communal nature of things, *but rather an acute sense of historical location*. This is an awareness so acute as to cut into the universal pretensions of a rationalism that presumes already to fully know itself and the history it proposes to reveal, and so acute as to render each and every tradition of interpretation, each and every hermeneutics, each and every knowledge, an unstable site of transit, of transformation and translation.[53] In this more agnostic and vulnerable version of history, without an objective reason able to guarantee the constellation of our lives, the very premises of the subject and historical agency, of occidental humanism, are what I am invited to reconsider in a radical recasting of historical understanding and cultural critique.

32

This brings me back to the question of the 'truth' in art. Opposed to a propositional understanding in which language and objectivity are supposed to coincide in a relationship secured by consensual rationality, here the prospect of 'truth' becomes an undecidable condition that speaks of more than any rational language can contain. This is not necessarily a theological or mystical proposal, even though Walter Benjamin, for example, entertained that possibility, but is rather an argument about time and locality, or history and being, as German Romanticism, Benjamin and Heidegger, in different ways, sought to suggest. And it is the question of art that most sharply maintains the aperture on this horizon.

Held in a historical constellation where meaning emerges from limits, and not from the timeless universality of the abstract language of concepts, the art work present us with the temporal indications of a horizon of language, worldly location and terrestrial framing, that lie *behind us*, *before us*, and *beyond us*. This is a sense of meaning that emerges from within the material constraints of historical configuration that is, precisely for such reasons, both locatable and ultimately without permanent or timeless foundations. In time and of time, such meaning constitutes a 'way' (Heidegger), a 'passage' (Benjamin) that registers positionality, a responsibility for a location, rather than the universal, accumulative, 'progress' that instrumental rationality seeks to collect around itself.

To think in this non-humanist manner, that is in a manner that precedes and exceeds the 'subject', does not mean to think in anti-humanistic terms: that would be equally arbitrary, equally despotic; that is, equally humanistic. To invert the sign, to turn the formula upside down, is only to reconfirm it. To take critical leave from the history of self-centred subjectivism does not mean to identify with the indifference of the inhuman. On the contrary, the non-humanist is that critical supplement that precedes and exceeds the imperialism of the subject.

For many this critical supplement is what language, understood in the widest sense of the term, holds in custody. Language preserves the performative potential of what exceeds the merely instrumental and the prescriptive. As an unfolding inscription, as a cultural and historical disclosure, language is not a linguistic matter, but a matter of becoming whose lexicon and grammar may be spoken in an ethical and a poetical syntax, by bodies and technology, by sexualities and sounds. The poetry of Hölderlin for Martin Heidegger, a science-fiction future in sound for Jimi Hendrix, the contemporary and future cyborg for Donna Haraway; for each a supplement that is irreducible to the consolations of humanism and the subsequent grounding and reconfirmation of the subject. In this suspension of the humanist disposition, the dispersal of its logic, the weakening of its voice, the displacement of its vision, there exists the invitation to accept the asymmetrical and incomplete world not as the consolatory destiny of a disenfranchised humanism but as the spur, the interrogation, of a non-identity that draws us on.

The sense of art that I am seeking to evoke here lies within proximity of this edge, announcing such a threshold, recalling what sustains us in our transit from the consensus of the known towards an elsewhere, and 'the roads not taken'.[54] This is an art that is irreducible to an ideological or communicative function; it is an art, a poetics, that installs an ethical insistence. At this point, the rationality of a specific formation of representation is required to register its limits. Here a particular sense of the world is confronted with a point of arrest. It is where a reason, an art, an aesthetics, an identity, nurtured in and by such a formation, is required to break with its premises and go beyond itself. To go beyond one's 'self' does not mean to lose one's self in a delirium of self-identification with one's history, technology and culture; it suggests, rather to take into critical custody such a self-centredeness.[55]

To register such limits is to step away from a self-absorption which turns language, history, culture and world over to a sterile, ultimately murderous, preoccupation with property: 'my' language, 'their' culture, 'our' history. To step away and pursue an art, a language, a history, in this dispossessed manner is to render proximate the promise of displacement and alterity, and with it the potential to reconfigure the sense of our selves. This is not an art of sublimation, something that seemingly allows us to relax secure in the contemplation of self-confirmation, but is rather an examination. It is not what allows us to escape our selves, but rather what renders us more susceptible to query and doubt. For it is to propose neither integration nor domestication, but rather a social and historical constellation that irritates and interrogates institutional understandings. Merely to recognise in alterity the relativity of previous claims to absolute sense, knowledge and truth, does not necessarily dislocate the subject's continuing pretence to self-realisation through the objectification of the other; the continuity of that relationship, even relativised and historicised, remains fundamentally untouched. It is rather the observer cured of her or his illusions and self-centredness that permits the observer finally 'not to speak of, but close by'.[56]

The artifice of intellectual distance comes to be replaced by historical and cultural contingency. It is at this point that the ideological imperative of modernity, desirous to render all transparent and subject to its rationalism, comes most acutely to be dislocated and reconfigured. This is why the 'post-' of 'postcolonialism', for instance, is more a spatial than a chronological metaphor. For it not only speaks after the event of colonialism, but also narrates history, above all, 'my' history, from elsewhere, from a site that is de-centred with respect to the socio-technical rationalism that seemingly governs modernity's 'reason'. To bear witness to that elsewhere is simultaneously an aesthetical and an ethical appropriation of the language and cultural identities in which I find my 'self'.

This imposes an *internal* interruption − exposure and critique − in the languages that empower *me*; the languages of occidental modernity that have historically permitted *me* to nominate myself as the *subject* of history and the others its 'objects'. To query and undo that 'critical distance', justified in the name of science, knowledge and 'truth', is to reconfigure the language in which I live and which provides me with my home. An intertwining and interrogation of horizons renders me, in my history and tradition, vulnerable, exposed to a worldling of the world in the search for a reply that is also the acceptance of a responsibility. Not only does this render a previous identity unhomely, but also the passion for murder, the historical, cultural, mental, ultimately physical, eradication of the other, without a secure ground. It would also be to think against the contemporary theoretical drift that valorises space and return thinking to the unstable, quotidian ground of place − to that rough, often resistant passage that absorbs and exceeds us. There, in the unruly exchange between language and land, gender and ground, ethnicity and ethics, exists a disturbing architecture that exceeds the monolithic home that rationalism continue to design. To be inscribed in a particular voice, body, time in which the abstract temporalities of 'modernity' and 'globalisation' are registered, is to be invited to reconceive, rather than merely evacuate, that place. In speaking from a political, historical, cultural and economic somewhere, as opposed to 'everywhere', time is folded in, brought to account, and its linear surface creased to reveal other ways of becoming. This invests not merely the contemporary moment but the overall historical formation that made me.

Beyond representation

History is not simply the excavation of the sedimented past; history is the institutionalised representation of the past. As monograph, book, documentary and developing archive, history is a contemporary activity that recalls the past in an ongoing configuration of the present. History is not what was, history is the testimony of what is: as knowledge, discourse, debate, representation, interpretation. The insistence of realism as the privileged modality of representation is particularly in evidence in Anglo-American cultural formations where language tends to be pragmatically considered as a 'neutral' tool and a fundamentally transparent means of communication. Only in the 'imaginative' sphere of literature and aesthetics is there left licence to contest these instrumental claims. Literary and poetical explorations of language are considered quite separate from the truth claims pursued elsewhere in the more objective or 'scientifically' inclined faculties of the humanities. But even in literature, as in the fundamental twentieth-century narrative of cinema, realism remains central to the subsequent confirmation of the world of the subject. This reduction of language to an objectifying syntax is neither accidental nor arbitrary, but rather lies in the history of the professionalisation of disciplines that 'established standards of nineteenth century science as epistemology and the realist novel as literary model.'[57] Such language, such realism, does nor reflect or embody everybody's world, only the world for some.[58]

It is this historical and cultural configuration of language that allows us to better understand the deep impact of 'French theory' in the anglophone world since the late 1960s. Lacan, Barthes, Foucault, Kristeva, Derrida, Irigaray, Lyotard and Cixous are all critical voices that announce and promote the ontological centrality of language in every understanding of the human enterprise. That side of 'theory' has rarely been considered in full. In English-speaking circles the ontological challenge of language has consistently been reduced to a 'linguistic turn', to a more technical and self-referring understanding, even if evoked as 'semiotic' or 'discursive'; an appropriation that is not too distant from considering language almost exclusively in the rationalism of 'doing things with words' (John L. Austin).[59] The pragmatic insistence in Richard Rorty's *rapprochement* with hermeneutics, not to speak of the hegemony of the self-referential logic of Oxfordian analytical philosophy, support and symptomatise the errancy revealed in this cultural translation of a 'foreign' theory, thereby muting and domesticating its impact in the mainstreams of Anglo-American academic life.[60]

However, not only do we speak, but also language, as historical testimony and repressed witness, speaks through us, ultimately providing us a with a home and a sense, a direction, a way in the world. This is to insist that language yawns open in a series of implications that are irreducible to linguistics or questions of logic and communication. The realist illusion that assumes we directly pass *through* language to observe, capture, describe and explain the *external* world has been directly challenged in historiography by Hayden White. In *Metahistory* (1973) and *Tropics of Discourse* (1978), White justly foregrounds the repressed language of historical narration, insisting on its literary composition and the epistemological ambiguity of its discourse. What this pioneering work unleashes is the consequential undoing of an objectivity secured in the subject–object relationship of humanism and its instrumental understanding of language. In turning to the *writing* of history, to the language and strategies of narrating the past, not only is the constructed nature of reality rendered accountable, but also structures of representation can no longer be subsumed in a merely formal or rhetorical problematic, as though 'reality' was out there, and back there, waiting to be recuperated by the subject. Writing history, at this point, comes to be directly inscribed in the historicity of language itself. Here, as Gregor McLennan perceptively points out, 'the customary distinction between history and the 'philosophy of history' is annulled.'[61]

Considered in this light, the insistence on realism as the privileged mode of representation reveals itself to be more a cultural construction than an ontological guarantee: the reality of representation *is the reality of representation*. This is not to make a modish argument about simulacra and the disappearance of the real (although the insistence on a lack of foundations alerts us to something potentially important); it is rather to argue for taking historical and ethical responsibility for the languages in which truth, knowledge and the sense of our selves is located and spoken. In the insistent coupling of representation and realism lies the presumption that there exists a unique and homogeneous truth. This is to suggest that while there may well be differences of opinion, debate and dissent, intellectual labour invariably progresses towards revealing the *telos* of an underlying and universal conclusion. This putative point of view is unique, it sustains a single rationality, a single truth seemingly guaranteed in the subject-centred protocols of a universalising humanism. But this ubiquitous point of view is itself a product, a prisoner, of a precise historical formation and cultural configuration which, in turn, sustains a regime of representation and its truth claims. If realism permits the possibility of avoiding a critical relationship with the language it deploys in explaining the world – the past, like the present, is simply waiting there to be discovered and represented – a critical historiography can surely no longer avoid confronting the disposition of language and representation in which history and its explanations appear. Caught in the language of time, and the time of language, there is no past in and for itself, there is only the passage of the present perpetually open to reconfiguration by the interrogation of the past: both the past that is interrogated and the past that interrogates.

This means that the past can neither be cancelled nor denied. Rather, recognising in the procedures of recall and the regimes of representation our unique access to the passage of time, the past distinctly remains the past. It can be revisited and rewritten in a limited and contested realism, but in its return it can also pose the challenge of the unrepresentable and the incommensurable. There are limits to representation, something most dramatically posed, for example, by the Holocaust, the *Shoah*.[62] Written in extreme figures and unimaginable horror, reason is unable to reveal exhaustively, or fully register, that historical event, whether in terms of the state institutionalisation of genocide or in the numbing bureaucracy and everyday banality of evil. In the radical incommensurability between the event and subsequent meanings the Holocaust surpasses and disrupts preceding frames of reference.[63] But viewed in this manner the Holocaust is no longer necessarily a unique *exception*, but rather a momentous modern historical event that throws a chilling light upon the limits of occidental reason to divulge and explain the forces of the world it has seemingly created. To the stunning singularity of the Holocaust is to be added what it reveals as a specific event in the formation and realisation of modernity itself.[64] To register the limits of reason, however, is not to install the refusal to think, even the unthinkable. As a minimum, to register the limits of reason is to interrogate the very rationalism that modernity is supposed to embody, and there to intersect its claims of 'progress' with the evident testimony of what exceeds its rationalisation. Rather than 'uniqueness', it is perhaps, as Bob Brecher points out, the *unprecedented* reality of the Holocaust that fractures thought, forcing us to think again.[65] If the Holocaust lies beyond the immediate appropriation of rationalism, and the temptations of explanation that slide, according to Primo Levi, towards justification, it does not lie beyond the historical constellation in which it occurred.[66]

This is to transpose the question of history beyond a liberal fanning out of possibilities whereby the universal adjusts itself to absorb particular and partisan points of view. The acknowledgement of feminist, black, gay and subaltern histories does not in itself necessarily challenge 'continued adherence to common-sense empiricism and realist notions of representation and truth.'[67] To remain within *that* regime of representation, seeking acknowledgement for a repressed narration of the world, is to remain a captive of its language while insisting on an unlikely redistribution of powers. To remain at this point is to repress precisely what the emergence of these diverse histories initially revealed: a regime of representation whose truth claims were dependent upon the systematic repression of others. This is to talk of something more radical and disruptive than simple adjustment. It is to render an inherited sense of representation and truth, a historical modality of picturing and framing the world, deeply problematic, perhaps obsolete.

The challenge to the authority of a discipline such as historiography, to what it purports to tell us about the past, is also a challenge to an understanding of the present and ourselves. To expose the execution of such a design and desire is not necessarily to render the historiographical project impossible, but it is to ask for another type of history and a more limited and circumscribed exercise of its authority.[68] Opposed to the abstract violence of historical objectivity, the problem of historiography comes to be how to represent an absence, how to work through that trauma. To reflect on what a particular history represents for whom, when and how, is to acknowledge Arthur Danto's just affirmation 'that there are no events except under some description.'[69] We always speak from somewhere; we are always located, bound in time, situated. This also evokes Heidegger's *Dasein*, or being-in-the-world without transcendental guarantees. The intellectual withdrawal from the world in order to return to it critically armed as a separate, autonomous being is the perpetuation of what Alain Robbe-Grillet once termed the 'terror' of humanism, 'characteristic of a universe where the answer to every question is "man".'[70] The transcendental subjective–objectivity of humanism gives way to a recognition of cultural locality, to being already subject to the world before we even conceive of it and our selves. The isolated 'I' passes into the temporal communality of the 'event', there experiencing the blurring of the boundary between body and language, subject and object.[71]

The disciplinary edifice of history, as the modern, continually renovated, archive of the uneven and contradictory trammels of an immanent 'progress', is thus transformed into the inconclusive and altogether more disquieting structure of a baroque ruin; a ruin that knowingly bears witness to the representations of the world, to its histories and 'truth', precisely in terms of the limits of language, locality, life. To re-evaluate the regime of representation that permits history to speak, to subordinate 'facts' and 'events' to the languages in which they appear, may well render the concept of 'primary sources', 'documents' and 'archives' unstable, as well as unleashing a disquieting proximity between the 'factual' and the 'fictional', but its central import lies in the insistence that knowledge emerges in the ongoing narration of the world seeking to cure the wound of memory.

Chris Marker's remarkable films provoke a lengthy meditation on the question of memory (and its media). In the film *Sans Soleil*, he relates:

> Who says that time heals all wounds? It would be better to say that time heals everything except wounds. With time the hurt of separation loses its real limits, with time the desired body will soon disappear, and if the desired body has already ceased to exist for the other then what remains is a wound, disembodied.

In the same film a seemingly shared frame, a series of stories, of images, held together in temporal and auditory flow, register the impossibility of reducing all to common understanding. Traces of stories, myths and memories transform history into inscriptions, history into a re-writing. Who is writing whom in this shared space of diverse places and temporalities? Who is looking at whom when the gaze is returned and the privilege of the camera to record life, the 'facts', is contested? In the visual passages from Iceland to Tokyo, to Guinea-Bissau, the Sahel, Hokkaido, Okinawa and the Ile-de-France, where is history made, and who, in the encounter of the political and the prosaic, makes history? Frames of expectancy and explanation are interrupted by 'things that quicken the heart'. These represent stories that weave in and out of official accounts, disturbing their logic. What emerges of history in this temporal account is a wound that bleeds into our lives, proposing a language born of insecurity: poetry.

The limits of politics and the poetics of limits

To contest the humanist view that considers the world, however unruly and turbulent, ultimately susceptible to a unique reason, is for many to abandon home. If politics represents the will to construct and achieve a manageable 'dwelling', then what it fails to grasp, what it expunges in the name of clarity and logic, might bring us to consider the poetical as being closer to the truth of our being in the world. In this key, art is not merely an idle ornament on the structures of the everyday, a stepping out of necessity, but an ethical insistence that invites us to think again. And in thinking again we might return to the presumptions of the 'political' and expose them to the liability of a world that does not necessarily respect or recognise its reason. In that gesture the history of the political is neither cancelled nor abandoned, it is rendered accountable to more than its explicit design. Truth, at this point, is not about mimesis, about the realism and transparency of representation, but is rather the quotidian site of revelation or disclosure.

Here the moral economy of political analysis is caught between a truth not yet realised and strategies of survival, between the purity of the project and the discontinuous results of mediation, negotiation and transformation. The politics of an instrumental rationalism, believing itself capable of rendering real a political will, is inevitably confronted by a supplement that refuses to conform, that frustrates and interrupts its desire. But that unruly supplement does not merely represent the limit of a political will or the other side of instrumental reason; rather it interrogates the very foundations upon which such a rationality depends for its exercise. In exceeding the world of the political this other side of reason, a reason that is not immediately susceptible to rationalism and transparent translation, maintains a necessary distinction between the known and the yet to be realised, between the prescriptive and the inscriptive, thereby *maintaining the limits of the political*. All may well be 'political', but all cannot all be reduced in a single historical instance to the instrumental logic of institutional politics. What shadows and flees that logic – the untimely, unexpected and unruly nature of our individuated and collective being in the world – is what might be called the poetical.

Perhaps there is no separate, autonomous, alternative to the existing capitalist structuring of the present-day world. Modernity, the western-isation of the world, globalisation, are the labels of an economic, political and cultural order that is seemingly installed for the foreseeable future. The capitalist framing of occidental modernity sets the political-econom-ical terms and conditions, not the results, of production and reproduction. Yet there clearly also exist the possibilities – no doubt more local in reach, transitory in effect, and modest in aspirations – of working in, through and across this historical formation. There exists the possibility to dislocate the prevailing 'logic', to frustrate its fetishism, to critique its culture, to deviate its decrees, to 'translate' its trajectories. Perhaps, and despite political proclamations to the contrary, the historical passage from one mode of production to another has never been self-consciously managed and directed.

In the wake of a complex and unfolding inheritance, a political choice emerges between faith (both teleological and theological) in an auto-nomous alternative yet to come and one that seeks redemption in the only place and history at our disposal. This is not to propose an abstract distinction between idealism and pragmatism; that would be too comforting and superficial a prospect. There is rather a distinction to be investigated between the presumption to reduce the world to a sub-jectivist humanism that parades as objectivity in the reconfirmation of the authority of the self even in the most utopic of projections, and an attempt to act, to think, and to be, in a more exposed manner, without the support of such promises. While the former attitude permits the consolation of ensuring moral authority and critical distance, the latter forsakes the comfort of intellectual confirmation, and seeks rather to construe a politics in which to listen to voices, histories, experiences ... silences, is to confront what is not immediately available to the listener's desire and design.

To confront what exceeds the 'political', in order to interrogate both its institutional practices and theoretical premises, is to render proximate and disturbing what cannot be rendered transparent, rational and manageable. Thus, to register the limits of the political is not only to reiterate the more obvious limitations of the organisation and deployment of the power of government and political parties in civil society, but also to preserve the historical insistence of what lies beyond their reach and understanding: the differentiated world and earthly framing that exceeds the particular passages in which they, you and I move, live and die. This appeal to what exceeds sustains Emmanuel Lévinas' noted insistence on the ethical impossibility of ultimate closure, control, totality and the accompanying agenda of rendering all – scientifically, technically, politically, culturally – transparent. What exceeds the ubiquitous desire for closure, conclusion and confirmation of the self, is what exceeds and challenges our understanding. A critical disposition is required to inhabit this threshold, on one side taking political pretensions seriously, forcing their multiple languages (emotive, rational, moral, technical, scientific) into the court of worldly accountability; on the other, registering the unrepresented and the unrepresentable. It is a site in which ontology itself – the assumed ground and foundation of political formulation and earthly acknowledgement – becomes susceptible to interrogation. Once thought and action are displaced from the abstract guarantees of rationalism they encounter a world in which the self is unable to completely possess the self.[72] Here criticism undertakes the apprenticeship of moving within the historical limits that sustains its voice, as thinking undermines a presumed knowing.

To refuse to neatly cleave poetics from politics opens up a path into the question of economic and state power that provokes another way of inhabiting these conditions while questioning their grounds, language and logic. Such a proposal is not pursued as a compromise, or liberal accommodation to the status quo, but as a radical undoing of the very premises upon which such a grammar of political agency depends. This is to seek deliberately to frustrate the intellectual demand for representation, to confuse and obliquely confute a language accustomed to the confirmation and subsequent closure of 'reason'.[73] To query the very possibility of inquiry is to weaken its premises through the resurrection of limits. Or is it really that simple? The recognition of limits can also strengthen the questioning through focusing the inquiry and more finely registering the pertinence of the subsequent critique. This, however, is an approach, a critical modality, practised without formal apparatuses or explicit methodologies.[74] For the concern here is not with the conclusive nature of concepts but with the power of articulation, with the agonistic formation and politics of knowledge, with the language, the grammatical violence, that creates the 'object' and subsequent explanation. In the pages and chapters that follow I have tried to sustain this unruly promise.

Notes

1 Roy Bhaskar, *A Realist Theory of Science*, Leeds, Leeds Books, 1975, p. 189.

2 Benedict Anderson, *Imagined Communities*, London, Verso, 1983.

3 Paul Gilroy, *The Black Atlantic: Modernity and Double Consciousness,* London, Verso, 1993.

4 Quoted in C. L. R. James' classic study, *The Black Jacobins: Toussaint L'Ouverture and the San Domingo Revolution*, London, Allison & Busby, 1980, p. 47.

5 Paul Ricoeur, *Time and Narrative*, vol. 3, trans. Kathleen Blamey and David Pellauer, Chicago and London, University of Chicago Press, 1988.

6 Or, and closer to my present home, in Enzo Striano's literary reconstruction of the life of Eleanora Pimentel de Fonseca, one of the 'martyrs' of 1799, in *Il Resto di Niente*, Cava de' Tirreni, Avagliano, 1997.

7 Hayden White, *Tropics of Discourse*, Baltimore, Md, Johns Hopkins University Press, 1985.

8 Emmanuel Lévinas, *Totality and Infinity*, trans. Alphonso Lingis, Pittsburgh, Pa, Duquesne University Press, 1969.

9 Irving Wolfarth, 'The Measure of the Possible, the Weight of the Real and the Heat of the Moment: Benjamin's Actuality Today', in Laura Marcus and Lynda Nead (eds) *The Actuality of Walter Benjamin*, London, Lawrence & Wishart, 1998, p. 23.

10 Hans Kellner, 'Language and Historical Representation', in Keith Jenkins (ed.) *The Postmodern History Reader*, London and New York, Routledge, 1997, p. 129.

11 Walter Benjamin, 'Theses on the Philosophy of History', in Benjamin, *Illuminations*, trans. Harry Zohn, London, Fontana, 1973.

12 This, as Heidegger argues in *Being and Time* (trans. Joan Stambaugh, Albany, NY, State University of New York Press, 1996), is 'nobody's time', the anonymous time of the 'they' that never dies; for, untouched by individual death, there is always more time.

13 Martin Heidegger in conversation with Richard Wisser, transmitted 24 September 1969 on ZDF and published in Günter Neske and Emil Kettering (eds) *Antwort: Martin Heidegger im Gespräch*, Pfullingen, Verlag Günther Neske, 1988. I am here using the Italian translation: *Risposta: A colloquio con Martin Heidegger*, trans. Carlo Tatasciore, Naples, Guida, 1992.

14 Salman Rushdie, *Imaginary Homelands*, London, Granta-Penguin, 1992, pp. 13–14.

15 Benedict Anderson, op. cit.

16 A. Wellmer, *The Persistence of Modernity: Essays on Aesthetics, Ethics, and Postmodernism*, trans. D. Midgley, Cambridge, Mass. and London, MIT Press, 1991.

17 Wendy Wheeler, 'In the Middle of Ordinary Things: Rites, Procedures and (Last) Orders', *New Formations*, 34, Summer 1998.

18 Quoted in the Italian daily *La Repubblica*, 19/8/99. Further details are available at: www.undp.org/poverty/publications

19 For further details on the ongoing pauperisation of the majority of the United States' population in the context of a growth economy, see Joel Blau, *Illusions of Prosperity: America's Working Families in an Age of Economic Insecurity*, New York, Oxford University Press, 1999.

20 See Daniel Lazare, 'America the Undemocratic', *New Left Review*, 232, November/December 1998. As Lazare persuasively argues, limiting government in a system of checks and balances also means limiting democracy and the 'development of coherent majority rule'. Institutional politics come to be restricted to interest groups and lobbies who have the economical and social means to render themselves visible, hence 'political', resulting in what Lazare bluntly defines a 'counter-democratic regime'.

21 All figures and quotes from Paul Gifford, *African Christianity: Its Public Role*, London, Hurst, 1998. The pessimism of considering that a continent has apparently 'gone missing' needs to be countered by awareness of a precise historical framing that 'simply does not recognise its debts and obligations to Africa', John Reader, *Africa*, Harmondsworth, Penguin, 1998, p. x. As if Africa's past and future is not, as postcolonialists and globalists teach us, also ours.

22 See Zillah Eisenstein, *Global Obscenities: Patriarchy, Capitalism and the Lure of Cyberfantasy*, New York, New York University Press, 1998.

23 Paul Gifford, op. cit., p. 13.

24 Michel de Certeau, *The Writing of History*, trans. Tom Conley, New York, Columbia University Press, 1988, p. 212.

25 Michel de Certeau, ibid., p. 2. See also James Clifford, 'Palenque Log', in Clifford, *Routes: Travel and Translation in the Late Twentieth Century*, Cambridge, Mass., Harvard University Press, 1997.

26 See Trevor Ranger's essay, '"Great Spaces Washed with Sun": The Matopos and Uluru Compared', in Kate Darian-Smith, Liz Gunner and Sarah Nuttal (eds) *Text, Theory, Space*, London and New York, Routledge, 1996. The multiple layering of cultures and powers, resulting in the mutability of landscape and the historical transit of perspective, is most thoroughly investigated by the same author in Ranger, *Voices from the Rocks: Nature, Culture and History in the Matopos Hills of Zimbabwe*, Harare, Bloomington and Indianapolis, Oxford, Baobab/Indiana University Press/James Currey, 1999.

27 Peter Garlake, *The Hunter's Vision: The Prehistoric Art of Zimbabwe*, London, British Museum Press, 1995.

28 Gianni Carchia, *La legittimazione dell'arte*, Naples, Guida, 1982, p. 177.

29 Clement Page, 'Pasolini's "Archaisms": Representational Problematics from Naples to Calcutta', *Third Text*, 42, Spring 1998.

30 For further considerations on representing the 'aboriginal' component of modernity, see Mary Ann Jebb (ed.) *Emerarra: A Man of Merrara*, Broome, WA, Magabala, 1996.

31 Clement Page, op. cit.

32 Michel de Certeau, op. cit., p. 219.

33 Anish Kapoor, quoted in Homi K. Bhabha, 'Anish Kapoor: Making Emptiness', in Bhabha, *Anish Kapoor*, Los Angeles and London, Haywood Gallery/University of California Press, 1998, p. 11.

34 José David Saldívar, *Border Matters: Remapping American Cultural Studies*, Los Angeles and London, University of California Press, 1997.

35 Ian McLean, 'Documenta X and Australians in Oxford: Thinking Globally from Europe', *Third Text*, 42, Spring 1998.

36 I have borrowed the concept of eclectic maps from the Italian architect Stefano Boeri. Such maps seek to suggest an oblique look that reveals what two-dimensional geometry (and its subsequent extension in three-dimensional computer assisted design) cannot 'see'.

37 Frantz Fanon, *Black Skin, White Masks*, London, Pluto Press, 1991, p. 229.

38 This is most eloquently expressed in the final pages of Edward Said's *Culture and Imperialism*, London, Vintage, 1994.

39 Rey Chow, 'Theory, Area Studies, Cultural Studies: Issues of Pedagogy in Multiculturalism', in Chow, *Ethics after Idealism*, Bloomington and Indianapolis, Indiana University Press, 1998.

40 Stuart Hall, 'New Ethnicities', in K. Mercer (ed.) *Black Film, British Cinema*, BFI/ICA *Documents* 7, London, Institute of Contemporary Arts, 1988.

41 Donna Haraway, 'A Manifesto for Cyborgs: Science, Technology and Socialist Feminism in the Late Twentieth Century', in Haraway, *Simians, Cyborgs and Women: The Reinvention of Nature*, London, Free Association Books, 1991.

42 Julia Kristeva, *Strangers to Ourselves*, Hemel Hempstead, Harvester Wheatsheaf, 1991.

43 Barbara Claire Freeman, *The Feminine Sublime*, Los Angeles and London, University of California Press, 1995, p. 71.

44 Immanuel Kant, *Critique of Judgement*, trans. Werner S. Pluhar, Indianapolis, Hackett, 1987, p. 99.

45 Barbara Claire Freeman, op. cit., p. 87.

46 Ibid.

47 Paul Gilroy, 'Art of Darkness: Black Art and the Problem of Belonging to England', in Gilroy, *Small Acts: Thoughts on the Politics of Black Cultures*, London, Serpent's Tail, 1993.

48 Erwin Panofsky, *Renaissance and Renascences in Western Art*, London, Paladin, 1970, p. 120.

49 Ibid., p. 123.

50 Catherine M. Soussloff, *The Absolute Artist*, Minneapolis, University of Minnesota Press, 1997.

51 Victor Burgin, 'Geometry and Abjection', in John Fletcher and Andrew Benjamin (eds) *Abjection, Melancholia and Love: The Work of Julia Kristeva*, London and New York, Routledge, 1990.

52 Gianni Carchia, op. cit., p. 17.

53 Ibid.

54 George Lipsitz, *Time Passages*, Minneapolis, University of Minnesota, 1990, p. 30.

55 Andrew Bowie, *From Romanticism to Critical Theory: The Philosophy of German Literary Theory*, London and New York, Routledge, 1997.

56 From Trinh T. Minh-ha's film *Reassemblage* (1982).

57 Hans Kellner, 'Introduction: Describing Redescriptions', in Frank Ankersmit and Hans Kellner (eds) *A New Philosophy of History*, London, Reaktion Books, 1995, p. 6.

58 On the historical hegemony of vision incorporated in realist narrative and its imperial perception and possession of the world, see Edward Said, *Culture and Imperialism*, London, Vintage, 1994.

59 John L. Austin, *How to Do Things with Words*, Oxford, Oxford University Press, 1976.

60 Richard Rorty (ed.) *The Linguistic Turn: Recent Essays in Philosophical Method*, Chicago, University of Chicago Press, 1967. The phrase 'linguistic turn' was probably first coined in Gustav Bergemann's 1953 essay 'Logical Positivism, Language and the Reconstruction of Metaphysics', reprinted in the Rorty collection. See Frank Ankersmit and Hans Kellner (eds) op. cit., p. 241.

61 Gregor McLennan, *Marxism and the Methodologies of History*, London, Verso, 1981, p. 85.

62 Saul Friedlander (ed.) *Probing the Limits of Representation: The Holocaust Debate*, Cambridge, Mass., Harvard University Press, 1992.

63 Jean-François Lyotard, *The Differend: Phrases in Dispute*, trans. Georges Van Den Abbeele, Manchester, Manchester University Press, 1988, pp. 56–8.

64 For an extensive discussion on the implications of the 'uniqueness' of the Holocaust, see Bob Brecher, 'Understanding the Holocaust: The Uniqueness Debate', *Radical Philosophy*, 96, July/August 1999.

65 Ibid.

66 Primo Levi, 'Afterword' to *If This is a Man* and *The Truce*, London, Sphere, 1987.

67 Keith Jenkins, 'Introduction: On Being Open about our Closures', in Jenkins (ed.) *The Postmodern History Reader*, London and New York, Routledge, 1997, p. 1.

68 A extensive overview of the question in the anglocentric world, written by a historian, and characteristically limited in its cultural and political implications to the linguistic, rhetorical and dialogic understanding of language, can be found in Robert F. Berkhoffer, Jr, *Beyond the Great Story: History as Text and Discourse*, Cambridge, Mass., Harvard University Press, 1995. For a more extensive and inter-disciplinary approach, see Frank Ankersmit and Hans Kellner (eds) op. cit.

69 Arthur Danto, 'Narrative Sentences', *History and Theory*, 2, 1962, quoted in Richard T. Vann, 'Turning Linguistic: History and Theory and *History and Theory*, 1960–1975', in Frank Ankersmit and Hans Kellner (eds), op. cit.

70 Alain Robbe-Grillet, *For a New Novel*, quoted in Elizabeth Deeds Ermath, *Sequel to History: Postmodernism and the Crisis of Representational Time*, Princeton, NJ, Princeton University Press, 1992, p. 119.

71 Elizabeth Deeds Ermath, ibid., p. 106.

72 Reiner Schürmann, *Heidegger: On Being and Acting: From Principles to Anarchy*, Bloomington, Indiana University Press, 1990, p. 1.

73 Ian Buchanan, 'De Certeau and Cultural Studies', *New Formations*, 31, Spring/Summer 1997.

74 Ibid.

2

EARTH FRAMES

Heidegger, humanism and 'home'

> ... what finally harbours us
> is our being shelterless and that we have thus
> turned it into the Open, when we see a threat
> in order to, in the widest compass, somewhere,
> where its law touches us, say 'yes' to it.
>
> Rainer Maria Rilke

> Thinking begins only when we have come to know that reason, glorified for centuries, is the most stiff-necked adversary of thought.
>
> Martin Heidegger

> Objectivity results from language, which permits the putting into question of possession.
>
> Emmanuel Lévinas[1]

Earth frames: the ambiguity of this phrase deliberately intersects the announcement of the earth as the common context of our being with a simultaneous insistence on the multiplicity and diversity of our terrestrial grounding. As persistent, and ultimately sole, sustainer, the singularity of the earth maintains the promise of further, manifold possibilities. Perhaps no other occidental thinker has devoted as much attention to this question as Martin Heidegger. Much in these pages emerges out of dialogue and debate with the thought of this German philosopher. In listening and responding to what this thinker has to say I am certainly not seeking to construe an apology for either the ominous confluence of his thinking with National Socialism in the 1930s or his shocking silence over the Holocaust after 1945.[2] Nor am I anxious to separate out these political and public manifestations from the presumed private autonomy of his philosophy: there are tensions and tendencies here that cannot be neatly delimited nor cancelled. These represent the dangers not only of Heidegger's reflections, but also of all reasoning that has been tempted by the lure of immediate, hence despotic, translation into an effective polity.[3] The century that has recently concluded also bears witness to other instances, carrying other names, tempted by other mandates. In all of this there exists the telling instance of proximity and distance: the proximity of Heidegger to Nazism and the seeming distance of other occidental prescriptions from other totalitarianisms (Stalinism and Maoism, for example).[4] It is tempting to consider such a disquieting relationship of philosophy to politics always occurring elsewhere, in another country, in a diverse political persuasion, as though somehow exonerating other philosophies, other politics, from thinking the unthinkable and bearing the burden of an interrogation that absolves no one from ethical responsibility.

If what Heidegger says to us warrants attention, and I believe that it does, then a thinking that once offered hospitality to the horror it could not come to name, is not likely to proffer the easy convenience of a calm conclusion. In listening to the troubled inheritance of Heidegger, which is also the troubled inheritance of the Occident thinking at the limits, thinking its limits and historical responsibility, I am following a path already frequented in recent decades by critical thought. This does not protect my choice nor sweep away the ethical difficulties, but perhaps simply confirms the verdict of the eminent European and Jewish philosopher Emmanuel Lévinas: 'who undertakes to philosophize in the twentieth century cannot not have gone through Heidegger's philosophy, even to escape it.'[5] For the questions Heidegger asked – the question of being, of technology, of dwelling, language, art and the earth – are questions, notwithstanding the terrible political solution he himself for a time entertained, that stubbornly remain as questions. In their disarming directness and insistence they take us to the heart of the matter: who are we, and what are we doing here? In their repudiation of logical imperatives and their refusal of non-terrestrial verification they undermine much of the self-edification of occidental philosophy. Here, too, danger is encountered. But this is not the danger of thinking surrendering to the immediate temptation of a political 'solution'. No, the danger is rather that associated with all thinking that renounces the reassurance of self-confirmation and insists on inhabiting thought, language and our earthly confines as an opening in which we are drawn beyond our selves, our habits, our histories, our world.

Thus, how I personally have come to be drawn into this opening may well betray a genesis that lies very much on the other side of the ideological confine that seemingly separates Heidegger from how I perceive the formation of my own thinking and being. It may also put in question the self-assured defence of such a divide, revealing a provenance to my thinking that I might consciously wish to disown. I confront a thinking, my thinking, without the comfort of an ideological guarantee. For it is the essential radicality of Heidegger's thought before the question of being, art, technology and language that has bequeathed a body of thought, however disquieting and uncomfortable, that can neither be easily disposed of nor merely banished by ideological condemnation. Despite his personal subscription to an ultimately murderous political project – in which the 'question concerning technology' and the realisation of occidental metaphysics disclosed itself in the physical elimination of alterity through programmed genocide – his thought ultimately exceeds this abysmal configuration.[6] Not only is he forced to think again, but in the end Heidegger's questions, as he himself would insist, do not belong to him.[7] They are questions that come to us through the language of being-in-the-world that precede and exceed each of us. The persistence of such questions indicates an inheritance that cannot simply be cancelled or renounced. Even if from his hut at Todtnauberg in the Black Forest Heidegger would probably have been loath to recognise himself in their present-day diction, these questions continue to speak to a request to change the conditions of thought and inaugurate a new relationship to what both sustains and succeeds us.

The limit, the other

We inhabit an epoch that Heidegger nominated as 'planetary'. It comes after modernity and installs a different affiliation to its history. Accustomed to dividing the globe into binary divisions that reference the distribution of geopolitical, economic and cultural power – Occident and Orient, 'First' and 'Third' worlds, North and South, centre and periphery – the insistence of thinking the planetary reveals a disturbing interrogation whose ultimate implications are likely to be intuitively resisted. For the 'space' that the 'planetary', what these days is often glibly nominated as 'globalisation', refers to is ultimately the compelling location of our historical being. This 'ground' or 'homeland' is neither a patriotic-political entity nor an immediate birthplace; it is not circumscribed by blood and soil: it surpasses and confutes such confines. It is in this obscured and elided extra-territoriality that our home is ultimately founded and secured. These are the historical co-ordinates of terrestrial existence that insist and interrogate us in a manner that does not offer the ready comfort of reproducing the local truths that we hunger for; those 'truths' that assure us in our egotism, that centre us in our world. It is this open region that Heidegger nominates as the site of our being. This is ultimately a home, however constant, which, denuded of guarantees, is without the comfort of foundations.[8] For:

> Being offers us no ground and no basis – as beings do – to which
> we can turn, on which we can build, and to which we can cling.
> Being is the rejection [*Absage*] of the role of such grounding; it
> renounces all grounding, is abyssal [*abgründing*].[9]

Here, in this earthly and exposed place, it becomes possible to conceive
of a thinking that abandons the necessity of the narcissism that sustains
my sense of 'home'. In the recognition of the contemporary epoch as
planetary lies a potential challenge to that self-reflection in the domestic
which is dependent upon a distinct and separated alterity. The historically insistent desire to ensure my voice and being, and confirm my
world, is what the recent development of postcolonial studies has
famously subjected to radical criticism. Yet, even the clarity of this
crucial intervention itself remains forever complicated by the continual
re-centring of the thinking that thinks its limits.[10] Here in the margins
of occidental metaphysics, seeking to step beyond the logic that domesticates and secures me in my world, I also enter a metaphysics of the
margins. For the 'margins' have now become the focus of attention as
they are called upon to bear the critique of the centre. Embracing the
questioning that comes from another world does not automatically nor
necessarily lead to my own intellectual dislocation. To affirm one's own
de-centring can also perversely re-centre it through the very act of abrogation. As the critique, before the seeming impossibility of complete
disengagement from the dictates of occidental 'truth', transmutes into
a metaphysics in its own right it is perhaps less the protocols of the
'postcolonial' and rather the globally disseminated disposition of Western
knowledge itself, parading as the 'universal', that comes under scrutiny.

In the disavowal of the occidental that frequently leads to the transformation of the non-occidental into a metaphysical property, the latter
is once again reclaimed and occidentalised, hence objectified, fetishised.
But, if not that, then what? Is it actually possible to refer to the non-
occidental without in some fashion drawing it into a eurocentric orbit;
without translating and transforming it so that it appears under Western
eyes and within hearsay of occidental discourse? Is it possible to speak
of a language, of representation, of resistance, even of indifference, coming
from elsewhere that is not already inscribed in the economies of the
occidental world?

We also know, however, that translation is always accompanied by
the silent supplement of what fails to be translated, of what is lost in
transit. If the subaltern speak then they already inhabit the space of that
inscription and there in mimicry double and displace the hegemonic
languages that nominate them. However, even if I polemically agree

that the subaltern have not yet spoken (Spivak), or have already spoken (Bhabha), and that in neither case are they transparent nor reducible to what translates, it is still only there, in this instance of (in)comprehension, that I in the West recognise and accommodate this alterity; that is, always in my terms; which is another way to say, as Rey Chow points out, always anthropologising the non-West as *my* possession, as *my* world.[11] To insist on this incommensurable ambiguity is not merely to register a structural difference and the asymmetry of power, as for example between the 'First' and the 'Third' world, between the ex-coloniser and the ex-colonised, but is to acknowledge an ontological gap that no amount of words or theory can fill.

Still, and remaining for a moment on the edge of this gap, it is also here that it perhaps becomes possible to learn not to speak, even if that means not speaking *for the silence* of the other. It may rather be the case to seek to reply, *in the wake of that silence*, to the possessive configuration of language, knowledge and rationalised being that is the West, that is my *self*. This deliberately weakens the logic of thought that, despite the liberal deployment of such seemingly dispossessing nominations as heterogeneity, difference, multiculturalism and hybridity, pathologically and structurally, that is in terms of a desirous power, tends to sustain the opposite. As with all theoretical will, 'postcolonialism' ultimately succours an institutional discourse destined to employ concept against concept, reason against reason, rooted in a language that is unable to abandon the plane of representation and which relentlessly reduces differences to mediations of its own self-same voice. This is not merely the limit of thinking the other, it is the very limit of thought.

Does all this mean that the West is destined to remain the privileged window from which to gaze on and assess the rest of the world? Or is the 'West' itself destined to be reconfigured, translated, and in the process both disseminated and dispersed? Surely, even within the limits of a thought rooted and routed in this particular distribution of power and knowledge, it is possible to tunnel into its pedagogy, to traverse it while seeking to transgress, and thereby attenuate its unilateral hold on the account. To take this step outside the habits of thought is immediately to encounter a more messy measurement of the world. It is one that invariably fails to find easy settlement in the institutional consolations of theoretical reasoning and critical distance.

Seen from afar working the artichoke and strawberry fields beneath Californian skies, or proximate in a Manchester bus queue and over the supermarket check out, I encounter the previously hidden hands, voices, bodies, that sustain my sense of place. These are the frequently dark faces, the mobile, migrant lives, of those whose daily work and structural exploitation ensure my stability. They now stand in my life, my language, the poems I read, 'unsatisfied'.[12]

> A dark woman, head bent, listening for something
> – a woman's voice, a man's voice or
> voice of the freeway, night after night, metal streaming
>   downcoast
> past eucalyptus, cypress, agribusiness empires[13]

We all, consciously or not, live modernity in the 'outraged light' of those who have not survived its imposed indifference, of those subjugated, frequently sacrificed, to the nihilism of its instrumental rationalities. The light of outrage is the light of history 'springing upon us when we're least prepared'.[14] This expression of Adrienne Rich's resonates deeply with the Lévinasian insistence on a sense of history open to judgement in every instance; that is, an ethics that precedes every calculation and verdict, that anticipates the act of thinking history, the act of thought. There is no hiding place, no 'little glade of time' in which we are sovereign enough to subtract ourselves from this judgement. We are profoundly unprotected. To claim protection is to refuse this opening. It is to pray to a God that negates an other. To the Rilkean affirmation of this law of the Open, Adrienne Rich adds:

> Outrage: who dare claim protection for their own
> amid such unprotection? What kind of prayer
> is that? To what kind of god? What kind of wish?[15]

In this 'atlas of the difficult world' such outrage reminds us of the constant exposure to the non-guaranteed space of life. Located in language and the proliferation of re-membering, no one can claim protection. Against the pedagogical prescriptions of abstract 'civility', 'society' and 'community', Homi Bhabha has justly opposed a poetical and political sense of performativity.[16] A pedagogical understanding already knows who the subject of history, and what the just society, is, and 'dare claim protection for their own'. Difference and diversity is inscribed only so far as it reflects the prescriptive, mirrored in the transparent communality of a bodiless, abstract individuality. The pedagogical shuns the possibility of uncertain becoming in, through and across the historical and cultural differences in which we are formed. If the pedagogical accumulates memory in the homogeneous time of progress and the speculative citizenship of humanism, and there forgets, the performative replays the shifting site of memories, of agonism, interruption and challenge, where voices refuse to fade away and continue to persist in their dissonance and dissatisfaction.

In the recent work of both Homi Bhabha and Judith Butler, the Foucauldian insistence on the pedagogical framing of identity formation and identification processes radically concentrates our attention on the constitution – both the physical, instrumental making and the legal, political insertion – of the subject.[17] Against the rigidity of a juridical and institutionally installed subjecthood, both critics endorse the unguarded instance of the performance in which a specific historical subject speaks a complexity that exceeds the pedagogical rule: the legally construed 'ought' is confronted by the historical 'is'. The abstract, metaphysical certitudes of identity – national, ethnic, gendered, sexual – are confronted, challenged and transgressed by the persistent perpetration of an uncertain becoming; a becoming that restates – and the critical tonality in both Bhabha and Butler, as well as its Foucauldian antecedents, here certainly justifies the adoption of a Heideggerean note – being thrown into a world that 'is revealed to be not fully one's own'.[18] It is in seeking to be at home within an ambiguous, uncanny world that is not one's own that directs us towards the potential freedom that arises from an understanding of limits.

Hence, the relentless interrogations in Adrienne Rich's poem 'Eastern War Time', although dramatically referenced though the Holocaust and a Jewish lens, can be further read as an invitation to enter into an understanding of memory (and identity) as the non-guaranteed space in which we make our home. It is memory that recalls a perennial exposure 'on earth and under the sky', reminding us of the contingency of our being in the world without protection. It is memory that discloses this open region by refusing to substantiate our desire for subjective clarity and the temporal suspension of an invariable truth. For when memory speaks it says:

I can't be restored or framed
I can't be still   I'm here
in your mirror   pressed leg to leg beside you
intrusive inappropriate bitter flashing
with what makes me unkillable though killed[19]

Everyone lives memory, but no one possesses it. The house of memory is not simply our customs, rituals and traditions, our bodies, institutions and monuments, nor even our innermost selves and individual unconscious. It is ultimately that place of concentrated being that is the historical hum of our earthly habitat.

It is here that forces speak out beyond the reach of the immediate instrumentality of the world and send me on my way to the other side of language. Here I am directed to the silent insistence of the terrestrial and the presence of an other. This nurtures a thinking that is adverse neither to listening nor to a subscription to limits. I find myself back on the edge of that ontological gap between the assurance of the same and the displacement induced by alterity. This is the gap traversed in the passage from the familiar to the unfamiliar, from the ordinary towards the extraordinary. It is marked by the irruption of a transforming and ecstatic time that, as an excess of language – in memory, in poetry, music, in art, in dread, in love . . . radically interrupts the continuum of the predictable, inviting me to reconfigure my relationship to the languages in which I reside.

The other side of history

The earth is distributed in space distinguished by boundaries – the recognisable and the opaque, the familiar and the foreign, the proximate and the distant: the demarcation of confines. These provide the co-ordinates of the *domus*, the habitat . . . our home and identity. Yet, in establishing these contours, these contexts for the domestic, the boundary invariably turns out to be boundless, the frontier flees rigid demarcation, and the absolute is revealed as a restraint arbitrarily imposed against the threat of the incomprehensible.[20] Borders reveal themselves as unwelcome questions, as sites of dislocation. In accounting for space, in domesticating the earth, there emerges the discipline 'geography': from the combination of the Greek *ge* (earth) and *graphe* (writing). Geography is the 'writing of the earth'. To insist on the contingent activity of the 'writing of the earth' is to double the theorem of a neutral 'science' with a desired and interested inscription. This is to exchange the presumed certitudes of epistemological mastery, here represented by the discipline of geography, for the uncertainty of an interrogation that travels, that wanders, without the guarantee of a final destination. The 'disinterested' geometry and grid order of spatial knowledge is supplanted by the partiality of inhabiting a provisional and animated place that evokes a passionate mapping.[21]

This, again, is to slacken, if not directly untie, the knots that have secured me in my sense of belonging, that apparently girded together the differences of the world in a unilateral appreciation and provided the ties that pulled me towards the continual confirmation of my home. The powerful links between historicism, scientism and imperialism, the disposition of knowledge that since the late Renaissance have institutionalised and propagated the hegemony of the occidental ego, here weaken and begin to experience the pressure of interruption. The purist desires these discourses sustained – the millenarian dream of realising the epistemological and political absolute – has been interceded and doubled by what that modernity repressed in the violent collectivisation and simultaneous oblivion of exploited, colonised, crushed, enslaved and exterminated histories, lives, bodies.

If my becoming is already and always under way then it can never be synonymous with the self-assured departure of rationalism seeking the house of theoretical conclusion. My becoming is more than the immediate causality that reason in the name of science, technology and progress is able to reveal and seemingly master. Becoming is rather the other side of this desired transparency and domination: it is the hidden source of the world, the other side of history, the ambiguous energy that dispatches us along an unmarked road into ways of being that have yet to be recognised. Heidegger nominates this as the 'ek-static' site of our being. It is what draws us beyond the habitual into the open region of terrestrial environs, into what exceeds and precedes our arrival. History at this point is not condensable to the accumulated record of progress – what assures us in our centrality – but is rather what provides and hides our being, what establishes and exposes our limits.[22] In this fissure between the chronology of time and our becoming, between the transparency of succession and the opaqueness of dwelling, emerges:

> what Heidegger calls *Ereignis*: 'the event of appropriation'. It is an event in which all that happens is the non-coincidence of History with itself; all that happens is the play of being and man. Or, rather, the coincidence of completed metaphysics with technology leaves a remainder, an unthinkable inverse, namely a more radical and ancient relation of being to man which governs all phases of History.[23]

As supplement, as the residual that technological rationalism, scientism and positivism fails to account for, *Ereignis* reveals the other face of the world, co-ordinating our historical condition in a manner that official history necessarily obliterates in order to permit the rationality of its explanations to hold sway. The escape from this latter narrative is an escape from the imposition of a knowledge that already knows in advance who we are and what we are doing; that has already defined the subject and object of its discourse and extended its grammatical dominion over the world in a deadly syntax of objectification.

Technology is humanism

It is here that the modernist knot of metaphysics, humanism and technology is most tightly bound together. Contrary to popular perception and superficial sentiment, technology and humanism coincide to become equivalent terms. They are not antagonistic, each is dependent upon the other. For technology represents the apex of occidental metaphysics and its appropriation of the world around a sovereign 'I'. Occidental metaphysics and technology co-exist in a common will to world the world in a subjective and subjugated image. The world is cognitively framed to appear before the subject as object, ready to be grasped and dominated, brought into its sovereignty and control. This subjectivism is the premise for the subsequent instrumental usage of our earthly surroundings. It is this metaphysical structure, the presumption that the world is subordinated to the will, language and domain of the subject 'who experiences his basic relation to beings as the objectification – understood as mastery – of what encounters him', which most succinctly clarifies the Heideggerian phrase that 'the essence of technology is by no means anything technological.'[24] But this is not merely a matter of thought that renders radically proximate the seemingly opposite poles of humanism and technology. Insisting on the subjectivism that passes for extreme objectivity, Heidegger dramatically concentrates our attention on that disposition of knowledge and power, widely associated with the work of Michel Foucault, which assures us in our centrality, in our world.

As Heidegger puts it in 'The Age of the World Picture': the transformation of 'the world . . . into picture and man into *subiectum*' constitutes the 'fundamental event of the modern age.'[25] Reduced to a common frame, to an object that reflects my presumed needs, the distances and complexities of my terrestrial habitat, its persistent, differentiated and incalculable forces, are rendered immediate in the calculations, techniques and technologies that represent me, and only me. Other modes of thinking and being are banished from the account. As Leslie Paul Thiele rightly notes: the 'world picture becomes humanity's chief measure of reality. Effectively, it becomes reality itself.'[26]

And, he continues:

> At this point, in an ironic twist, the objectivity of the world itself vanishes. All that exists now comes to exist, from a technological perspective, because it is represented or produced by us. As Heidegger notes, 'whatever stands by in the sense of standing-reserve no longer stands over against us as object'. We are, therefore, no longer speaking solely of an anthropocentrism

that objectifies its world in order to exploit it. We are speaking of an 'unconditioned *anthropomorphism*' that creates a world in its own image.[27]

Whatever is not enframed in this 'unconditioned anthropomorphism', whatever fails to represent and reproduce this logic, is excluded from thinking and banished from understanding.[28] My becoming is supplanted and ultimately displaced by my being the world: humanism is disclosed as occidental subjectivism. But when the world becomes mine, reduced to a unique logic that serves only to reflect me, there occurs a dramatic reduction in my freedom. This is not the imperious freedom that delivers the world over to me to do with as I please, but the freedom of being in the world and there finding my way. This is not the freedom to dominate, but rather the freedom to be in the world, experiencing limits and the wonder of what exceeds my egotism. This is the freedom to respond to, and take responsibility for, worldly dwelling not as its master but as its caretaker.[29] This is to propose a sense of being that is neither a godhead nor a religious force, although it may pertain to the sacred, but as something that exists beyond the subjectivist humanism of individual beings and remains irreducible to it.

For what exists, and continues, beyond the imposition of a *ratio* intent on calculated revelation and the subsequent realisation of what by now is a planetary design, poses a persistent interrogation. It provides occasion for the interruption of a language whose particular differentiation in history, science, technology and the market place is secondary to its common metaphysical desire and design. It is to query an abstract logic that believes itself capable of transcending every particularity, every place, every body and experience, in order to arrive at a complete picture, a full and exhaustive explanation. To refute the mapping of the world along a single grid plotted from the perspective of a unique point of view, requires us to acknowledge, even better, to listen to, the other side of the particular history that installs this desire and drive for homogeneity. It is to confront the arid comfort of homecoming – the confirmation of the premises that map and insure the metaphysical journey and its technological realisation – with what sticks out, deviates and disturbs the explanation, with what cannot be easily accommodated, with what in this particular order of things remains homeless. It is here that what is referred to as history, the ideology of knowledge that believes it can globally grasp the dynamic of our being, encounters its confines.

How does one live in this 'open region'? Confronted with a world that is seemingly organised by the overwhelming will of an instrumental rationality bearing the names of reason, science, technology, progress, and their global configuration in contemporary capitalism, is there simultaneously an ethos, a terrestrial call, a ground, that overflows and is irreducible to such a logic? For Heidegger, as for the poets, the musicians, the artists and the custodians of the extraordinary and the ecstatic, an answer is sought in the errancy of language. Language opens on to the enigma of what resists and withdraws from the merely rationalist organisation of the world, of what permits the question to survive as a question, to live on, returning again and again bearing the promise of an interruption.

As the historical missive of this covenant between the earth that houses us and the world we construct, it is in the extreme exposure of the languages we speak, and which speak us, that, rendered in the work of art, discloses the wonder of this constant, yet ever-changing, tension between the opening of the earth we inherit and the closure of the world we inhabit.

> In setting up a world and setting forth the earth, the work is an instigating of this striving. This does not happen so that the work should at the same time settle and put an end to the conflict in an insipid agreement, but so that the strife may remain a strife. Setting up a world and setting forth the earth, the work accomplishes this striving.[30]

It is art, according to the 'post modern primitive' Cherokee artist Jimmie Durham, that is 'looking for connections that cannot, may be, should not, be made'.[31] It is the working of art that returns us to our lives, our language, our poems, 'unsatisfied'.[32] This is to come to a threshold in which the poetical, the unexpected turn of the languages we inhabit, might in the end reveal more than the instrumental politics of the rational.

The poetic supplement

In the gap between the global reach of the occidental *ratio* and the terrestrial frame that permits that very possibility to take place, between a world conceived in the singular where all differences are measured along the axis of progress, profit, calculation and information, and an earthly habitat that also houses what diverges and remains incommensurable to such evaluation, I spill out of the frame that my 'origins', my home and history, ultimately my prescribed identity, has sought to provide me with. It is perhaps the poetical transgression of instrumentality that best reveals my temporal relationship to the ground that supports my body, my voice, my history, by both confirming and confuting it, by simultaneously investing and exceeding it, by taking it to the limit and there consigning it to the safekeeping of the possible. Held in this time, co-ordinated in this earthly location, my under-standing is torn between the regimentation of representation – what I have been taught to refer to as the 'truth' – and the opening that supplements while all the time sustaining the arbitrary closure of this *logos*. To be attuned to this interval, to listen to what emerges in this gap, is to receive a sense in which my world can neither be subjective nor sovereign.

It is in this space that the languages of music, literature and the unconscious constitution of memory surge forth; here the poetic discloses its potential, and the marvel of an expression that thwarts and mocks instrumental reason takes place. It is here that our wonder before an inheritance finds temporary shelter. Synchronised to this discontinuity, to this ambiguous being in history that both marks me in time while calling me beyond it, propels me to breach instrumental reason – the will to will, the replacement of questioning by calculation – with that supplement that lives on in dreams, myths, songs, dance, language . . . This is a poetics that, notwithstanding the planetary realisation of occi-dental metaphysics in the global rationality of capital and technology, narrates survival. It is such a rationality, this universal configuration of occidental logic, *not the tools and techniques themselves*, that returns us to Heidegger's insistence that 'the essence of technology is by no means anything technological.'[33]

In 'The Origin of the Work of Art' (1936), Heidegger speaks of the tension or 'strife' in the work of art between the possibilities of being in the world and a particular historical appropriation and configuration of such possibilities. In the disarming simplicity and rude insistence of these premises, Heidegger proposes a radical transvaluation of Western aesthetics. Our concern before the work of art is here drastically returned to the material constant or originary ground, the earth, whose confining limits insist and inscribe themselves in every epoch, constraining every world. Beauty, perfection, genius – the habitual and abstract terms of aesthetics are radically renounced for a consideration of art in terms of what sustains and extends our existence. This is not to talk of art in terms of communication, it is to resist such functionality for an ethical insistence. The measure of beauty is replaced by the astonishment before what surges before us, through us, and beyond – what is here glimpsed but is habitually in abeyance: the very question of being. Michel Haar comments:

> Indeed what is dislodged is both the primacy of intellectual enjoyment of the sovereign subject-spectator as well as the primacy of the artist or 'creator' and his or her creative states, which subjectivism holds to be the absolute origin of art.[34]

A rapid characterisation of the present epoch, the epoch of the planetary, of the global, would suggest two diametrically opposed tendencies: that of the domination of occidentalism which is simultaneously accompanied by the proliferation of diverse worlds. Nowhere can this be better illustrated than in the modern-day art world. Here the dominion of the Western art market − its institutions of criticism, galleries and museums − is constantly forced to overreach itself in housing works of art that reveal other worlds (in which the very idea of 'art' and the 'aesthetic' as an autonomous quality may well be absent, or else secondary to another agenda). In this attempted domestication, the very categories − ethnic, primitive, 'Third' world, minority − that previously sought to catalogue (and contain) these works, rendering them subaltern to the disposition of the Euro-American art discourse, become increasingly brittle. Aubrey Williams, David Medalla, Jimmie Durham, Chila Buman, Uzo Egonu, Sonia Boyce, Guillermo Gómez-Peña, Rotimi Fani-Kayode, Anish Kapoor, Claudette Holmes, are artists who belong to more than one category, more than one world. Not only do their art works, seemingly from elsewhere but actually and profoundly proximate, often directly relay a relationship to the grounding of the earth in their symbolic materiality (while not necessarily ignoring the Western, academic, avant-garde discourse into which they are inserted), but also their very being requires a response that breaches the confines of the hegemonic logic that is apparently explaining them. By resurrecting in our midst not merely a plurality of worlds this art, once labelled 'primitive', 'native', 'aboriginal' or 'ethnic', but now equally cosmopolitan in its marketing and execution, dramatically draws us into the interval between the earth and a world, offering both a diverse configuration of that encounter and with it a diverse sense of being in the world.[35] This 'other art' is not a wholesale alternative existing to represent a primordial 'authenticity' that challenges the presumed inauthenticity of modernity, but is rather an 'other' view that opens up a gap, an interval, between the accustomed and unknown, between a world and another, permitting the question of our becoming to continue to continue. It is an art that simultaneously interrupts and interprets modernity.

In this opening, in the rift installed by the act of painting, by a film, a snatch of music or piece of prose or poetry, the perceived alterity of the art work and its particular 'origins' splices the assumed singularity of a planetary logic with the thread of the trans-national which, as the site of *mutual translation*, is where idealised 'authenticities' are inevitably travestied. The apparent homogeneity of the institutional discourse of art – the gallery, the exhibition, the journal, the museum – is here intricated and interrogated by the same work simultaneously occupying diverse modalities: as object of the occidental, academic gaze (aesthetic and commercial fetishism), as a ritual, mythical or religious sign (ontic difference), as a cultural and historical way of being (ontological difference). The composite effect of such differences, irreducible to a single explanation or site, works to promote a multifarious 'dynamics of change' rather than the flat index of 'progress'.[36] Experiencing and exploring the rift between the potential of terrestrial becoming and the immediate limits of the local world I inherit and inhabit, the art work here becomes central. It no longer pertains either to a distanced exotica, or to an idealised aesthetics, but is proximate and interrogative. For it discloses the interval between the ordinances of the world and its interruption by what both exhumes and eschews the fragility of its order. That is why true art, as opposed to the consolatory techniques of reproducing the familiar, is invariably shocking, even terrible. It refuses to be domesticated, it arrests our world and in rendering it extra-ordinary sharply underlines its restrictive nature by enhancing the promise of our 'capacity to be' (Heidegger).

> Art is the setting-into-work of truth. In this proposition an essential ambiguity is hidden, in which truth is at once the subject and object of the setting. But subject and object are unsuitable names here. They keep us from thinking precisely this ambiguous nature, a task that no longer belongs to this consideration. Art is historical, and as historical it is the creative preserving of truth in the work. Art happens as poetry. Poetry is founding in the triple sense of bestowing, grounding and beginning. Art, as founding, is essentially historical. This means not that art has a history in the external sense that in the course of time it, too, appears along with many other things, and in the process changes and passes away and offers changing aspects for historiology. Art is history in the essential sense that it grounds history.[37]

Modernity other-wise

Now, to cast light into the historical and aesthetical tradition out of which I most directly emerge, and turning the previous considerations inwards, would be to recast European modernity in a more vulnerable light. To reiterate that most subtle commentator on the Baroque, Christine Buci-Glucksmann, this involves listening to the shadows where the interior ear of history catches the unsaid and the unsayable as time devours itself while seeking an unattainable deliverance in the prosaic minutiae of the world.[38] It is perhaps in the shadowed modernity of the Baroque, a counter-tradition that constantly seeps into my considerations, that an alternative aesthetic, subject to an emergence between terrestrial enframing and worldly becoming, can be both glimpsed and heard. The volatile engagement between body and mind, between the finite sensuality of the passions and the dreamed infinity of reason, between the physical insistence of dance and the abstract geometry of rationalism, what classicism was later to resolve in favour of the latter, is here consistently and dramatically sustained.[39] In this exploration of worldly contingency where vision – El Greco, Caravaggio, Giordano, Ribera, Rubens, Rembrandt, Velázquez – is always less than transparent, and sound summons ungovernable sensibilities, there exists a notable resonance with the experience of late modernity. Drawn from either end of this historical epoch, from its putative beginnings and presumed conclusion, it is a proximity suggestively caught in the alliterative slide between 'Baroque' and 'rock'. In John Dowland's lute and Jimi Hendrix's guitar, a temporal insistence in the promise of terrestrial enframing sounds sharply against the other-worldly abstraction of classical aesthetics for whom form is timeless, the detail merely feminine, the ornament decadent.[40] Further, listening to the Baroque, just as listening to jazz, is to catch the intimation of a critical passage from the unilateral sight of the imperious gaze to the dispersal of pitch, from reveries of transparency where all is revealed to the interminable journey of sound and the infinity of the inconclusive.

Playing Baroque music today, listening to it, discussing it, is to participate in a mediation between past and present, between diverse pasts and presents. Antoine Hennion, to whom I owe the suggestive coupling of Baroque and rock, has pointed out that the techniques employed in the musical execution of the Baroque – all those debates over how to play Bach 'correctly', for example – are part of a cultural syntax, an enunciation, a performance.[41] As such the musical object is never an object, that is some 'thing' that is neutral and scientifically sustained, no matter how much technique and technology is applied to the relationship, but is always a historical mediation, always the 'world's world-ing'.[42] Further, to insist on an 'exact' or 'correct' rendition of the musical score is to negate the performance, the style, the accidental or ornamental, the contingent: all elements that are not marginal, but were deeply central, to the Baroque aesthetic. The act of interpretation, of translation and appropriation, takes us beyond the formal and peda-gogical devices of the Baroque into something more, into that excess of performance which is the custody of the present. It is ultimately our modernity that permits the Baroque to return and to be. For although inevitably denigrated it is modernity itself that paradoxically permits us to return to other 'Bachs', that permits us to interrupt the linear inher-itance of a music whose presumed 'degradation' and fading authenticity is proportional to its distance from its historical point of 'origin'. It is modernity that permits us to enter the multiple sites, appropriations and configurations of the Baroque.[43] These are the fruits of a musical re-membering that interrupt the classical development of an assumed continuity and tradition with elements that deviate and reroute the sounds through the material traces (musical treatises, commentaries, evidence from the visual arts, from literature, from critical thinking and costume) that mediate and configure both the then and the now. It is these traces, deposited in the ontology of sound, in the languages we inhabit, that permit us to return in order to reconfigure our present and re-call our pasts.

Further, to listen to Baroque music is to apprehend in its timbre and tone a history of the abject. Composed around the mortal fall into a decentred, flawed and contingent province, into a post-Copernican universe that was beginning to test its limits in colonialism and the anguished freedom of a seeming limitless reason, it is a music that plays at the confines of a precarious world that is no longer either unique or unequivocal. Over three centuries later, the sound of Jimi Hendrix also proposes a music that plays at the border; a sound at the cross-roads of musical genres and cultural identities, caught between worlds, confronting their consolations. In both cases, listening draws us into an aesthetics of ornamentation, an aesthetics of excess, that overflows the frame of prescribed reason and cultural restraint, and strains across the frontier, seeking an elsewhere, an encounter with alterity. Here, to consider the ornament – the trill or mordent on the lute, the arabesque patterns etched in electricity by Hendrix – is to consider that instance of decentring in which the unilateral drive for clarity and conclusion is thwarted by a transversal cut that sends sound spiralling out of ordained structures into the unmapped insistence of the corporeal and the contin-gent; there to encounter the promise of the possible.

On earth, beneath the sky

Hendrix encounters Heidegger in an insistence on the 'thingness' of sound, 'by granting the thing, as it were, a free field to display its thingly character directly.'[44] Sound, as an event in the history of being, betrays the metaphysics of the beautiful, exposing it to a worldly vulnerability; opening it up to a terrestrial imperative that refuses the assumption that the greater the distance from the event the deeper the critical and aesthetic appreciation. Turning that prejudice around, and suggesting that the augmentation of distance increases the fetishism, we can then listen to John Cage's silent musical composition 4'33' as the loudest critique of such distanciation and the object it desires to construct. 4'33' was performed for the first time on the 29 August 1952 at Woodstock. An individual sits before a piano for the duration of the piece. What is heard is not the execution of a musical score, but the sound of the event, the silence that represents unorganised sounds. What is brought to the listener's attention is not merely the arbitrary cut in the continuum of sound that configures a performance, as an apparently autonomous work, even a performance without deliberately executed musical notes. What is brought to our attention is also the semantic importance of the nothingness against which the sonorial 'situation' is foregrounded as an event in a particular time and place, susceptible to the incidental and chance, unique: not as an object but as an event.

The structure of transcendence, the final word, the critical judgement, is mocked by the proximity of the incipient mortality of the temporal imperative. Music becomes an object that never is. Sound surges beyond a 'propositional way of understanding.'[45] The analyst is cast loose into a mediation in which the conclusions of 'critical distance' are perpetually postponed by a language that simultaneously constitutes both the subject and object of its discourse. Here the critique of the sociology of music, like the critique of all sociologies, becomes the critique of a desire to construct an 'object' outside the languages of appropriation, of mediation . . . outside its worldly existence.

I find myself confronting the dissolution of 'critical distance', and of learning to live without an exterior point of view; of having to construe and construct a sense from within, of having to argue and articulate a mediation – hence also to contribute to the configuration of sound as a cultural and historical event. Here, the 'sociologist' also becomes part of the 'sociology'. Whether researching and playing a Weiss prelude on an eighteenth-century lute (invariably a reconstruction), or exploring the tonal qualities of the electric guitar, sound is being configured as an event in the history of being. It is mediated, translated . . . performed, made to speak, becomes a cultural utterance. It is where the celebrated Nietzschean aphorism on the ontological illusion of the facticity of being is most clearly accented; there are no facts, only interpretations are testimony to the 'fact': music exists (and persists) in its interpretation. Here to play – both to listen to and to perform – the Baroque is less to insist on a historicist and 'authentic' interpretation, and is rather to celebrate its passage, thereby opening up a space in language in which its traces live on in further configurations.

In the work of art what is simultaneously revealed and withdrawn is this insistence of being: what we are aware of but rarely attend to or fully consider. Being is not something that stands over and above us, outside time and place; it is rather something that precedes our individuality and consigns us to our temporal habitat.[46] Being is not an object of which the subject is able to have an adequate understanding. To consider the implications of this prospect is to invoke an invitation to think in a manner in which the centrality of he or she who thinks can no longer be automatically assumed; that is, to think in a manner in which the thinker is consigned to the custody of the language in which she or he appears. Here historical and cultural agency can never be validated from a theoretical conclusion, but only in an ongoing, worldly becoming.

Accordingly Heidegger nominates as true history not the mere accumulation of time in facts, figures, institutions and events, but the unfolding of being that comes to meet us, and which never disappears. To turn to history, as to turn to the work of art, is to concentrate on the centrality of recollection (*Andenken*) and remembrance (*Erinnerung*).[47] What comes out of the past to meet and envelop us is a historical memory greater than the individual act of remembering: 'I can't be restored or framed'.[48] Here, what cannot be contained in the representation lives on as a shadow or trace that confutes and exceeds the subject-centred economy of appropriation and its pedagogy of identity. What comes out of the past bears more than any individual can contain or explain. Further, it reveals the past as a future. For what precedes us is the potentiality that permits us to turn to face the unhomely and confront the enigma of our being. In the danger of the present we are drawn to the past that discloses the history that has brought us here. As though in a flash (what for Walter Benjamin 'flares up' in a moment of danger) a sense of being that outshines its oblivion in the calculations of its present appropriation is returned to the care of memory and the inheritance of the possible.[49]

Heidegger suggests that what teaches us to live within this inheritance of the possible is the over-determination of the earth; this he nominates with the expression *Übergewalten* or its 'over-powers'. The earth as a frame, as a 'delimiting current', maintains the vital tension between the exposure to an opening and the closures imposed by a particular world. Art, memory and language do not merely reflect their time. Like the earth they are both within and beyond every epoch, sustaining that 'open region in which man dwells'. The apparent oblivion of the question of being in the rational calculus of modernity's 'progress' is not an excuse for nostalgia. For, as Heidegger himself insists, there is no choice, no possibility of subtracting ourselves from this world and somehow turning back to an imagined truer or more authentic state. The recovery of a fuller sense of terrestrial dwelling can only occur here in the time, technology and history we inhabit. Even in the empty soul of the machine there still beats the heart of a world that is never fully autochthonous. It depends and calls upon the extra-worldly, upon the terrestrial ground and the language that both precedes and sustains its suspension in a specific historical epoch. In that most modern of sites – the digital mapping of existence in information and cyberspace – the cry of being, which is never exhausted in the voice of technology, and the call for what exceeds and sustains us, lives on and coexists in the same circuits, bodies and world.

What cannot be contained

Such a critical voice intersects the occidental privileging of the disembodied logic of the gaze (*theoria*) that disseminates in language the instrumental calculus of technological representation. The latter is what Heidegger calls *Gestell* or 'enframing'.[50] Letting things be, rather than only appear within the calculated representations that mirror our desires and design, means to leave a space open to the autonomous call of what exceeds me. Through his insistence on the priority of listening to the unrepresented but irrepressible side of language, Heidegger performs an epochal critique on the hegemony of vision in occidental thinking. The tension between seeing and listening, between imposing a view on the world and receiving the disclosure of language, is embedded in the very nature of being. This poetic supplement, although hidden, unseen, is always there awaiting us. To listen to this side of language, is to transgress the rigid body of logic in which we are apparently held. It is a historical reply that speaks in terms that cannot be strictly limited to its own particular epoch.

Dead generations press in. To speak is always to speak in the wake of language. Language records and speaks of this abeyance. In this interval emerges our home. Language provides the shelter and, as poetry, as music, as muse, as memory, sings 'the accord – always the same, always changing – which at each moment traverses being-in-the-world in its entirety, modulating the difference between things and world, between Earth and world.'[51] In the opening of language I encounter the fragrance of what I cannot ever fully know: the unfathomable heart of dwelling 'in the house of the world on Earth and under the sky'.[52] This is the site of ethics.[53]

This unforeseen and unexpected arrival returns history to listening to that side of the narrative, often silent, or else heard as an incomprehensible murmur, that receives and recognises an other. This extension of 'my' history to an other is also the acceptance of such a supplement in its own irruptive terms. It is where the abstraction of alterity is rendered vital, concrete and my own temporal account rendered responsible. This means to confront tradition with what it cannot contain, for the guest is clearly the envoy of 'the vicissitudes of translation.'[54] A history, that exposes itself in the anticipation of such an arrival, is a history of the interruption introduced by the stranger, by the other. This is a history of transit and translation in which the continuity of the regime of representation through which I understand the 'political', tradition and democracy, citizenship and state, limits and law, is brought into an unguaranteed critical focus.[55] The other introduces the other side of politics, or an other politics: the repressed side of my representation. What inserts itself into this discourse, into this precise historical, cultural and political situation, is that there no longer exists the other *for* me, but only the other *beside and beyond me*.

If it is in the languages of the present planetary epoch that this particular 'worlding of the world' occurs, then to produce and view an art work, to perform and to listen to music, to read, to work, travel and inhabit this world, is to live the discrepancy between apparent ownership and the unremitting resistance to such a codification and control. For language bursts beyond instrumental arrest in calculated representation to forge a way in the world. The truth that is encountered in language is not a truth that is reducible to a reflection between the subject and its object; rather it is what, through the rift between our earthly framing and worldly existence, emerges to refuse such 'grammatical' solutions. For what issues forth is precisely what eclipses and necessarily confounds the expectations of a rational will seeking immediate resolution. It is the radicality of thinking through and beyond the occidental tradition of rationality and its mapping of western subjecthood over the world that lives on and survives along the paths of Heidegger's inheritance, despite the reactionary political exit which he himself entertained in the 1930s.

After Nietzsche it has been Heidegger who has taught some of us to turn away from the abstract accumulation of subjective understanding. A thinking that presumes to withdraw the world into the parameters of the rationalising self is challenged by a thinking that occurs in the unprotected passage of time, finitude and limits. In the *an-archic* disposition of a thinking without foundations which contests an imperious rationalism – both the abstract architecture of rationalism and the bludgeoning pragmatics of empiricism – there exists the dangerous temptation of a voluntaristic leap into the historical certitude of effective action, the desire to leave a decisive mark, a permanent signature in time. Against this devouring insistence the work of Emmanuel Lévinas provides a critical deferment that permits the possibility of limiting such thinking to the advantage of something else, something further: the custody for what exceeds the very act of thinking and its tendency to render coherent, equal, homogeneous, whatever it encounters. In the face of this alterity, intellectual, political and moral certitude, whether located in the transparent logic of rationalism or the opaque constellation of the history of Being, is perpetually disturbed. In this lies the passage between what Lévinas refers to as the 'said' and the 'saying', between the 'grammar' of being and its eventual speech, between the theoretical and its active unfolding in the encounter with others.[56] This is the interval between ontology and ethics, between being for oneself and being for an other whose alterity can never be circumscribed within the confirmation of one's own position. In this radical and disturbing shift from the dominion of identity to the prospect of difference, the impossibility of closing the circle of identification and knowledge brings occidental reason to its limit.

To move from the logic of the said to the potential opening of the saying is to register in the presence of another the possibility of speaking otherwise. This is to fold a tradition, a thought, back over against itself, and there to extract from its limits a new sense of departure. To interrupt the law of habitual reasoning is to insert the time of alterity that cannot be absorbed in the identity of the speaker and the already spoken; it is to insist upon an understanding of history not as the site of identification, but as the memory of a wound that can never be closed, that remains 'open to the wind from outside' (Georges Bataille).

In this step beyond subjectivity we find ourselves in the company of both Heidegger and Lévinas. But whereas the former dispatches the claims of subjective rationalism to the all-encompassing preoccupation of Being, Lévinas definitively breaks out of the confines of that thought to deposit the question of identity in the language of the non-identical that draws us beyond ourselves. While the question of Being may travel with others, it ultimately returns to its source, confirms the circle of identification and, even if having nominated an essential alterity, closes the corporeal and the unruly in the reassuring enclosure of abstract repose. To cast my sense of being outwards towards what both exceeds and sustains me, is, on the contrary, to travel without return towards infinity.

The 'tragedy' of listening, as opposed to the comfort of the closed perspective, is, as Edmond Jabès noted, that it opens up a relationship with the infinite, the unthought, proposing a measurement of silence by the unknown and the unknowable.[57] It is where the aesthetical and the ethical become one. To install a responsibility inflected towards infinity is what Lévinas proposes. In the proximity of an other, the fragile circle of self-confirmation snaps, and language escapes the semantics of the self. For Lévinas it is not from our limits and finitude, ultimately our death, that our thought should issue forth, that is ontology, but from what we can never fully experience nor explain. While the former reaffirms the unicity of thought and its power even over the unthought and unthinkable, the latter requires a response that is never reciprocated, that is unable to speak for, and yet accepts responsibility for, that disquieting difference and irremediable distance. This is to return to reason, to thought, the alterity it seeks to obliterate in order to confirm its sovereignty.

What emerges at this point is most obviously not a conclusion, a planned edifice of theory managing practice, but a course in the world that persistently turns away from such closures towards the open region in which we learn that our capacity for understanding is always less than the history we inhabit, and that the language we inhabit exceeds our expectations. A sense of being that both sustains and exceeds me as an individual, courses through and beyond the thought that seeks to grasp it; it remains irreducible to instrumental will. It is this condition, to return to the lines by Rilke that open this chapter, seemingly so delicate and precarious, that can nurture us. As an apprenticeship in limits, a way of thinking and being, this framing of the questions that configure me proposes a radical and irreversible postponement in the understandings I have inherited from modernity. Sense abandons a rigid semantics for the apprehension of direction, movement and the incomplete.[58] This will now be explored in the context of both Baroque and contemporary musics, in questions of architecture, in diverse literatures . . . in the memories of modernity consigned to the custody of language, sound, buildings, and our living in their midst.

Notes

1 Rainer Maria Rilke, 'Für Helmuth freihern Lucius von Stoedten', quoted in Michel Haar, *The Song of the Earth: Heidegger and the Grounds of the History of Being*, Bloomington and Indianapolis, Indiana University Press, 1993, p. 122. Martin Heidegger, 'The Word of Nietzsche: God is Dead', in Heidegger, *The Question Concerning Technology and Other Essays*, trans. William Levitt, New York,

Harper & Row, 1977, p. 112. Emmanuel Lévinas, *Totality and Infinity*, trans. Alphonso Lingis, Pittsburgh, Pa, Duquesne University Press, 1969, p. 209.

2 Heidegger's stunning silence needs also to be listened to alongside other silences, otherwise he becomes merely the convenient totem of occidental guilt in the disavowal of intellectual responsibilities before the event of totalitarianism, mass murder and genocide. While Herbert Marcuse's private letters to his former teacher, and the generic response of Horkheimer and Adorno's *Dialectic of Enlightenment* (New York, Seabury Press, 1972), are not to be overlooked, Heidegger's post-war silence on the Holocaust is nevertheless joined, with the explicit exception of Hannah Arendt, by much of the left-wing German emigration of the 1930s. As Alfons Söllner, speaking in the conference 'Exiles and Emigrés' at the Los Angeles County Museum in April 1997, pointed out, this silence was not really broken in Germany until 1968.

3 The story is told by Hans-Georg Gadamer of Heidegger, after his resignation in 1934 from the Rectorship of the University of Freiburg, encountering a colleague on a tram who quipped 'Back from Syracuse?' The reference is to Plato's voyage to Syracuse in Magna Grecia (Sicily) to advise the tyrant Diogenes II on matters of government, and rightly reminds us that the recognised foundation of occidental thinking was itself deeply embedded in the desire to impose an absolute illumination on the world. Knowledge of an authentic truth hidden behind the immediate (and false) appearance of the world justified the Platonic will that, ironically, Heidegger's *oeuvre* irreversibly dismantles.

4 Hannah Arendt also made this point in her essay 'Martin Heidegger at Eighty', in Michael Murray (ed.) *Heidegger and Modern Philosophy: Critical Essays*, New Haven, Conn., Yale University Press, 1978.

5 Emmanuel Lévinas, *Ethics and Infinity: Conversations with Philippe Nemo*, trans. Richard A. Cohen, Pittsburgh, Pa, Duquesne University Press, 1985, p. 42. A more recent signal is to be noted in the obdurate centrality of Heidegger – 'a thinker, whose great, early unfinished work (*Being and Time*) remains so fertile a source of both theoretical inspiration and political disquiet' (p. xiii) – within a rigorously argued materialist conception of history and time in Peter Osborne's *The Politics of Time: Modernity and Avant-garde*, London, Verso, 1995.

6 The idea that the West, not merely Nazi Germany, but the histories of the European confinement of alterity, also discloses itself in the modern technology, state bureaucracy and political totalitarianism that rationalised genocide in the Holocaust has been reiterated by Zygmunt Bauman (*Modernity and the Holocaust*, Oxford, Polity Press, 1989) and Philippe Lacoue-Labarthe (*Heidegger, Art and Politics: The Fiction of the Political*, Oxford, Basil Blackwell, 1990). It is an argument that has been explicit for decades in Lévinas's critique of the aggressive imperialism of occidental philosophy – including the abstract uniqueness of Heidegger's own concept of 'Being' – for reducing all to the 'primacy of the same' (*Totality and Infinity*). It is also a central motif in the poetry of Paul Celan. Nevertheless, nominated as a shocking German 'exception', or solely a Jewish 'experience', the Shoah is still contested, and not only by conservative critics, as a dramatically unqualified interrogation of modernity and its 'reason'.

7 This 'turn' in Heidegger's thought can be most significantly delineated around his changed understanding of 'home' in the 1930s and 1940s as it shifts from location in nationhood and sanguinity (F. R. Leavis was writing in a similar

vein, complete with references to 'race' and 'national genius' in his noted 1930 volume, *Mass Civilisation and Minority Culture*, Cambridge, Gordon Fraser) into the homelessness of Being encountered 'on the way to language'.

8 This is Heidegger writing in 1946 in the 'Letter on Humanism'. Thirteen years earlier the political and genetic sense of a German homeland, explicitly addressed to the triumph of National Socialism, was publicly endorsed by the philosopher in his assumption of the Rectorship of of Freiburg University in April 1933 (he resigned ten months later); see Martin Heidegger, 'The Self-Assertion of the German University', in Günther Neske and Emil Kettering (eds) *Martin Heidegger and National Socialism*, New York, Paragon House, 1990. Needless to say, the radical conservatism of Heidegger's thought neither commences nor concludes with these two moments.

9 Martin Heidegger, *Nietzsche*, vol. 4, trans. Frank A. Capuzzi, San Francisco, Harper & Row, 1982, p. 193.

10 For a decisive discussion of thinking this limit see Stuart Hall, 'When Was "The Post-Colonial"? Thinking at the Limit', in Iain Chambers and Lidia Curti (eds) *The Post-Colonial Question: Common Skies, Divided Horizons*, London and New York, Routledge, 1996.

11 Rey Chow, 'Film as Ethnography; or, Translation between Cultures in the Postcolonial World', in Chow, *Primitive Passions: Visuality, Sexuality, Ethnography, and Contemporary Chinese Cinema*, New York, Columbia University Press, 1995.

12 Adrienne Rich, 'Eastern War Time', in Rich, *An Atlas of the Difficult World*, New York and London, W. W. Norton, 1991, p. 44.

13 'A dark woman, head bent, listening for something', in Adrienne Rich, ibid., p. 3.

14 Adrienne Rich, 'Eastern War Time', op. cit., p. 49.

15 Ibid.

16 Homi K. Bhabha, 'Unpacking My Library ... Again', in Iain Chambers and Lidia Curti (eds) op. cit. In this essay Bhabha performs an exemplary reading of Adrienne Rich's 'Eastern War Time' (to which I am in debt here) that contests both the abstract civility of liberal moral philosophy and the localised affiliation and focus of communitarian politics.

17 Homi K. Bhabha, *The Location of Culture*, London and New York, Routledge, 1995; Judith Butler, *Gender Trouble: Feminism and the Subversion of Identity*, London and New York, Routledge, 1990.

18 Leslie Paul Thiele, *Timely Meditations: Martin Heidegger and Postmodern Politics*, Princeton, NJ, Princeton University Press, 1995, p. 177.

19 Adrienne Rich, 'Eastern War Time', op. cit., p. 43.

20 For a stimulating discussion of this theme, see 'Marking Boundaries/Crossing Lines', in Syed Manzurul Islam, *The Ethics of Travel: From Marco Polo to Kafka*, Manchester, Manchester University Press, 1996.

21 Ibid. In her book-length discussion with Heidegger – *L'Oubli de l'air*, Paris, Editions de Minuit, 1983 – Luce Irigaray considers this grounding of being in the earth to be the ultimate site of metaphysics. What, in her opinion, remains in oblivion is the air that sustains us and permits us to be. It is the unrequited gift of air, of the breath of woman, of a mother, that permits the entrance and erection of man. That this observation opens up a further and crucial path through the world signalled by gendered difference I have no desire

to negate. However, I am not convinced that the framing of the terrestrial in Heidegger necessarily excludes this possibility, or that the concept 'air' is necessarily any less metaphysical than 'Earth'; unless we are appealing to the guarantee of diverse physical properties: invisible/visible, ethereal/solid, etc. Both air and the earth, in their centrality to our being-in-the-world, have been equally occluded from the edifice of occidental thought. And then, as has been so frequently observed, the dismantling of metaphysics can never fully escape the metaphysical language it is undoing.

22 Michel Haar, op cit., p. 2.

23 Ibid., p. 3.

24 The first citation is from Martin Heidegger, 'φυσιζ in Aristotle's Physics', quoted in Leslie Paul Thiele, *Timely Meditations: Martin Heidegger and Postmodern Politics*, Princeton, NJ, Princeton University Press, 1995, p. 198; while the second is from 'The Question Concerning Technology', in Martin Heidegger, *The Question Concerning Technology and Other Essays*, New York, Harper & Row, 1977.

25 Martin Heidegger, 'The Age of the World Picture', op. cit., pp. 133–4.

26 Leslie Paul Thiele, op. cit., p. 199.

27 Ibid., p. 200, emphasis in original.

28 The expression 'unconditioned anthropomorphism' comes from Martin Heidegger, *Nietzsche*, vol. 3; *The Will to Power as Knowledge and Metaphysics*, trans. J. Stambaugh, D. Krell and F. Capuzzi, New York, Harper & Row, 1987.

29 Or, as Heidegger puts it, as caring shepherd. This also opens up the question of the relationship between metaphysics, technology and capitalism in the making of the modern world system. While much critical attention has been given to the third term, understood as the fundamental mode of production of the modern epoch, the former two have been relegated to the sphere of the superstructure and the social relations of production, both subservient to the omniscient drive of capital. Yet technology does not emanate from a unique mode of production. Lenin's dream of marrying electricity to socialism in a future collectivity, and Ford's mass production of individualised mobility, were ideologically separate but technologically (and metaphysically) proximate. Even if the cynical screw of history were to insist that it was all capitalism, state socialism being but another name for its installation, it seems to me that listening to Heidegger on the question of metaphysics and technology allows us to better understand the will of capital in order to interrogate, prospecting to interrupt, its seemingly seamless history of 'progress'.

30 Martin Heidegger, 'The Origin of the Work of Art', in Heidegger, *Poetry, Language, Thought*, trans. Albert Hofstadter, New York, Harper & Row, 1975, p. 49.

31 Jimmie Durham, *The East London Coelacanth*, ICA video, London, Institute of Contemporary Arts, 1993.

32 Adrienne Rich, 'Eastern War Time', op. cit., p. 44.

33 Martin Heidegger, 'The Question Concerning Technology', op. cit., p. 287.

34 Michel Haar, op. cit., p. 97.

35 On the complex negotiated entries to, and exits from, the institutional frame of occidental art discourse, see the decisive discussion on Australian Aboriginal art in Eric Michaels, *Bad Aboriginal Art: Tradition, Media, and Technological Horizons*, Minneapolis, University of Minnesota Press, 1994.

36 Gilane Tawadros in Jean Fisher (ed.)., *Global Visions: Towards a New Internationalism in the Visual Arts*, London, Kala Press, 1994.

37 Martin Heidegger, 'The Origin of the Work of Art', op. cit., p. 77.

38 Christine Buci-Glucksmann, *Tragique de l'ombre*, Paris, Galilée, 1990, pp. 16–17.

39 Anne-Laure Angoulvent, *L'Esprit baroque*, Paris, Presses Universitaires de France, 1994.

40 Naomi Schor, *Reading in Detail: Aesthetics and the Feminine*, New York and London, Methuen, 1987. Schor is referring to the classical ideals of Sir Joshua Reynolds and a misogyny of the aesthetic in which the coupling of maleness to form, and femaleness to formlessness, are central to its vision.

41 Antoine Hennion, *La Passion musicale: une sociologie de la médiation*, Paris, Edition Métailié, 1993.

42 Martin Heidegger, 'The Thing', in Heidegger, *Poetry, Language, Thought*, op. cit.

43 Michel de Certeau, *The Writing of History*, New York, Columbia University Press, 1988.

44 Martin Heidegger, 'The Origin of the Work of Art', op. cit., p. 25.

45 Ibid., p. 24.

46 It is on this point that after 1945 Lévinas takes his distance from Heideggerean ontology, arguing that the anonymity of Being has forgotten the question of the human which is secured in being-for-another. This is an extremely delicate and complex point that does readily separate out into a choice between Heideggerean ontology and Lévinasian ethics. The critique of 'humanity' and 'humanism', iterated in Heidegger's noted letter on the argument, and later extended by Michel Foucault ('Man is an invention of recent date. And one perhaps nearing its end', *The Order of Things*), does not imply espousing the inhuman. For Heidegger's incisive critique of the artificial rigour of such binary oppositionsal logic, see pp. 225–6 of the 'Letter on Humanism', in Martin Heidegger, *Basic Writings*, op. cit. For an enthusiastic presentation of Heidegger's thought by Lévinas himself in 1932, see Emmanuel Lévinas, 'Martin Heidegger and Ontology', in *Diacritics*, Spring 1996. The essay is preceded by a useful introduction that plots both the resonance and subsequent divergence between these two thinkers, see Committee of Public Safety, '"My Place in the Sun": Reflections on the thought of Emmanuel Lévinas', ibid.

47 Michel Haar, op. cit., p. 71.

48 Adrienne Rich, 'Eastern War Time', op. cit., p. 43.

49 While, for obvious ideological reasons the differences are rapidly identified, the affinity of Heidegger and Benjamin's thinking in their respective understandings of memory, tradition and language is rarely noted. For an exception see the section 'The Pearl Diver' in Hannah Arendt's 'Introduction' to Walter Benjamin, *Illuminations*, trans. Harry Zohn, London, Fontana, 1973. Peter Osborne has also reflected at some length on the 'uncanny resemblance' of Heidegger's and Benjamin's understanding of historical time, an understanding that 'relies upon the interruptive force of some notion of the ecstatic to disrupt any straightforward narrative continuity': Osborne, op. cit., p. 175. However, this proximity, apart from Benjamin's own expressed antipathy to Heidegger, is fiercely contested by Fabrizio Desideri. In *La Porta della Giustizia: Saggi su Walter Benjamin* (Bologna, Edizioni Pendragon, 1995), he writes: 'The Benjaminian *Jetztzeit* (the

presence and actuality of the instance of a temporal constellation) radically demonstrates through the use of the very same term to be polemically opposed to Heidegger's *Jetzt-Zeit* (which indicates the worldly instances of the 'now' that pass indifferently from one to another). In such a situation only a strong dose of philological and theoretical recklessness permits the possibility of identifying the two concepts' (ibid., p. 180). It is certainly the case that for Benjamin memory revealed the redemption of the vanquished that opened up a gate on the future, while for Heidegger it provoked the remembrance of the oblivion of being. Yet, despite a sharp distinction between conceiving human history as a catastrophic, disjunctive, time, and terrestrial being in terms of radical continuity, I feel that a potential resonance – heard above all in a shared commitment to listening to language – cannot be simply surmounted or rapidly discarded by philological and theoretical fiat.

50 Martin Heidegger, 'The Question Concerning Technology', op. cit.

51 Michel Haar, op. cit., p. 114.

52 Martin Heidegger, quoted in Michel Haar, op. cit., p. 115. The considerations in this present paragraph are deeply indebted to Haar's evocative reading of Heidegger and Rilke.

53 This also explains why in Heidegger we find no explication of ethics as a body of thought or conduct: the ethical is always, already inscribed in the question of dwelling and the being of language that secures us. This ground, although historically experienced, is neither local nor fixed. It is what, in permitting us to be, sends us on our way. Lévinas' critique of Heidegger at this point for being rooted in the 'pagan moods' of the soil is perhaps an overtly reductive response to the sweep that Heidegger implies.

54 James Clifford, *The Predicament of Culture: Twentieth-Century Ethnography, Literature, and Art*, Cambridge, Mass., Harvard University Press, 1988, p. 24.

55 Jacques Derrida speaking at the Institut Français, Naples, 4 November 1996.

56 Emmanuel Lévinas, *Totality and Infinity*, trans. Alphonso Lingis, Pittsburgh, Pa, Duquesne University Press, 1969.

57 Edmond Jabès, quoted in Christine Buci-Glucksmann, *L'Enjeu du beau: Musique et Passion*, Paris, Galilée, 1992, pp. 179–80.

58 'not the "meaning" of being, but its directionality; the "sense" as the direction in which something, e.g., motion, takes place (the acceptance of both the English "sense" and the French sens – "sense" of a river, or of traffic – stems, not from Latin, but from an Indo-European verb that means to travel, to follow a path)': Reiner Schürmann, *Heidegger: On Being and Acting: From Principles to Anarchy*, Bloomington, Indiana University Press, 1990, p. 13.

HISTORY, THE BAROQUE
AND THE JUDGEMENT
OF ANGELS

There is no health; Physitians say that wee,
At best, enjoy but a neutralitie.
And can there bee worse sicknesse, then to know
That we are never well, nor can be so?

John Donne[1]

Donne's words echo with the 'fall into secular time', with the fall into a world that 'is fractured into a series of discrete entities, dissolved from some supposed transcendent state of primal and eternal unity.'[2] An anthropomorphic universe, whose ultimate and inaccessible truth was once secured in the revelation of God, is decentred by an indifferent heliocentrism. Humankind finds itself consigned to a permanent exile, exposed to the raging sickness of the world, where time, truth and the body are ravaged by history and the error of its ways.[3]

It resonates with its perceived place in the universe as the art of witnessing, as the art of testimony. Lost in space (Kepler, Pascal), decentred, the uniformity of logic and nature is punctuated by the accidental: the ornamental, the decorative and the monumental. The continuum of urban space is interrupted and deviated by the ephemeral and the surprise that threatens the persistence of its order.[4] As 'mere appearance', as a *facciata*, the ornamental reveals the essential 'structure of feeling' of the Baroque. Here in the aesthetics of the embellishment, in the refusal to conclude and acknowledge a natural order, in the insistence of a temporal witness and the accidental provocation of the event, we behold the senses at work as they unfold, interrupt and deviate the predestined and the ordained.

The *facciata* and the ornament

Santa Maria del Giglio in Venice was unveiled in 1683. It presents us with a *facciata* in which religious references have been completely substituted by a sculptured paean – 'strutting statues in the common stage postures of the day' (John Ruskin) – to Antonio Barbaro and his family.[5] The façade by Giuseppe Sardi is dominated by the statue of this Venetian admiral. Beneath his feet are scenes from six naval battles against the Turks, statues of his brothers, and the maps of six cities (Zara, Candia, Padova, Roma, Corfu, Spalato) that featured in the military and diplomatic life of this Venetian commander. The whole affair is crowned with the statue of Glory flanked by the Cardinal Virtues, and accompanied by Honour, Virtue, Fame and Wisdom. In this public display of historical triumph an apparent transcendence is knowingly undermined by a pomp and vanity built on the transient emblems of mortality.[6] We view a façade, a spectacle, a canvas, a screen, in whose glance the Baroque reflects upon itself. Caught in history, guaranteed by nothing but its own death, this sensibility extracts a sense of being from a continual dialogue with its limits. Its purpose lies within itself: the erotics of the gesture, the designed frustration of form and function that supplements and subverts the closure of *logos* and makes of language an event whose artificial, historical truth echoes throughout the grammar of the epoch.

Between the melancholy melody and sombre chords of John Dowland's *Semper Dowland, semper dolens* (1604) and the echoing bass ostinato and haunting arpeggios of Silvius Leopold Weiss's *Tombeau sur la mort de Mr Comte d'Logy* (1721), between these two lute pieces, we traverse the musical arc of the Baroque. The lute itself, delicate and intricate in its construction, tuning and the execution of its music, is an allegory of the fragile bridge that spans the extremes of the rational and the unrepresentable that so characterises the age. Already by 1750, the year in which both Weiss and Bach died, it was destined for the antiquarian, its place taken by the altogether more robust, rational simplicity of the guitar.

The lute masters of England, France and Germany cast their sonorities in the shapes and tempos provided by existing dance patterns subsequently collected into suites: the galliard, the alman, the gigge, later the courante, the minuet, the gavotte, the bourée and the sarabande. Such borrowings were not merely imitative as innovative. They drew attention to the making of music in the borrowed measure:

> The characteristic approach by which the various metric, melodic and harmonic models provided by contemporary dance are adapted by the virtuoso instrumentalist to exclusively, non-choreographic ends is, however, only too open to the temptation of artful elaboration, subtle dissimulation of the original model and its sublimation in the interplay of idiomatic figures and passages.

In this way, the instrumental composer-performer takes possession of the tradition of dance music, reproducing it on his
instrument and subjecting it to further compositional and/or
'practical' elaboration-which itself becomes the centre of artistic
interest in the new composition.[7]

Alongside the exploration of such existing structures, of equal importance was the musical freedom of style and execution cultivated from
Dowland to Weiss, from René Mésangeau to Denis Gaultier and Robert
De Visée, in the fancies, preludes, fantasies, and their sombre culmination in the funeral oration of the tombeau. What pulls me to the lute,
and to the latter group of compositions, is the insistent inscription of
the melancholic in these scores. Dowland's titles are, as always, emblematic reminders of this sensibility: *Lachrimae antiquae*, *Forelorne Hope Fancy*,
Farewell; but it is with the seventeenth-century tombeau of the French
and German lutenists that this tendency reaches its apotheosis. These
compositions mark time – *Monsieur Bianrocher* (Dufaut), *Monsieur de Lenclos*
(Gaultier), *Baron d'Hartig* (Weiss) – in a perpetual dialogue with the
dead. To interpret the past is also, as Michel de Certeau points out, to
inter it: to honour and exorcise it by inscribing it in the possibilities
of language.[8] To name and mark past time and recover it for the present
is to produce a *tombeau*, a funeral commemoration that simultaneously
celebrates life.[9] For it 'is to make a place for the dead, but also to redis-
tribute the space of possibility, to determine negatively what must be
done, and consequently to use the narrativity that buries the dead as a
way of establishing a place for the living.'[10] It is, perhaps, from this
encounter, along the borders of different worlds, of life and death, where
certainties are transmuted into circumscribed limits, and the ego mocked,
destabilised, and temporarily held in melancholy before being irreversibly
undone by a mean mortality, that the poetics of the Baroque draws its
greatest resources.

In the ornamental the Baroque reveals the corner-stone of its structure:
'Artefice, as sublime meaning for and on behalf of the underlying, implicit
nonbeing, replaces the ephemeral.'[11] A sustained appoggiatura in the
melody, rhythmic variations in the bass, a lingering dissonance hovering
between notes (acciaccatura), a rapid trill or accidental note, the tremolo,
the mordent or the bite, are all ornaments that register tonal uncertainties; shades of potential discord that conduct us into the folds in sound.
Although seemingly auxiliary they reveal themselves to be obligatory.[12]
The ornamental, Lorenzo Bianconi writes, is 'a term which is appropriate
only if one recognizes the decisive structural role of the ornament in
instrumental music.'[13] As if a jewel, the ornament or 'grace note' is not

an afterthought, a subsequent embellishment added to the finished work, but is rather the essential point towards which the work strives.[14] Like the small windows high up in the Baroque cupola the ornamental notes cast light down into the interior. They direct us into the creases in the body of sound. We traverse the melody and descend into the *basso continuo* of the world.[15] A sombre incertitude, hovering over the formless abyss that lies at the bottom of being, pulls us down through the sound to release a tragic vision of the world and a musical redemption of truth.[16] Over our heads the 'centre' continues to oscillate in the arabesque of an elaboration that is never an 'extra', but is essential to the execution, to the unfolding that disseminates the tonality.[17] As an opening in the sound, usually improvised, it surprises the form with the individual responsibility and freedom of the performance.

The body, in particular the hand directly inscribed in music by lute tablature, sustains the production and sustenance of sounds between fingers and strings, and provides an immediate and intimate code for the initiated. As Marin Mersenne observed: 'They perhaps thought that they would gain greater glory by keeping this Art secret than by divulging it: this is why the pieces coming from their hands are never played as they were intended, unless they are first heard and learned by themselves.'[18] This forcefully reminds us that the language of the Baroque is elliptical. It neither pretends to be transparent nor presumes to be eternal. Sense is unfolded into a sensibility, is in-corporated in a temporal 'here' where language becomes the art of the interruption.

Magic, mortality and the distrust of mimesis

The Platonic idea of a perfect form, the circle which functions as the transcendental guarantee of a harmony to which the heavens were expected to correspond, is displaced by Kepler's discovery of the ellipse traversed by the planets. The circle is breached. The centre is duplicated and dispersed within the ellipse. The archetype fractures, the orbit vacillates, the mind migrates. The closed order of cosmology gives way to the infinity of astronomy.[19] Suspended between anterior and posterior certainties — the precedence of Renaissance humanism and the subsequent convictions of scientific logic and rationalism — the Baroque involves a self-conscious act of throwing a construction over nothing. Alone, and responsible for our actions and the place of our making, we acknowledge Giordano Bruno's 'heresy' in Zarathustra's joy.

In the parable of Bruno's heresy lie the seeds of a dilemma that will cast its shadows over the century that opens with his public execution in Rome, February 1600. Alongside the popular mythology of the persecuted man of reason and science speaking out against Papal obscurantism, is the perhaps more significant claim to be made on his behalf against the Inquisition for a freedom that permits a highly erudite magician to speak his mind without being reduced to ashes at the stake. This, of course, is the argument so brilliantly sustained by Frances Yates in her book *Giordano Bruno and the Hermetic Tradition*.[20] But where she sees in Bruno (and Campanella), for example, the public termination of an esoteric Renaissance discourse before its disappearance underground into more obscure settings (the Rosicrucians, the Freemasons), and its inevitable replacement by the scientific, post-Copernican formation of the modern epoch, I prefer to think that Bruno's thought constitutes a perennial disturbance. The provocation of Bruno thinking the infinite draws our attention both to the ambiguous languages of the Baroque and to the repressed shadows of rationalism. Giordano Bruno, after all, was condemned as a 'man of letters'. His 'errors' stemmed from textual hermeneutics, from his interpretation of certain Gnostic texts, particularly those carrying the collective name of Hermes Trismegistus. He was a sixteenth-century semiotician who proposed an erudite, however mystical, reading of a decentred infinity that happened to formally coincide with the emerging, scientific geometry of space.

Yet the magical manner of reading the logic of the universe does not simply disappear, it haunts and shadows subsequent enquiry. Before his death, and well into another century, Isaac Newton consigned his manuscripts to a trunk. The trunk was discovered by Keynes in 1936. The writings in it are concerned with Biblical exegesis, and with works on alchemy and magic. They starkly illustrate how 'the primary physicist was also the ultimate magician'.[21] We are here dealing, as Loup Verlet points out in his book on the contents of that trunk, with the occlusion of an initial discontinuity, with the hiding of the fractured foundations of a discourse. We are presented with a version that excludes breaks and ruptures, with a version in which the contents of the trunk are ignored and denied. Newton's years of study of 'mystical language' are invariably separated and subsequently cancelled from his scientific production. But, as Verlet points out, the mathematisation of reality with which Newton's model established the basis of modern science, perhaps finds its genetic moment within a religious problematic that is inspired by and continues to seek responses in other, 'non-scientific', forms of knowledge. Here, suspended between the co-ordinates of mathematics and magic, we are back with Bruno.

The sense of loss, the rude displacement, the fall from grace into the immense landscape of an incomprehensible and infinite (dis)order, in which humankind 'rolls away from the centre towards X' (Friedrich

Nietzsche), surely inaugurates the geography of Baroque melancholia, the installation of irony, and the modern sensibility of historical secularism. Trapped in the fragility of a desire for transcendence, for completion, for the homecoming of truth, the Baroque acknowledges in the very fabric of its language, in its voluptuous accommodation of loss, a destiny of interminable peregrinations that reveal in every instance, in 'all the mornings of the world', the folly of such a presumption.[22] Every statement, gesture or expression is immediately doubled by doubt, every resolution by the uncertain shadows of an imminent dissolution. It is this realisation 'of a truly temporal predicament' that so profoundly animates the Baroque dissemination of allegory and irony.[23]

In this doubling, where the subject refuses to stand unequivocally by its own statements, irony displays both the refusal to give up expository discourse and the impossibility of assuming it totally. The interplay between statements about objects and reflection about these statements as objects is ambiguous. The subject is placed in a transcendent position with respect to discourse, but only to deny the possibility of being the guarantor of transcendence.[24]

The empty sockets of a skull, fresh flowers between its teeth, gaze blankly upon the everyday street.[25] The world, words, women . . . truth, have become fickle, unstable tokens of a destitute cosmology: falling stars, children begot with mandrake root, the sound of mermaids singing – signs destined to reveal their falsehood 'ere I come, to two or three'.[26] The temporary abeyance of transcendental guarantees, prior to an imperious rationalism once again claiming the universe for humankind, permits the recognition of the full autonomy of representations whose only reason lies within themselves. Fallen to earth, language, images and signs, 'stunningly joined to nothing', can only respond to their passage and presence on this mortal coil.[27] The acknowledgement of the image in and for itself, of the temporal construct of the artifice, of the simulacrum, 'implies the closure of metaphysics and the complete acceptance of the historical world.'[28] Yet this is compounded, rather than contradicted, by a simultaneous intolerance to loss. For the fierce consolation of Protestantism and the aggression of the Inquisition are only seemingly opposed symptoms of a deep reluctance to forgo: both institutionalise an intolerance to loss. In refusing to give up the lost object, the primal thing, the assurance of timeless truth, the terrestrial signatures of signs and sounds continue to gesture across the abyss of time in a perpetual mourning that contributes directly to the Baroque affect:

> Like a tense link between Thing and Meaning, the unnameable and the proliferation of signs, the silent affect and the ideality

that designates and goes beyond it, the imaginary is neither the objective description that will reach its highest point in science nor theological idealism that will be satisfied with reaching the symbolic uniqueness of a beyond. The experience of nameable melancholia opens up the space of a necessarily heterogeneous subjectivity, torn between the two co-necessary and co-present centers of opacity and ideal. The opacity of things, like that of the body untenanted by meaning – a depressed body, bent on suicide – is conveyed to the work's meaning, which asserts itself at the same time absolute and corrupt, untenable, impossible, to be done all over again. A subtle alchemy of signs then compels recognition – musicalization of signifiers, polyphony of lexemes, dislocation of lexical, syntactic, and narrative units – and this is immediately experienced as a psychic transformation of the speaking being between the two limits of nonmeaning and meaning, Satan and God, Fall and Resurrection.[29]

So, the world is not only decentred but also doubled by the coeval insistence on dogma and doubt in every discourse. Open to construction and determinism, the world is also susceptible to a poetics of ambiguity, to a cleft in reason where rational design can slip into the alliterative contours of a dream.[30] The straight lines employed in astronomy and architecture for the geometrical rationalisation of time and space are shadowed, mimicked and mocked by alchemy and necromancy, by magical equations, emblematic insignia and the terrestrial trappings of life, before it all evaporates in the deceptive order of music: the note hangs in the air, and then falls away. In the fall . . . in that transient, slipping away, in that exceeding of representation, the functional and the rational are exposed as fragile faiths: logics, despite their declared neutrality, that are always circumscribed by human desire. Nowhere is there more starkly displayed than in the insistent application of 'science' to music found in the writings of Pierre Gassendi, Marin Mersenne and René Descartes. Seeking a universal harmony in the geometry of sound and an arithmetic of the passions, they employed mytho-mathematics of Greek and Byzantine provenance that invariably betray the alchemical, astrological and magical drives that continually shadows Baroque reason.[31]

If the shortest distance between two bodies is a straight line, it is the shock of the allegoric that provides the most rapid transport from the obvious into the hieroglyphic and the other, obscured centre of the ellipse. Nicholas Dyer, architect, responsible for the building of seven new churches in the cities of London and Westminster in 1711, here reveals a logic that accords with an unsuspected design:

And thus will I compleet the Figure: Spittle-Fields, Wapping
and Lime-house have made the triangle; Bloomsbury and St Mary
Woolnoth have next created the major Pentacle-starre; and, with
Greenwich, all these will form the Sextuple abode of Baal-Berith
or the Lord of the Covenant. Then, with the church of Little St
Hugh, the Septilateral Figure will rise above about Black Step
Lane and, in this Pattern, every straight line is enrich'd with a
point at Infinity and every Plane with a line at Infinity. Let him
that has Understanding count the Number: the seven Churches
are built in conjunction with the seven Planets in the lower
Orbs of Heaven, the seven Circles of the Heavens, the seven
Starres in Ursa Minor and the seven Starres in the Pleiades. Little
St Hugh was flung into the Pitte with the seven Marks upon
his Hands, Feet, Sides and Breast which thus exhibit the seven
Demons – Beydelus, Metucgayn, Adulec, Demeymes, Gadix,
Uqizuz and Sol. I have built an everlasting Order, which I may
run through laughing: no one can catch me now.[32]

In his classic account of the English intellectual thought of the period,
The Seventeenth Century Background (1934), Basil Willey returns again and
again to the deep seated ambiguity in its voice. He carefully tempers
talk of the dawning of the age of reason and the triumph of science by
insisting on the Janus-like quality of the epoch, with its ability to live
'in divided and distinguished worlds' (Sir Thomas Browne).[33] For what
was new did not necessarily imply an irreversible cut in time, but rather
a novel configuration of elements that simultaneously encouraged
and deviated the possibility of an indivisible truth to be located in a
mechanical rationalism 'which supposes that which is fluctuating to be
fixed' (Francis Bacon).[34] Writing in an epoch in which, with Werner
Heisenberg, uncertainty had become a principle within the paradigm of
the natural sciences, Willey justly queries a rationalist vision of the
earlier period. He notes:

> The distinctions were only beginning to be made which for later
> ages shut off poetry from science, metaphor from fact, fancy from
> judgement. The point about these different worlds was not that
> they were divided, but that they were simultaneously available.[35]

This framing of thought, and life, was suspended in a fluctuating and
ambiguous balance between light and shadows, between the flat, tabular
frame of reason and the infinite spread and inter-layered folds of explanation. Fernand Hallyn writes:

we can consider the seventeenth and eighteenth centuries as the period of transition from the predominance of the vertical axis, linking several levels of reality, to the predominance of the horizontal axis, reducing everything to a single level.[36]

Between a *spiegare* (to explain, expound, unfold) and a *piegare* (to fold, wrap, crease), emerges the *spiegamento* (the explication, the spread, the unfolding). Contrary to the fixed point of the rationalist a priori sought by Descartes lies the mutable point of view found in the body, where to explain is to unfold a complexity and to trace the in-finite in the folds, creases and envelopment of the world; in the finitude of our physical frame, time and place, in the world of our possibilities.[37]

> To explain does not simply imply to extend, expand and lay out an argument, but is rather to be involved and evolve with it. Although the organism defines itself through its capacity to endlessly bend and fold its parts, it explains them not by referring to infinity but with reference to the limits available to the species.[38]

This reveals that the centrality of rhetoric to the Baroque is not an idle or 'ornamental' matter. The art of seeing and comprehension has to be assembled and fabricated, it is diverse from information. In the violent instability of the Counter-Reformation and the uncertain world of a new social order, knowledge demands articulated conviction rather than mere consensus.[39] Sometimes the construction, both in architecture, the theatre, and thought, leaned more towards the light, sometimes more towards the shadows; invariably it recognised its hybrid provenance in both. The constraints of mortality were inscribed as much in its rational flights as in the vivid movement of bodies and light that are obliquely pictured in Caravaggio: temporarily caught but not centred, falling away, out of the frame.[40]

And it is in the art of Caravaggio that we most dramatically encounter this uncertain sense of centre and certitude. Here the perspective of mimesis is subverted and the death of representation announced. The neo-classicist Poussin declared that Caravaggio had come into the world to kill painting.[41] In frustrating a rationalist appropriation and the pleasurable measure of classical order and interpretation, Caravaggio's manner of painting 'from life' threatened the nobility of the gaze (*theoria*) by offering what is seen rather than what reason composes and condones. The 'deadly beauty of theory', the crypt-like configuration of discourse, and the rationalism of a representation that renders the world legible and possessable, is destroyed by Caravaggio turning the gaze inwards on itself and the mortal frame it announces.[42] As Louis Marin points out, in Caravaggio we encounter not the truth of the object represented, but the truth of the representation. Eliminating distance and trapping the eye in the appearance, all occurs on the surface of the painting, the

> plane where the outside and inside coincide in a blurred and undecidable boundary. It is here that the outside and inside are at their most intense and attain their greatest power, a power so overwhelming it cannot be resisted.[43]

The 'idea' of painting as faithful mimesis, as 'true' to nature, as a historical judgement and critical prospect, is replaced by the act of painting where 'the moment of sight erupts within representation.'[44] Marin concludes: what looms out of the black space of these canvases is that 'the self-reflexive moment within Caravaggio's paintings reveals painting to be a representation without basis, without foundations.'[45] In Caravaggio, 'the glance is a gesture of pointing, a wordless 'this' that does away with supplementary discourses and description, striking here and now.'[46]

Like the dying note on the lute or viol de gamba, texture and tonality is decentred, transient, melancholic. This passionate view of things emerges from the event of suffering history – 'bound upon a wheel of fire' – and not from the secluded security of logic. In its violent affirmation this temper also announces the precarious space of the emergence of the modern urban world, and anticipates what in later centuries will be referred to as 'mass culture'.[47]

The style and sensibility of the excessive and the ornamental is increasingly rendered public with the rise of absolutism. Throughout the seventeenth century there emerges in music, for example, a growing distinction between private and court performance. The miniature musicality and domestic reception of French lute music fades away before the authority of absolutism. A growing patronage of music by an urban bourgeois – often in antagonism to styles favoured by the court – further leads to the displacement of the theatre from private, palatial contexts to the public sphere. Nowhere is this public growth more manifest than with the spectacle afforded by opera. If opera as musical convention begins in 1600 in Florence with Ottavio Rinuccini's *Euridice*, it emerges for the first time as a mass spectacle in Venice in 1637 with the opening of the first public theatre. In the shift from court to public opera, there is the passage from a unique event, a one-off creation, to a performance designed to be produced in series; that is designed for reproducibility almost three hundred years prior to the same definition that Walter Benjamin was to apply to the cinema.[48] Opera was a public event, with all the ideological, economical and political resonance that go with being 'public'. It depended upon a public in both aesthetic terms – to complete the drama by participating in its unfolding – and economic ones: buying tickets, seats, boxes. In the period between 1600 and 1637 opera changes from concern with the ancients (the presumed music of antique Greece) to modern, commercial, theatrical productions in which the ancients were forgotten.[49] This represents a move from the dusk of humanist culture (and with it Florence) towards a modern, urban, public one (Venice). Here society is able to contemplate itself.[50] This is all further accentuated in the breaching of earlier aesthetic categories with opera's hybrid mixture of the vernacular and the sublime, increasingly driven home in a general lack of respect for the previous canons of composition, drama and representation. This is not to suggest, as Lorenzo Bianconi points out, that seventeenth-century opera was a popular medium – this did not occur until the nineteenth century – it was rather a medium that was popularised and publicised as an active, public manifestation of cultural and secular power.[51] As such, together with its unstable sentiments, structures and excess, opera was the model of the Baroque.

Along with the systematic installation of centralised government and court life (Madrid, Versailles, London), and the public rationalisation of financial, juridical, educational and military control, renewed imposition of seigniorial rights on the land induced, sometimes physically enforced, the rural migrations of peasants, sharecroppers and small landowners from the countryside towards the cities. It led to the growth of the landless and propertyless street dweller: the anonymous faces of the future urban 'mob', 'crowd' and 'masses', as well as the urban criminal underworld. Added to these violent dislocations were interminable religious wars and persecution resulting in rural regions being scoured by bandits and roving armies of disbanded soldiers and ex-mercenaries. To this were aggregated regular outbreaks of witch hunts and the plague. In an 'age drunk with acts of cruelty both lived and imagined', these were all immediate exemplars of the 'Baroque pedagogy of violence', terrifying reminders of a fragile world and a precarious mortality.[52]

In the first half of the seventeenth century London was ravaged by plague – 1603: 33,500 deaths; 1625: 35,500 deaths; 1636: 10,500 deaths – and in 1665–6, the Great Plague: 69,000 deaths, followed by the Fire.[53] Similarly, Baroque Naples is studded with allegorical *guglie* or obelisks built to exorcise plagues, earthquakes and volcanic eruptions: the eruption of Vesuvius in 1631, the plagues of 1656 and 1657, the earthquakes of 1688 and 1694.[54] What was once held at a distance through the promise of another world, life and salvation, is dramatically brought close; it is re-presented (*vor-stellen*) and re-membered, in-corporated and rendered flesh. It becomes some 'thing' (*res*) that concerns and disturbs us.[55] So the last things – death and judgement – become immediate things.[56] The Italian philosopher Mario Perniola associates this Baroque acknowledgement of the historical and ontological import of death in life, as opposed to something separate and extraneous to terrestrial existence, with Loyola and the Jesuits. It is not a head full of reason, but a body inscribed with terrestrial constraints, dwelling in the perishable shelter of the Earth and destined for the worms of time, that provides the constant and tragic corpus of Baroque drama, of the epoch's aesthetics and ascetics.

Melancholy and colonial space

Yet in this powerful proximity, in the marked inscription of mortality into truth, there also emerges a remarkable confidence.[57] As though in compensation for a lost centrality, the century of the Baroque is also witness to the violent and extensive elaboration of an expansive egotism that seeks to model and mould the rest of the world in its image and imaginary. In the moment that European thought considers itself to be a prisoner of time, cast into the unprotected vicissitudes of history, it discovers a terrible freedom. The 'colonial anxiety' that invariably accompanied encountering radical alterity in Africa, Asia and the New World was rapidly scripted into the dominion of European language and reason.[58] In the wide avenues, the giant plaza and imposing church façades that the Baroque realised in urban Mexico and South America, there was erected an architecture in which non-European bodies and histories were included only to be ruthlessly negated, just as they were in the plantations, forest clearings and trading posts further north. Silence, the intractable and the untranslatable was forced to bear testimony to a European narcissism which sought 'to represent even those experiences that resist it with a stubborn opacity.'[59] This invisible presence was traced in the labour, slavery, blood, torture and death of those beings that colonial government, military repression and the Inquisition administered and occluded. Maintained on the colonial periphery by force, fear and terror, the limits of a European possession, and position, were simultaneously installed and repressed as the West brutally insisted on becoming synonymous with the world.

In Europe the initial plunder and bullion of the New World, and its subsequent exploitation by slave labour, provided the immediate infrastructure for the emergence of the centralised state, modern urban culture and the economical-financial system that was to promote European modernity. This lacerating encounter with alterity has inevitably left its signature in the ambiguous signs, sounds and shadows that characterise both the political *and* cultural economy of the time. One can even hazard to suggest that the epoch's male melancholia (Donne, Dowland, Hamlet . . .) stems less from the dusk of Renaissance humanism and more in response to the redrawing and subsequent limiting of the known world, now displaced by heliocentrism and the novel disturbance of America: the latter invariably portrayed as an untamed, monstrous, virgin, female body whose threatening presence is to be subdued, conquered and domesticated. There is no necessary nor immediate correlation between a Peruvian silver mine and Caravaggio's *The Resurrection of Lazarus*, between an Iroquois war council and a pavane on the Elizabethan lute. But in the disenchantment that speaks of humankind's fall out of a unique cosmic order into the unprotected heterogeneity of worldly differentiation there emerges a language that ineluctably registers the disconsolation of limits: there European subjectivity is brought up short, potentially displaced. In the anatomy of melancholy no doubt lies the concentration that permits occidental humans to recentre themselves. Here there is registered a profound shift in the perception of historical time, accompanied by the emergence of the individual as a circumscribed subject. In the acknowledgement of limits, reason and time respond to finitude.[60]

In this constellation it is, of course, commonplace to refer to the age of the Baroque as an age of melancholia. From Robert Burton's noted treatise on the matter of 1621 to Walter Benjamin's study of its 'mourning theatre' three centuries later, the theme is ubiquitous and most succinctly amplified in the music of the period. But if melancholia represents the unfinished business of grieving, a loss that is never accepted as complete loss, what exactly does Baroque melancholy seek to retain and incorporate in its unceasing projection of sorrow? Why, in all its theatrical excess is the final note a diminished one, a dissonant echo of fading deprivation? If the accomplishments of the Baroque are generally etched in male melancholia, what transpires in this announced but incomplete mourning? In the repudiation of cosmic certitude, a stable godhead and religious conviction, there is certainly a loss that can never be publicly registered nor privately elaborated. For the prohibition is of a cultural and historical order. There is no public space, outside heresy, for its announcement. Melancholy, as the deferred recognition of loss, invokes the suspension between a lack and a state yet to be attained. To move in an emerging secular order that continues to negate the possibility of burying its predecessor is to remain caught in the trauma of the 'miming of the death it cannot mourn'.[61] But here there is also something about male melancholia and the Baroque body that has to do with the circumscription of borders and limits, of being framed by an irrevocable mortality, by the potential horizon of death and alterity, that is most dramatically entwined in colonial space.

This body, however, is also a body that transgresses earlier limits, that overflows and exceeds its positionality in an earlier epoch; it is no longer obviously constrained by geography or an unique authority. This European body is now also the object of the stranger's gaze, and therefore simultaneously becomes a *centred and a limited* subject: 'I see only from one point, but in my existence I am looked at from all sides.'[62] In the borders and contact zones of this 'new world', such a body is also 'othered' by the 'native'.[63] In this liminal site of anxiety the European gaze – however imperial its presumptions – is folded into the more fractured and uneasy exercise of colonial hegemony in an oscillating theatre of power: 'we are beings who are looked at, in the spectacle of the world. That which makes us consciousness institutes us by the same token as *speculum mundi*.'[64] In this oscillation, in the space in which every subject is a potential object, and in a return to its anxieties, the Baroque proposes 'the performative rituals of cross-cultural first contact'.[65] As such, Paul Carter continues, the Baroque announces:

> a counter-tradition within Western reason, and we have suggested that this counter-tradition is intimately implicated in the poetics of colonization – and thus, perhaps, in the continuing critique of Western Logos that will characterize the emergence of a post-colonial polity and poetry.[66]

Here in the return to, and the return of, the native's gaze, the mythical origins of occidental modernity, its myths of knowledge, return home bearing a critical edge that stages the reversal of anthropological scrutiny, now looking backwards towards its 'origins'. The violent intrusion of the 'stranger' is dispatched to its home in the West, disseminating a critical disposition that relocates a previous accommodation in another history. Inevitable in this unsolicited return is a re-view of the history and disciplines that once administered the colonial space and now seek to explain the consequences.[67]

In the ostentatious public display of the Baroque – its theatre, fireworks, fountains, obelisks, churches and, above all, opera – there is the cultural orchestration of an excessive presence registered in a power negotiating for the first time a mass, urban public.[68] This disposition is not something that is merely laid on an inert public: for the spectator, the listener, is drawn in to release the spring of the drama, the emotional force of the music, to complete the event and not merely to witness its unfolding. Such public and extravagant displays can be read as symptoms of the political and cultural anxiety attendant upon stepping beyond a previous known order. A religious and epistemological covenant was shattered by dissension, war and counter-knowledge; it all amounted to the uneasy elaboration of a decentred polity seeking a new absolute. Here, even in the theatrics of the emerging centralisation of the state and its absolute monarchy, the Baroque reveals an anxious disposition of power, hence violent excess and dramatic enactment in a world that threatens to evade custom and control. This threat is both internal – science, secularism and a burgeoning urban modernity – and external: the disturbing ingression of other worlds. Cortés before Tenochtitlan, later known as Mexico City, and prior to its destruction, speaks of 'the most beautiful city in the world'. The Baroque space is also the colonial space, and the intrusion of new worlds, both from within and without, is central to the Baroque aesthetic of wonder, dread, fear, awe and the spectacular.[69]

The style of time

The Talmudic legend assigns to each instance of time a specific angel, that is to say its specific quality, or, in other words, its irreplaceable messianic virtuality . . . this figure of paradoxical thought, according to which the end can be realised immediately 'in the very heart of history', subverts the very foundations of historical Reason. It implies that time is no longer to be considered as a directive axis, where one thing inevitably follows another, or as a river that flows from its source towards its mouth, but rather as a juxtaposition of instances, each of them unique and irreducible to a totality, and which therefore do not follow one another as if they were stages in an irreversible process. Here the past, the present and the future no longer succeed each other along a direct line as though viewed externally, but coexist as three states of permanent consciousness.

Stéphane Mosès[70]

all manifest discourse is the repression of what is not said which, in turn, undermines all that is said.

Noreen O'Connor[71]

The complex play of the lights and shadows of the Baroque, its limits and interrogation, opens up a critical space that returns to inhabit our present. It raises a question, creates an opening in the construction of our understandings, a rent in the fabric of our knowledge. It draws us into the shadows of illumination, into the repressed zones that our sense of being seeks to avoid. For it forces us to confront and converse with what we most avidly seek to ignore: our limits and our mortality. The Baroque critique of permanency and essentialism, complemented by the simultaneous de-centring and re-centring of sixteenth-century Europe in colonial directives, returns as a ghost – 'Remember me' – to haunt the dusk of Western modernism. It erupts in the heterotopic challenge to the rational, utopic design of the latter. It calls out for an ethical reply to the needs of another scene, another story, another possibility, reminding us that historical reason is itself to be judged. For behind the 'perverse absolutism' (Lévinas) of Western knowledge, and its universal desire for an unfractured, unitary logic, a rational teleology of time and causality, there lies the evasion of such judgement. To refuse to register the enigmatic, the discontinuous, the repressed and hungry shadows of oblivion, and to eradicate them in the violent insistence on coherence, is to flee from life and the anguish of death, and is to repudiate responsibility for those conditions.[72]

When the earth is refused and violently reduced to an ethereal pact between thought and transcendental logic, when the world is abrogated and distilled into the pure spirit and transparency of a rational sentence, all those unresolved, mutant, incomplete, uncanny, cracked, silent and undone languages that contribute to the insistent 'worldling of the world' come to be denied.[73] As we draw back from that blinkered perspective, turn away from that narrow path, and reinvest ourselves with the responsibility for our lives and what sustains them, other lives, we catch the echoes of Baroque antecedents in the duplicity, disturbance, excess, folds and opacity of knowledge, while at the same time listening to the counter-point of cultural amnesia and European narcissism. We re-member in that mortal mess-age and its history of shadows, the questions that permit us to continue to question, that permit us to be.

This is why for some the ragged and incomplete *chiaroscuro* patterns of the Baroque are far closer to present sensibilities and worldly configurations than the subsequent faith in instrumental reason and confident subjectivity. To recall that earlier interval is to remind ourselves of the complex, sometimes indifferent, contingency of the world before positivism stepped in to reassure us with the secular gods of 'science' and 'information'. The proximity of the allegorical landscapes of the Baroque to the radical and disruptive experiences of late modernity has been finely apprehended by Christine Buci-Glucksmann:

Here one can see, well before modern art, allegory as the testimony of the domination of the fragment over everything, of the destructive principle over the constructive one, of passion, as the excavation of an absence, over the mastery of reason. Only the fragment is able to demonstrate that the logics of the body, of feeling, of life and death do not coincide with those of Power or the Idea. In the fragment there appears precisely that which is mute (hence music), that which is new (even if it is death), that which is unmastered and profoundly ungovernable: catastrophes that embody the very act of representation.

Reality is here consigned to a perennial antinomy, to the deceptive game of reality as an illusion, in which the world is simultaneously evaluated and devaluated. 'The profane world, considered from the point of allegory, is simultaneously evaluated and devaluated.' In it there lies the specific seduction of the Baroque, in which the pre-eminence of the aesthetic – of play, of appearance – is united with metaphysical loss against a background of affliction and melancholy. The metaphor of the theatre – of the world as theatre and the theatre as world – portrays the particular temporality of the Baroque . . . Over this eternal displacement of appearances there lies the presence of an omniscient, but now distant, spectator: God. The abyss between reality and illusion, however, is insuperable: the theatre now knows itself to be theatre.[74]

This exposes and advances the contemporary baroquisation of the world in which the rationalist drive, and a facile faith in the linear accumulation of 'progress', is now perhaps to be considered an abnormal interval. In an altogether wider constellation, the seventeenth-century Baroque, with its fragile allegories of excess and mortality, with its melancholy acknowledgement of the limits of reason and life, is affinitively linked to the reappearance of neo-Baroque styles in the late twentieth century, where 'style', like the earlier Baroque ornament, is not a trivial extra but rather exemplifies the self-conscious pathos of the languages we inhabit.

It is in the insistence of our being captured in time, subjected to history and mortality, rendering sense from the crisis and fragility of human existence, that the Baroque sensibility flares up into an image that projects light into our world. Like the illumination from dead stars, the Baroque arrives to become part of our lives, as something that is simultaneously present and absent.[75] The palpable instability of what we are accustomed to refer to as 'knowledge' and 'truth' provides a telescopic link between two historical constellations. It leads to the suggestion that historical specificity does not lie in the factual annotation of the passage of time, but in receiving and acknowledging a discontinued moment by interpreting it and ourselves in its present light. That moment is both unique and repetitive, 'irreversible and recurrent'.[76] For its truth does not lie in a 'foreclosure through facts', but in the event and resonance of language.[77] Truth is not my personal property, restricted to the range and intention of my will.[78] It is something that both invests and escapes me: it is discontinuous.[79] So the transient past, apparently lost forever, can and does return to activate another, even novel, sense of the present, and, with it, an opening towards the future.

This is to suggest an ethical and involved, rather than a positivist and distanced, paradigm of knowledge.[80] In this mode, the past is never recaptured 'as it was', as though, in a reversal of time, we could simply retrace our steps back along the path of homogeneous evolution to an earlier moment. The past does not come down to us smoothly across the passage of time. It erupts and resonates in our time as a disconcerting and discrete event: as the voice and body of the other that challenges our own bodies and time. The past is the scene of persistent traces. As signs, silences and resonance, we are directed towards what is irredeemably lost to us yet which continues to haunt our language and thoughts, and thereby interrogate our sense of the present. To translate (and transform) the past in this manner may well be to betray how things 'actually were', but it is also to refuse to discard its body. If we were to reduce the Baroque to the uniform tread, and ultimate oblivion, of 'progress', we would be cancelling the possibility of its return: the possibility of past generations to continue to interrogate, disturb and challenge our time and our custody for their times.

To temper and test time in this manner is to punctuate it in order to hear the respiration of other ways of being in time. It is to acknowledge our own precariousness in which the past is not given and the future is not predictable: all is to be undone, inter-preted, contested, again and again and . . .

To open up the body of history, and expose it to the vindication of the world, involves the adoption of a figure of time, of knowledge, that is also a figure of speech, of writing, able to hold in suspension the ambiguous 'truth' that language sustains in our continual rewriting of the past as we research the historical potential of the present. For style is the body, the physicality of language. So, we acknowledge in the gesture of a style – of thought, of writing, of speech – the co-presence and responsibility for past, present and future. There the intractable, rebus-like quality of Baroque allegory, as the speech and writing of a sensibility, as epochal expression, suggests something more than merely a literary technique or archaic poetics. Walter Benjamin writes:

> in allegory the observer is confronted with the *facies hippocratica* of history as a petrified, primordial landscape. Everything about history that, from the very beginning, had been untimely, sorrowful, unsuccessful, is expressed in a face – or rather in a death's head. And although such a thing lacks all 'symbolic' freedom, all classical proportion, all humanity – nevertheless, this is the form in which man's subjection to nature is most obvious and it significantly gives rise not only to the enigmatic question of the nature of human existence as such, but also of the biographical historicity of the individual. This is the heart of the allegorical way of seeing, of the Baroque, secular explanation of history as the Passion of the world; its importance resides solely in the stations of its decline.[81]

In the interregnum between religious faith secured in the divine stability of the pre-Copernican universe and later consolation in the idolatry of science, the Baroque exposed a naked, unprotected being, in which any 'person, any object, any relationship can mean absolutely anything else. With this possibility a destructive, but just verdict is passed on the profane world'.[82] Stripped of an obvious symbolic function, caught in the fall of the world, in the profanity of decay and ruin, the Baroque points elsewhere by tunnelling into the body, the physicality, of language. As Benjamin points out, the typographic extremes and charged metaphors of the Baroque are only the most obvious symptoms of a language that tends towards the visual, towards the illumination that emanates from an independent and autonomous image. But it is a marked, a wounded autonomy, for:

> In the field of allegorical intuition the image is a fragment, a rune.[83]

The image is both a fragment, a ruin, but also a rune, a hieroglyph.

> The false appearance of totality is extinguished. For the *eidos* disappears, the simile ceases to exist, and the cosmos it contained shrivels up. The dry rebuses which remain contain an insight, which is still available to the confused investigator.[84]

Beneath its flourish of pomp, the Baroque insists on the imperfection and incompleteness of the world, it insists on our physical and terrestrial enclosure, on the inevitability of decay and ruin, and so wins for itself, out of the depths of its language, an insight destined to endure: 'Where man is drawn towards the symbol, allegory emerges from the depths of being to intercept the intention, and to triumph over it.'[85]

The idea that historical time might be multiple and discontinuous, that history is an allegorical construction exposing the ruins of time, is not only what links Benjamin to the excessive and poetic underside of modernism (Baudelaire, Kafka), but it is also what links this German Jewish thinker to the Baroque and his own marvellous and deeply allegorical reading of modernity. The key texts here are the volume on the mourning theatre (*Trauerspiel*) of the German Baroque (published in 1928), the only book that Benjamin actually completed, the massive and incomplete project on the Parisian arcades that he worked on in the last years of his life in exile, and the 'Theses on the Philosophy of History' (1940).

To subvert and discard the links in the temporal chain of irreversible causality, in order to turn time back against itself and release another story, and another way of telling, is what animates Benjamin's continual engagement with the languages of time and being, with the writing of history. It is to give a name to the defeated and deceased, to return again to the overlooked and the shadows, and there to reveal in a diverse scansion of time the detailed instances that make up the eternal pathos of terrestrial existence in the repetitive discontinuities of mortality. In the ambiguous gesture of the collector – simultaneously salvaging and reifying the past – Benjamin seeks to actively re-member, rather than merely recall, such traces and fragments.[86] Like the Baroque *tombeau*, he seeks to open up a space in language and time in which another history can appear and, with it, an alternative future in which each historical moment can be sundered to reveal an opening towards paths and possibilities not yet taken. Hence historical time, as opposed to the linear tyranny of physical time, becomes reversible. It permits a re-membering, a return, that produces the 'open' time of writing, of politics, of aesthetics and ethics, ready for judgement in every instance (Emmanuel Lévinas).[87] It is the history of the 'untimely, sorrowful, unsuccessful', in the discontinued, discarded and dispersed histories of the vanquished, that Benjamin continually sought to snatch from the hands of the victors, to snatch from the oppression of the continuity of *their* time and 'progress'. For such 'progress' is founded upon the continuity of catastrophe, on the defeat of the denied bodies and stories of those excluded: the ruins of history.

This is to establish a new type of historical intelligibility that binds us to the time of the other, that binds us to a response and a response-ability (Shoshana Felman) for the excluded, for oblivion.[88] In the transient act of writing under the eternal sign of ethical redemption, Benjamin, like Franz Rosenzweig, but the Heideggerian echoes here should also not be overlooked, sought an intelligibility that was not closed, 'scientific', or metaphysical, but was rather consigned to the custody of language; to the vital unfolding of my being in language, and of my language in being, in which the breath of the living fans the ashes of the past that flare up to cast light on the future.

Unspeakable sounds

A passing note. In the centrality of music to the black Atlantic experiences of modernity we encounter not simply a historical and cultural archive, a vital storehouse of memories, but also a counter-history and constellation of potential redemption.[89] Here past, present and future fuse in an abrupt interruption – the blue note on the bent guitar string, the shout, the saxophone growl, the bass story, the rap – that challenges immediate circumstances to reveal the presence of other histories. For rap invokes an interruption of language, a cut which folds language in upon itself, and then unfolds it in variations of the English tongue, Anglo-American rock music, other worldly soundtracks and urban style. It constitutes the act of testimony, of bearing witness, that reveals a diverse scansion of historical time, a different cultural inscription and musical signature. Unchaining such languages from their presumed referents, the supplement of rap proposes another centre. Usually considered to be an addition, an ornament, to the centrality of rock music, viewed from elsewhere rap registers an essential relocation and resiting of the musical (and cultural) score.[90] In this separation of sound from the earlier signified, we enter the 'topos of Unsayability'.[91] Like the Baroque insistence on the ornament that permits us to look into the interior and bear witness to the 'underground of language', rap's decoration and decentring of readily available languages and styles suggests that music reflects more than is accessible to the categories of reflection, and invokes the 'effort to say that of which one cannot speak.'[92] On this point Andrew Bowie notes:

> The importance of music in the history of modernity seems to me in part at least explained by its role as part of the counter discourse of modernity, that discourse that in the face of the determination to ground the subject in rules, codes and systems

always reveals the extent to which these systems cannot be self-grounding.[93]

A home

Reason is entitled to a home in the world, but the world is just
that: a home; it is not totality.

Franz Rosenzweig[94]

To return to the lost harmony of the circle. In the circle of investigation we set out confident that we will return to our point of departure complete with our survey and solutions. In the ellipse we discover our decentring, and never return to our point of departure. Like a Baroque column spiralling upwards in a twisting formation, we find ourselves caught in a movement in which beginning and end do not correspond. We encounter other centres, other perspectives, disseminated along the spiralled ellipse of our trajectory.

Caught in the scissors of time, a space opens up between past and future that reveals the ever-present body of language: 'The being of language – the language of being.'[95] I 'live here, forever taking leave', called upon to lend my ear and body to the miracle of the terrestrial call:

Wasn't all this a miracle? Be astonished, Angel, for we
are this, O Great One; proclaim that we could achieve this, my
    breath
is too short for such praise. So, after all, we have not
failed to make use of these generous spaces, these
spaces of *ours*. (How frighteningly great they must be,
since thousands of years have not made them overflow with our
    feelings.)[96]

The Baroque announces a border, most obviously in a line drawn between the 'ancients' and the 'moderns', between religious cosmology and secular science, but also in its dramatic establishment of an ambiguous threshold between what is familiar and what remains foreign. Its presence is an unsettling one within the narratives of modernity, a modernity that it seemingly simultaneously founds and disavows. For the Baroque's excessive energies and diverse directions cast an unruly commentary across the unilateral 'progress' subsequently installed by modern mythology. All knowledge pertains to narrative, to a way of telling that returns us to the familiar, in which the new, the discovery, the 'there', is returned to the 'here', is rendered recognisable in a shared economy of sense. But it would be foolish and denying, ultimately life-threatening, to ignore the uncanny, the unstable and interceptive voices that call upon us to tell the story again and again seeking to accommodate what the previous telling ignored and repressed. So, the account is never complete. The 'truth' it bears is forever open to further interrogation. History thinks it has come home, only to discover that it has established a new point of departure.

Notes

1 John Donne, 'An Anatomie of the World: The First Anniversary', 1611, in *The Poems of John Donne*, edited by Herbert Grierson, London, Oxford University Press, 1951.

2 Thomas Docherty, *John Donne, Undone*, London and New York, Methuen, 1986, pp. 37–8.

3 On the Baroque as a period of 'general crisis' which monarchical absolutism sought to control and direct, see José Antonio Maravall, *Culture of the Baroque*, Manchester, Manchester University Press, 1986.

4 Severo Sarduy, *Barroco*, Paris, Seuil, 1975; I am using the Italian translation: *Barroco*, Milan, Il Saggiatore, 1980, pp. 50–3.

5 John Ruskin, *The Stones of Venice*, quoted in Mary Laura Gibbs, *The Church of Santa Maria del Giglio*, Venice and New York, Venice Committee, n.d. Ruskin considered the church 'so grossly debased that even the Italian critics . . . exhaust their terms of reproach', ibid.

6 See Mario Perniola, 'L'essere-per-la-morte e il simulacro della morte', in M. Perniola, *La società dei simulacri*, Bologna, Cappelli, 1983.

7 Lorenzo Bianconi, *Music in the Seventeenth Century*, Cambridge, Cambridge University Press, 1987, p. 98.

8 Michel de Certeau, *The Writing of History*, trans. Tom Conley, New York, Columbia University Press, 1988, p. 101.

9 For the resonance of the idea of the tombeau in historical reasoning see Iain Chambers, *Migrancy, Culture, Identity*, London and New York, Routledge, 1994.

10 Michel de Certeau, op. cit., p. 100.

11 Julia Kristeva, *Black Sun: Depression and Melancholia*, trans. Leon S. Roudiez, New York, Columbia University Press, 1989, p. 99.

12 Robert Donington, *A Performer's Guide to Baroque Music*, London, Faber & Faber, 1978. Note the revealing resonance in Edward Said's comments on classical Arabic music in the next chapter.

13 Lorenzo Bianconi, op. cit., p. 93.

14 For a discussion of the origin of the term 'Baroque' in the context of jewellery, and Portuguese (*barrucco* – an irregular shaped pearl), see Severo Sarduy, op. cit.

15 See the description of Leibniz's multi-storeyed 'house of resonance' in the opening pages of Gilles Deleuze, *Le Pli: Leibniz et le Baroque*, Paris, Editions de Minuit, 1988; I am using the Italian translation, *La Piega: Leibniz e il Barocco*,

Turin, Einaudi, 1990, p. 17. The English edition is *The Fold: Leibniz and the Baroque*, trans. Tom Conley, Minneapolis, University of Minnesota Press, 1993. The ever-present, and ever-evolving, basso continuo can be compared to the modern-day 'rhythm section' of guitar, bass, keyboards and drums in both jazz and rock music; see Thurston Dart, *The Interpretation of Music*, New York, Harper & Row, 1963, p. 78.

16 Christine Buci-Glucksmann, *Tragique de l'ombre*, Paris, Editions Galilée, 1990, pp. 229–30. 'De la musique, comme art de l'émotion sans concept, comme Affect de tout affect', ibid., p. 230.

17 Ibid., p. 202.

18 Quoted in the CD notes for *Denis Gaultier – La Rhétorique des Dieux*. Suites pour le luth I, II, XII, Astrée, 1989, lutenist: Hopkinson Smith.

19 For the detailed nuances of this 'cosmological break' in the making of the Baroque sensibility, see in particular Severo Sarduy, op. cit.

20 Frances Yates, *Giordano Bruno and the Hermetic Tradition*, London, Routledge & Kegan Paul, 1964.

21 Loup Verlet, *La Malle de Newton*, Paris, Gallimard, 1993.

22 The reference is to Pascal Quignard's *Touts les matins du monde*, and its subsequent realisation as a film, with Quignard's screen-play, by Alain Courneau in 1992. On 'sad voluptuousness', see Julia Kristeva, op. cit.

23 Paul de Man, 'The Rhetoric of Temporality', in Paul de Man, *Blindness and Insight*, London, Methuen, 1983, p. 222.

24 Fernand Hallyn, *The Poetic Structure of the World: Copernicus and Kepler*, New York, Zone Books, 1993, p. 22.

25 The church of Santa Maria delle Anime del Purgatorio (1604), Via Tribunali, Naples. The flowers are changed daily.

26 John Donne, 'Song', in *The Poems of John Donne*, op. cit.

27 Hélène Cixous referring to Shakespeare, in Hélène Cixous and Catherine Clément, *The Newly Born Woman*, Manchester, Manchester University Press, 1987, p. 98.

28 Mario Perniola, 'Icone, visioni, simulacri', in Perniola, op. cit., p. 122.

29 Julia Kristeva, op. cit., pp. 100–1.

30 Kepler's *Dream*, published posthumously by his son in 1634, describes celestial phenomena as they would have appeared from the moon. Earlier versions had circulated in manuscript form and Kepler thought it was known to John Donne; see Fernand Hallyn, op. cit. 'A Dream' is also the title of a fine fantasy for the lute by John Dowland.

31 See Marin Mersenne, *Questions Inouyes*, Paris, Fayard, 1985, and Pierre Gassendi, *Initiation à la théorie de la musique*, Aix-en-Provence, Edisud, 1992. Descartes wrote a *Compendium Musicae* that was published posthumously in Utrecht in 1650. It is available in a French translation as *Abrégé de musique*, Paris, Presses Universitaires de France, 1987.

32 Peter Ackroyd, *Hawksmoor*, London, Abacus, 1985, p. 186.

33 Sir Thomas Browne, quoted in Basil Willey, *The Seventeenth Century Background*, New York, Doubleday, 1953, p. 50.

34 Francis Bacon, quoted in Basil Willey, op. cit., p. 43.

35 Basil Willey, op. cit., p. 50.

36 Fernand Hallyn, op. cit., p. 20.

37 'The point of view is found in the body': Leibniz, letter to Lady Masham, June 1704, cited in Gilles Deleuze, op. cit., p. 17.

38 Gilles Deleuze, op. cit., p. 13.

39 This is to agree with Marc Fumaroli that the diversity of the European Baroque tends largely to flower under the Italianised umbrella of the Counter-Reformation: see Marc Fumaroi, *L'Ecole du silence*, Paris, Flammarion, 1994.

40 Severo Sarduy, op. cit. p. 50.

41 In his history of painting and architecture of 1725 André Félibien wrote: 'Poussin could not bear Caravaggio and said that he had come into the world in order to destroy painting', quoted in Louis Marin, *To Destroy Painting*, trans. Mette Hjort, Chicago and London, University of Chicago Press, 1995, p. 15. My account of Caravaggio here is deeply indebted to Marin's suggestive reading.

42 Ibid., p. 15.

43 Ibid., pp. 102–3.

44 Ibid., p. 107.

45 Ibid., p. 110.

46 Ibid., p. 164.

47 See José Maravall, op. cit.

48 Much of this discussion of opera is drawn directly from Lorenzo Bianconi, op. cit.

49 Ibid., p. 165.

50 Catherine Clément, *Opera, or the Undoing of Women*, Minneapolis, University of Minnesota Press, 1988.

51 Lorenzo Bianconi, op. cit., p. 190.

52 The first phrase is Benjamin's: Walter Benjamin, *The Origin of German Tragic Drama*, London, Verso, 1990, p. 185; the second is from Maravall, op. cit., p. 163.

53 Figures from Christopher Hill, *The Century of Revolution, 1603–1714*, London, Sphere, 1969, p. 278.

54 Gaetano Cantone, *Napoli barocca*, Bari, Laterza, 1992.

55 Martin Heidegger, 'The Thing', in Heidegger, *Poetry, Language, Thought*, trans. Albert Hofstadter, New York, Harper & Row, 1975.

56 Martin Heidegger, 'The Origin of the Work of Art', in Heidegger, *Basic Writings*, New York, Harper & Row, 1977, p. 152.

57 I am extremely grateful to Kathy Biddick for reminding me of this 'confidence'.

58 Peter Hulme, *Colonial Encounters: Europe and the Native Caribbean 1492–1797*, London and New York, Routledge, 1992. On the diverse ceremonial inscriptions of English, Spanish, Portuguese and Dutch possession and conquest in the Americas, see Patricia Seed, *Ceremonies of Possession in Europe's Conquest of the New World, 1492–1640*, Cambridge, Cambridge University Press, 1995.

59 Rey Chow, *Writing Diaspora*, Bloomington and Indianapolis, Indiana University Press, 1993, p. 38.

60 See Ludger Heidbrink, *Melancholie und Moderne: Zur Kritik der Historischen Verzweiflung*, Munich, Wilhelm Fink, 1994.

61 Judith Butler, *The Psychic Life of Power*, Stanford, Ca., Stanford University Press, 1997, p. 142.

62 Jacques Lacan, *The Four Concepts of Psychoanalysis*, Harmondsworth, Penguin, 1991, p. 72. The idea of being simultaneously centred and limited is most tellingly explored in Michel de Certeau's account of Jean de Léry in Brazil in the 1560s who, as a figure of modernity, witnessed, as it were, 'a primal scene in the construction of ethnological discourse', see Michel de Certeau, 'Ethno-Graphy. Speech, or the Space of the Other: Jean de Léry', in de Certeau, *The Writing of History,* op. cit.

63 Rey Chow, op. cit.

64 Jacques Lacan, op. cit., p. 75.

65 Paul Carter, *The Lie of the Land*, London, Faber & Faber, 1996, p. 229.

66 Ibid., p. 302.

67 See Gregory Lambert, 'The Culture of the Stranger: Reflections on European Aesthetic Ideology in the "New World"', Ph.D. dissertation, University of California, Irvine, 1995.

68 See José Maravall, op. cit.

69 In the absence of domestic return, and remaining lost in the El Dorado of a new horizon, the self can be carried away in an infinite economy of signs, where language runs out and the senses run ahead, unchecked, towards death. This is perhaps best exemplified in the futile expeditions of Sir Walter Ralegh, and Werner Herzog's film, *Aguirre, Wrath of God.*

70 Stéphane Mosès, *L'Ange de l'histoire: Rosenzweig, Benjamin, Scholem*, Paris, Seuil, 1992, pp. 19–20.

71 Noreen O'Connor, 'The Personal is Political', in R. Bernasconi and D. Wood (eds) *The Provocation of Levinas*, London and New York, Routledge, 1988, p. 59.

72 E. Robberechts, 'Savoir et mort chez F. Rosenzweig', *Revue Philosophique de Louvain*, 90 (May), 1992.

73 Martin Heidegger, 'The Thing', op. cit.

74 Christine Buci-Glucksmann, *La Raison Baroque: de Baudelaire à Benjamin*, Paris, Editions Galilée, 1984, pp. 71–2; *Baroque Reason: The Aesthetics of Modernity*, London, Sage, 1994. The author is quoting Walter Benjamin.

75 Walter Benjamin, *Charles Baudelaire: A Lyric Poet in the Era of High Capitalism*, London, New Left Books, 1973.

76 Stéphane Mosès, op. cit., p. 139.

77 Dori Laub, in Shoshana Felman and Dori Laub, *Testimony: Crises of Witnessing in Literature, Psychoanalysis, and History*, New York and London, Routledge, 1992, p. 73.

78 Emmanuel Lévinas, *Totality and Infinity*, trans. Alphonso Lingis, Pittsburgh, Pa, Duquesne University Press, 1969.

79 Stéphane Mosès, op. cit., p. 132.

80 Ibid., p. 127.

81 Walter Benjamin, *The Origin of German Tragic Drama*, op. cit., p. 166.

82 Ibid., p. 175.

83 Ibid., p. 176.

84 Ibid., p. 176.

85 Ibid, p. 183. José Maravall also insists on the centrality of the interruption and the incomplete to the Baroque, suggesting that it offers, for example, a key to the reading of Shakespeare's later 'unfinished' plays: see Maravall, op. cit.

86 On the political ambiguities of collecting, and its place in the articulation and disarticulation of modernity, see Rey Chow, op. cit., pp. 43–4.

87 I have borrowed the concept of 'open time' from Stéphane Mosès, op. cit., p. 177.

88 Shoshana Felman, in S. Felman and D. Laub, *Testimony: Crises of Witnessing in Literature, Psychoanalysis, and History*, New York and London, Routledge, 1992.

89 Paul Gilroy, *The Black Atlantic: Modernity and Double Consciousness*, London, Verso, 1993.

90 Ted Swedenburg, 'Homies in the Hood: Rap's Commodification of Insubordination', *New Formations*, 18, Winter 1992.

91 Carl Dalhaus, *Die Idee der absoluten Musik*, quoted in Andrew Bowie, 'Music, Language and Modernity', in Andrew Benjamin (ed.) *The Problems of Modernity: Adorno and Benjamin*, London and New York, Routledge, 1989, p. 70.

92 The 'underground of language' comes from Shoshana Felman, in Shoshana Felman and Dori Laub, op. cit., p. 15; while the second voice is that of Theodor Adorno, quoted in Andrew Bowie, op. cit., p. 80.

93 Andrew Bowie, op. cit., p. 83.

94 Franz Rosenzweig, *The Star of Redemption*, trans. William W. Hallo, New York, Holt, Rinehart & Winston, 1971, p. 13.

95 Martin Heidegger, 'The Nature of Language', in Heidegger, *On the way to Language*, New York, Harper & Row, 1982, p. 76.

96 Rainer Maria Rilke, from the Seventh Elegy of the 'Duino Elegies', in *The Selected Poetry of Rainer Maria Rilke*, trans. Stephen Mitchell, London, Picador, 1987, p. 191. The phrase 'we live here, forever taking leave' comes from the concluding line of the Eighth Elegy, ibid., p. 197.

4

A VOICE IN THE DARK,
A MAP OF MEMORY

> música
> dormida en el caracol de la memoria.
> music
> asleep in the shell of memory.
>
> Octavio Paz

> car tout étant aujourd'hui 'recorded' et la mémoire, la même
> toujours, n'étant plus tout la même.
>
> since everything today is recorded, and memory, always the
> same, is no longer the same at all.
>
> Jacques Derrida

> 'So a musical phrase', I said, 'is a map reference?'
> 'Music' said Arkady, 'is a memory bank for finding one's way
> about the world.'
>
> Bruce Chatwin

> Music rests on accord between darkness and light.
>
> Trinh T. Minh-ha[1]

I could begin

I could begin with a late winter evening in England in 1967. In a cream
coloured Georgian city on the river Avon, set among the rolling hills
of Somerset, I had gone to the weekly pop concert at the Bath Pavilion.
It was a regular venue for groups and singers touring the country. There
I had already seen Gene Pitney, Cliff Bennett and the Rebel Rousers,
the Animals, the Byrds ... Tonight I was paying five shillings to see
the still relatively unknown Jimi Hendrix Experience.[2] 'Hey Joe' had
just been released and I had seen the first, extraordinary, television performance on *Ready, Steady, Go!* featuring a beautiful, bedevilling, black
man playing the guitar with his teeth and producing the most
mesmerising sound. That evening, in a forty-minute set, the three-piece

group ran through many of the numbers that would go into their first LP, *Are You Experienced?* The image fades, details of dress and performance become hazy. What remains is the sensation of shock, surprise and excitement, condensed in the visceral intensity of Hendrix's guitar. To bear witness to that startling electricity, to that momentary disruption of local cultural co-ordinates, is what still burns in the memory.

That event, like so much of the music at the time, opened a door on the possibility of other worlds. It revealed that there could be more exciting cues and more intensive rhythms to draw upon in imagining one's life. The allure of the city, not necessarily the real one but the imaginary one with its streets of transgressive freedom, beyond school, beyond your family, beyond what you had been taught and constrained to be, also happened in the mid-1960s to coincide with the triumphant installation of youth in 'swinging London'. The body, my body, yearning for sex, but also aching for something more than the narrow horizons of institutional smugness and complacency could offer, was willingly tuned to such possibilities.

So, Jimi Hendrix, like so much of the pop music at the time, summoned up the sexed and sexual body, particularly, although not exclusively, for young men, proposing an avenue of cultural meaning where sounds, desires and rebellion could coalesce into a life style ready to scramble and contest the codes of imposed conduct. But why Jimi Hendrix, and not the suave Otis Redding or the explosive James Brown? Was it just because he was here in England, adopted by the London rock coterie, and was finding his initial success in Britain, as though a native son, before being exported back to the United States? He was certainly a black man who was not like any other black man. He was not like the, very few, black males I had met in my local life in southwest England, nor like the black American performers I had seen and heard on television playing the blues, rhythm and blues (R&B) and soul music. Perhaps only the transgressive camp style of Little Richard could be considered an extravagant hint of the future possibility of Hendrix, but certainly not Otis Redding, Sam and Dave or Wilson Pickett. Although, if I had chosen to linger longer in the vicinity of the sounds of 1960s soul music I would have inevitably encountered several of the sonorial trajectories and musical maps that also made up Hendrix's own itinerary.

Listening to Hendrix today opens up a manner of existence in which music testifies to an alternative scansion of time – the time of modernity, of the city and the West – that carries me into a narrative, a song, a cry, where sound reveals a history that questions the disposition ready to reduce music to a moribund lineage of stylistic influences. If language constitutes the house of being, then musical styles are themselves onto-logical statements: a sounding out of circumstances that betray more than a mere modification in musical syntax. At the time I experienced only a glimmer of this wider possibility. Nevertheless, it has continued to attract my attention, to bleed into my subsequent concerns. Jimi Hendrix continues to shadow my life. Beyond the tragedy of its abrupt termination lies the interrogation of a sound that I have inherited, which persists, survives, lives on, bearing a question that calls on me to respond.

To many in his predominantly white audience in that period, with his unrestrained music and unrestrained hair, Hendrix was the 'wild man' that has always haunted the European imaginary threatening its order. Coming from beyond immediate experience his musical style and sexuality revealed for some the seduction, for others the horror, of the id. But, I think there was also a more subtle exoticism (and eroticism) evoked around this black, American guitarist from Seattle that helped to confuse both eurocentric stereotyping and black imagining. Up on stage, in public coitus with his guitar prior to a climax in which the instrument was ignited in symbolic sacrifice, the excess of rock flared up in the night to temporarily hint at musical and cultural miscegena-tion. This touched the deepest chords of the unspoken cultural ambivalence in modern popular music and contemporary urban life in which the love of black music often, even violently, negated a love of black people.

Hendrix attired in kaftan, headband and bell bottoms, was initially associated, however, with the pale bodies of psychedelia, with the flow-ering of the hippies and summers of love. By the late 1960s in North America and Europe youth and its music had publicly triumphed. There was pop music, pop fashion, pop culture, pop art . . . a pop life. Although still frequently contested, American popular culture outside the United States, in a word, 'Americanisation', was ubiquitous. It was synonymous with the triumph of youth and its patterns of consumption. Nevertheless, there was another side to these shiny surfaces and optimistic tomorrows, all ironically reflected in the artistic speculum of Warhol's serial paint-ings and Lichtenstein's comic-strip canvases. When, in the intense pursuit of self-realisation, the languages of youth, consumerism and individu-alism were pushed to the point of fracture then the political economy of these very same categories came to be abruptly interrogated by the ambiguous reach of their cultural potential.[3]

Between the festivals of Monterey (1967) and Woodstock (1969), the arc of a rebellious journey into the heartland of 'Amerika', into the psychic, aesthetic and political configurations of overdeveloped capi-talism, was delineated. It sought an alternative and more 'authentic' life style that was simulated in an archaic symbolism borrowed from the pre-industrial worlds of the native American, Zen Buddhism and an imaginary Arcadia evoked by a return to the natural rhythms of the land. The doors on this alternative were paradoxically unlocked by the industrial fruits of chemical elixirs and the technical reproduction of sound. In its totalising and self-conscious reach, in its subjective evocation of utopia and an erotics of liberation, this counter-culture marked an unmistakable shift beyond the earlier subcultural snatching of stylised moments from the edges of the working week. Insisting on the utopic, the trajectory of the student movement in Europe, campus radicalism in the United States, and the generalisation of a culture that had 'dropped out' to embrace experience 'on the road', were destined to be interrupted by other versions of their dream. These, located in the everyday exclusion of racialised and gendered bodies, initially erupted in the long, hot summers, when pressure spilled out of the south, and out of the ghettos. It was here that black musics – particularly the insistent request of Soul – created the most potent 'junction of the erotic and the political' (Henri Lefebvre).[4]

It is in this unforeseen intersection of occidental utopianism with the return of its repressed past that Hendrix's music invites us to consider a scene that exceeds its counter-culture representations.

It is commonplace, yet still significant, to refer to Hendrix's 'psychedelic' guitar style as having its origins in the post-war black American tradition of urban blues and rhythm and blues. This was a tradition that constantly frustrated traditionalists as it apparently moved irreverently from what many white observers considered to be the 'authentic' to the 'inauthentic': from the personal immediacy of acoustic instruments to the anonymous mediation of electric amplification. Freely explored this black tradition refused to be prisoner of a prescriptive past and thereby exposed itself to the languages of change, to the cultural catalyst that the city and its urban cultures and technologies proposed.

A radically innovative urban aesthetic emerged. Whether in the meandering, improvised streets of jazz or the direct, electric highways of rhythm and blues, this aesthetic openly replied to the metropolis and modernity in a fashion that was quite distinct from the nervous closure of a European-derived canon that consistently turned its back on the city and obstinately sought the house of culture elsewhere. It was white musical commentators and cultural critics, anxious to preserve their concept of 'authentic' black musics (and the subaltern position it represented), who persuaded, for example, Big Bill Broonzy to abandon his contemporary electric guitar and Chicago band sound for an earlier solo acoustic style when he toured Britain in the 1950s. 'Authenticity' at this point was clearly of more significance for the overseers of hegemonic, white culture, and its aesthetics, than for those who were supposed to incarnate it.

To turn to rhythm and blues is to turn to a music in which the presumed antithesis between 'authentic' black music (the rural blues of the pre-war period) and the 'artificial' trickery of the city (the electric guitar and the amplified voice) was largely ignored by most of its practitioners. As an ongoing practice and cultural interrogation of historical possibilities, such music formulated an aesthetic that had little time for cultural neurosis over the city and the possibilities of technical reproduction. It refused to be limited by such preoccupations. The sounds and styles of the urban women blues singers – Ma Rainey, Bessie Smith, Memphis Minnie, Billie Holiday – all using microphones, and having their music amplified in the medium of records, radio airplay and publicity, were the pioneering part of the making of this modern urban culture.

Although often brutally stigmatised by race and class, the blues was not an isolated, autochthonous, 'folk' phenomena, but rather an integral part of modernity, central to the making of contemporary, urban culture. But while Hendrix's own foray into rock music sometimes seems to evoke a technologically sustained return of the wandering male blues singers of the 1920s and 1930s (Charlie Patton, Robert Johnson), black women – witness the altogether more difficult trajectories of Chaka Khan with Rufus, or Nona Hendryx – had a rather different, and less successful, tale to tell. Again, the romantic undercurrent of authenticity – the itinerant bluesman – provided a narrow opening, while the centrality of black women's voices to modern, urban music continued to be restricted to the predominantly racialised categories of soul music, or else to the glitzy show business success of Tamla Motown, both genres that were largely ignored by the white rock music fraternity and its critics.

Hendrix, as an isolated black guitar hero in the very white world of rock music, was initially doubly exiled: displaced both from the black, African-American context of the late 1960s, and simultaneously isolated in the temporarily adopted habitat of Anglo-American rock music. As a black performer acknowledged in the white world of rock, Hendrix was a disturbing, but largely exotic, presence who in his lifetime was marginalised from a potential identity in the historical agendas of both these potential homelands. His sound, his iconoclastic sonic signature, his guitar graffiti, represented a disturbing interruption in the prescriptive cultural script. His was a cultural and musical constellation that challenged the assumptions of readily available identities. Whatever cultural telescope you employ, Hendrix's presence distorts views of the cultural landscape. Like the simultaneous presence and absence of his wah-wah guitar doubling, displacing and ghosting the rock music feast as an uninvited guest, his music is an oblique mark that has left a restless and disturbing sign on the history of our times.

The double scandal of Hendrix's music was that it drew upon all the resources of a black musical inheritance to take rock further than its progenitors had foreseen, and, in breaking bounds and going beyond the pale, it simultaneously opened up a further set of possibilities for contemporary black music. Like the cultural interrogation and disorientation posed by the paintings of Jean-Michel Basquiat in the white rooms of the art world, Hendrix provided a cultural masque (and mask), a putting into play of the simultaneous expression and repression, of his own cultural configuration.[5] As a radical interruption, a slash of disturbance across the expected soundtracks of both white and black musics of the time, he transformed those languages into a moment of freedom.

It is for this reason that I feel called upon to listen to Hendrix's music not in terms of nostalgia, or by simply registering his historical significance in the narrative of popular music, but rather to hear in his sound, as it acquired shape and timbre in the extensive, cultural daze of the late 1960s, a series of sonorial and cultural passages that continue to cast a resonance, and a dissonance, both back upon that past and onwards over my present into possible futures.

While cast backwards towards his blue roots, Hendrix was simultaneously considered to have spawned the legion of male guitar neophytes who came after him and roamed the high plains of 1970s rock music – from Led Zeppelin's Jimmy Page to Eddie Van Halen – establishing the divisive genre of heavy metal. But his experimental sound, his freeform and electronically extended techniques (wah-wah, feedback, reverberation, echo) were also to become ubiquitous in urban black musics: from soul, to jazz, to cinema soundtracks; from Sly Stone and Bobby Womack to Isaac Hayes; to Miles Davis, Ornette Coleman, Sonny Sharrock and James Blood Ulmer; and then on, via a tributary of James Brown, to George Clinton and Bootsy Collins; to Prince and Living Colour. If, after Hendrix, white rock music was radically transformed, so, too, were black sounds. Hendrix was not so much an oddity wandering in the white rock world as a complex and fragile bridge, gathering together new possibilities that previously travelled in different and seemingly quite separate cultural configurations.

Listening to his music with this ear not only permits me to talk about Jimi Hendrix in the apparently separate contexts of African-American musics and white rock, but also allows me to return to the theme of modern urban cultures and to the questioning and refashioning of contemporary aesthetics. This provides the means to break with the closed circle of exotic positioning – Hendrix the black gypsy, the nomadic 'wild man' – while simultaneously appreciating the richness of his musical and cultural spirit. This extends the provocation of Hendrix to challenge existing cultural authorities on both sides of many cultural divides. The ambiguity of Hendrix's musical gift blocks and deviates the facile adoption of binary oppositions, not only of those between 'authentic' and 'inauthentic' musics, but also of those between 'authentic' and 'inauthentic' identities.

An almost contemporary provocation along similar lines, and directly influenced by Hendrix's example, was the challenging position that Miles Davis occupied between black, urban music and white rock after the release of *In a Silent Way* (1969). As if in defiance of the 'appetite for sameness and symmetry' (Paul Gilroy) Hendrix and Davis are part of a black musical vanguard, to which could be added names and styles as diverse as those of Sun Ra, John Coltrane, George Clinton, Sly and the Family Stone, Prince, that has confused the obviousness of such distinctions, turning the music loose from earlier cultural (and ethnic) claims without loosing the bass line, the *nero continuo*, of their story, their histories, and its particular way of telling. This becomes a music that is suspended in the historical and cultural configurations of ethnicity, for it is undeniably African-American, but that is no longer the point of arrival, *rather the point of departure* into a series of openings leading to a radical reconfiguration of urban aesthetics and ethics. Received along this axis, Hendrix's fascination with extra-terrestrial sounds and sci-fi worlds – in such pieces as 'Third Stone from the Sun', 'Up from the Skies', '1983 . . . A Merman I Shall Turn To Be' – echoes along a spectrum that certainly stretches from the cosmic voyaging of Sun Ra's Solar Arkestra to John Coltrane's *Interstellar Space*, and then on through George Clinton's cybernetic funk to 'roots' being digitally reviewed and synthesised in the contemporary reroutings of urban rap and hip hop.

In the striking lyricism of Hendrix's musical 'voice' we are constantly drawn into a language that speaks in other-worldly accents of a cultural redemption that is seemingly always postponed to tomorrow and elsewhere. Drawing on this disenchantment – the blues in the deepest sense of the term as a 'structure of feeling' (Raymond Williams) rather than merely a musical figure – Hendrix constructs an electric poetics that successfully breaches his musical and cultural inheritance to release not only a promise but also an effective reworking of the conditions that constitute his complex positioning. It touches its musical zenith in his famous deconstruction of the American hymn of identity, 'The Star Spangled Banner', on stage at Woodstock.

The adoption of extra-terrestrial persona and scenarios in Hendrix, Sun Ra and George Clinton might therefore be considered to suggest a two-way flight: away from rigid ethnic and historical grounding, but also a flight further and deeper into the possibilities of inhabiting a modern, urban sublime. Here there exists an elaboration of an ironic musical disposition in which the prescriptive is overtaken by the inscriptive, tradition by translation and transformation, as the music travels elsewhere, beyond the boundaries of your presumed identity and cultural position. Such sounds collate the heterogeneity of experiences. They recast historical and cultural encounters in the particular body and breath of the event, thereby simultaneously confirming and breaking the inherited rules of music, culture and history. In pursuit of your place in the world, imposed standards – musical motifs, aesthetic values, ethnic positionalities – are necessarily punctured, parodied, deviated and displaced. There is no tradition, no language, that is immune from this process. So, when Hendrix plays the blues – 'Red House', 'Voodoo Chile' – he invariably digs deeper while simultaneously sounding further out, extending the orbit, prolonging the interrogation of the journey.

Here, on the brink of cultural memory, I find myself considering music not only as a sound that marks and commemorates past time, but also as a moment in a continuing narration that permits a re-membering and re-telling that allows new configurations of sense and sensibility, able to engage with my times, to emerge. In fact, on the way to listening to the music of Jimi Hendrix, it might perhaps be even necessary to temporarily suspend some of the questions that initially positioned and interrogated the figure of Hendrix in his lifetime in order to hear better what was silenced or even excluded from such a framing. Whether identified as a black minstrel whose wild antics confirmed the worst white stereotyping, or as an Uncle Tom who had sold out his race, in the excess of language bestowed upon him what breaks through the cultural masque he enacted and the ritual masks he wore, what lives on is the sound, is the poetic testimony that remains irreducible to the point his commentators and critics were seeking to make.

Of course the noise of those past controversies is not simply to be turned off as though it were now anachronistic historical static. But instead of holding Hendrix hostage such controversies can now be transformed into a further opening: for those circumstances, those contingencies, are inevitably also inscribed in Hendrix's eclectic musical speech, in what he was musically saying and how he was speaking. What ultimately remains is the burden of the sound, its historical weight, which bears testimony to a time and to a figure that continues to speak to us.

Hendrix's music is unequivocally to be located in the developments of an avant-gardist, urban black aesthetic that has consistently challenged inherited understandings of culture, technology and the historical and aesthetic possibilities of inhabiting the modern city. At this point, his music becomes central to any understanding of the emergence of a contemporary urban sublime. Posed in this manner, Hendrix's music is pivotal in the shift from marginality – the musics of an ethnically identified, urban dispossessed (blues, jazz, R&B, soul, rap) – to becoming central in the dispersal of an abstract aesthetics and its ahistorical understanding of culture.

It is at this point that the passage from the hypnotic rhythms of Bo Diddley's electric guitar to the futuristic soundscapes etched out along the neck of Hendrix's instrument a decade later might begin to be considered as part of a shared repertoire. In both cases, there is a coming to terms with the city, urban life, a metropolitan imaginary and technical reproduction. There was probably no other choice but to seek to make that space your own. But what is significant here for the history of modernity is how a subaltern and discriminated culture successfully managed to turn the languages of presumed alienation – those of the city, of its technologies and techniques – into an unsuspected affirmation. In its sonorial codification of urban space, rendering it an intimate and sustaining place, black musics have taught us to experience and live it other-wise; that is, beyond the obsessive condemnation of patriarchal critical closure and its refusal of urban culture and associated technologies.

Listening to this music with these ears it becomes possible to consider the history of modern African-American musics as a form of perpetual dialogue with the possibilities (and limits – which in being recognised come to provide new openings or cracks in the existing form) of the modern city: from the blues to jazz, from soul to rap. Are not all these musics diverse modes for exploring modernity – as lament, as protest, as joy as well as anger, as a poetics – rather than outrightly rejecting it? Most significantly, to listen to this history in this way is to invert the frequently romantic marginalisation of its voices. Here black musics no longer occupy the site of exotic marginalia but come to be centred and central. Rather than be considered as an embellishment of the urban soundtrack, an exciting ornament that revives and jolts the predictable grooves of post-war white rock music and the popular mainstream via a series of 'borrowings' and 'inspirations', in these black sounds, in this 'blackstream', we can hear something more. There emerges a displacement, another cultural version or historical 'cut', that reveals another centre to metropolitan music making, another way of being in the city

111

and inhabiting the modern world. At this point African-American musics overturn the assumed model of subcultural marginality and their cultures of resistance – eternally destined to subalternity and negation – and become instances that decentre and recentre the historical score. The ubiquitous global insistence of reggae and rap musics, reaching out into local variants and translations, is perhaps the most eloquent and resilient symptom of this cultural realignment in metropolitan musical grammar.

But even when this structural adjustment is acknowledged, resulting in a diverse mapping and understanding of the cultural scene, the presence of Hendrix remains disturbing. In a diverse centring of modern metropolitan music he remains an enigmatic figure. Like the wandering gypsy persona he adopted, it is sometimes difficult to focus, or configure, his position in both the cultural texts of the 1960s and the ones that are being enacted today. Perhaps it is precisely this difficulty – the impossibility of being readily configured or easily discarded – that is most instructive?

For Hendrix's music evokes a complexity and multiplicity of ways that spill over readily available distinctions. It plays at the crossroads, and while it has travelled a particular road, a highway violently shaped by slavery and racist subjection, it refuses to be contained by that route. It elaborates an urban and urbane aesthetic that is not limited to the construction of particular musical genres, but which plays on the borders, living between musical and cultural worlds, reworking and rerouting their possibilities within the historical inheritance of modernity. If we want to insist on a 'rooted' sense of culture, and tradition as a continuum of autonomous identities and experiences, then Coltrane, Hendrix, Davis and Prince are all 'exiles'. Their musics envelope us with shifting, nomadic configurations, an ensemble of inter-, or trans-, cultural sounds that explore, or 'sound out', inherited limits while all the time transporting us elsewhere.

The political and ethical understandings that can be drawn from these histories, from these sounds as they course through our lives and resonate in our sense of becoming, is not only that they cast the shadows of their influence across modernity, but also that they simultaneously reveal a diverse and more experimental manner of inhabiting and testing its possibilities. As they sound off against, and yearn across, the divisions of our time they open up spaces within the inherited to stretch and tear the accepted, to disturb and undercut the ordained, to sound the world in a diverse key.

To cite the past

To cite the past is to resite the present and reveal in it the instance of contingent paths that lead us back while taking us forwards. Memories . . . of a Berlin childhood, of a zoological garden, of a city where 'to lose oneself, as one loses oneself in a forest, is an art to be acquired' . . . of a Belfast adolescence 'where you could feel the silence at half past eleven on long summer nights as the wireless played Radio Luxembourg, and the voices whispered across Beechie River'.[6] December 1993, at the Masonic Auditorium in San Francisco, Van Morrison sings 'In the Garden'. This segues into an earlier song – 'Real, Real Gone' – which, in turn, recalls Sam Cooke's 'You Send Me'.

Here a male body modulates beneath, and then broadcasts itself through, the music: the rasp of a voice recalling limits while simultaneously stretching across them as the vocal descends into the respiration of being, sense into the infinity of sound. Still in California, south of Big Sur looking through the pines out at the ocean at the promise of whales, in my inner ear I hear a further song:

Foghorns blowing in the night
Salt sea air in the morning breeze
Driving cars all along the coastline
This must be what it's all about.[7]

Attempting to describe such music is to embark on a doomed activity, destined to fall short of the desired object; it is to be left mumbling before the ineffable. So why write? Perhaps merely to launch a sign, leave a trace, hook myself to a sound and the dream it disseminates in its wake, and there seek a path through the world. And then the song itself is not necessarily about anything. It is an event in sound in which the accidental and the intentional are conjoined. So, it is not a case of verbal approximation, of explaining the sound, as though it contained the kernel of a stable sense and intent, but rather to seek in it a response that provokes my sense of being.

Another time, at the end of a dark alley in the Quartieri Spagnoli in Naples in an eruption of light stands the Galleria Toledo Theatre. I have come tonight to see and hear the Algerian dancer El Hadi Cheriffa accompanied by the voice and percussion of Moussa Belkacemi. The sounds, the body, the poetics of a visual and aural grace harvest traditional music and forms in a volatile mix (Bedouin, Berber, Tuareg) whose distinctions and composition are equally part of the modern Maghreb. The question of their composition, and the composition of such a question, shadows the dance, echoes in the song . . .

The voice that sings
like the hand that writes
is the body in language
responding
to the call
and
care
of being

To think

To think. Most of us have inherited a manner of thought that relies on the primal separation of the subject from the objects of the world; a sharp division between subjecthood and the things it subsequently claims and secures for itself. Through this distinction reason escapes the finitude of the thinker, knowledge escapes time. Although thereby prone to the liberty of speculation and self-assessment, this is paradoxically a manner of thinking, even in its most attentive and reflexive moments, that can never really question itself. Thought orbits around the unexamined premise, and presumptions, of the *cogito*. Interrogation is reserved for what lies outside the immediacy of subjectivity: the external world of objects and alterity. Critical thinking, as opposed to consolatory thought, however, necessarily disavows a desire for this subjective completeness. In disrupting the drive to be 'overwhelmed by coherence', critical thinking is not conceptual at all.[8] Its rigour is neither egocentrical nor geometrical, for it comes to be disciplined by an altogether more extensive and ambiguous imperative: that of always and already being in the world. It is from there that understanding emerges. Redemption does not lie further on up the road but at our feet, in the steps we take each day, in the language we inhabit, in the finitude of our bodies, in the limits of our being. To contest the existing ways of the world cannot involve postponement, a knowledge yet to come. Where we have each arrived, the place each occupies, is the result of an ongoing engagement, stretching across generations, with those ways. Our power, our being, comes out of that past to meet and configure our future.

The asymmetry of powers, of their political and cultural representations, and of their inscription in differentiated discrepancies and discriminations, structures a world in which coherence, and the knowledge it espouses, is invariably the metonymy of a violent imposition. Even if explicitly linked to the linguistic evocation of the plural, this social and political disposition is invariably a subtle net that systematically captures and marginalises difference, often, symptomatically enough, in the name of liberalism, identity politics and multiculturalism. To draw from the conditions I inherit and inhabit a language that invites me to think other-wise encourages me to interrupt and interrogate such inherited prescriptions, even those of a radical provenance. This permits me to admit, maybe even to inhabit, a diverse configuration of the 'political'.

Musics and memories: the perpetual translation of space – the space of a language, a sound, an image, a life – into the peculiarities of a place, into the shaft of existence constituted by the passing 'now', inevitably invokes the translation of geography into ontology, of the syntax of sound and images into the event of singing and seeing, of the abstract into the body. To consider these questions in the context of sound, even in the epoch of global technological reproduction, is to lend attention to the metaphorical and metamorphosing power of music giving voice to the enigma. As a language, as an economic institution and set of cultural practices, a way of listening to and sounding out the world, music contributes not only to the making of soundscapes, but also to the variegated culturalscapes in which we move. As such it is also 'a repository of our knowing and our memory.'[9]

We could consider music

We could consider music as one of the languages we inhabit, dwell in, and in which we, our histories, cultures and identities, are constituted. As a language it is seemingly immaterial and yet profoundly terrestrial.[10] Language is the constellation of presence and absence, of loss, that provides the invisible co-ordinates of our being; what, after all, remains as the wound of reality, is language; that no more and always more that propels us forwards along rarely discernible lines of movement exposed to the winds of the world where there is no unique point of reference or origin. This, perhaps, as Foucault towards the end of *The Order of Things* puts it, is our 'origin without origins'. At this point to ask what music is, is to ask what our culture is, who we are, and what are we doing here? As Antoine Hennion justly notes: 'music is a sociology'.[11]

To propose this moment of reflection, this silence before the song, is to oppose theoretical seizures of the world intent on reducing language, be it of music or everyday discourse, to a transparent medium, deployed after our arrival, simply the servant of our subjectivity. Language does not come after the subject; it is already waiting and calling us. For languages, whether literary, musical, or quotidian, and even if often dependent upon quite precise techno-cultural systems, are not turned on and off by the flick of a switch. They persist and permeate our world. They ghost our presence and circulate beyond our individual volition. As part and parcel of the economy of our lives they exist prior to our knowing and thus inform our being and becoming. They are irreducible to a medium or technology. They are part of our understanding.

Where, for example, does the image or the sound end and the social begin? Or, in another lexicon, where does the commercial commence and the aesthetic conclude? The impossibility of defining such boundaries draws us beyond the narrow distinctions that seek to maintain such mediums, such languages and technologies, at a distance, whether critical or social. We cannot withdraw from them, they are always at hand. We are forced to recognise their ontological centrality to who we are, and to what we might desire to become.[12]

Perhaps this lack of distance, resulting in a propensity to be enveloped and made over in these languages so that, beyond the obvious instrumental reach of economic and political profit, they also come to resonate deeply with the ambiguous journeying of our being in the world, is most acutely signalled, though rarely considered, in the dominion of sound. The passage of sound, and the sobering thought of the inconclusive, betrays our pretensions to grasp and reduce our surroundings to a common frame. It is here where the immediacy of visual regimes and the surveillance of ocular sense is usurped by the infinite relay of song and silence, where to listen can become as significant as to sing.

> What I mean by 'transgression' is something completely literal and secular at the same time: that faculty music has to travel, cross over, drift from place to place in a society, even though many institutions and orthodoxies have sought to confine it.[13]

Although continually embedded in appearances, in the visual economy, the body continually exits from this daily frame through the migrations of sound. Memory clings to the former while following the itineraries of the latter. Sounds chaff against the unilateral constrictions of ocular hegemony and constantly threaten to break bounds and circulate without regard for address or direction. The visual fetishisation of the object is consistently carried away by sound – notes, shouts, respiration, the rap, the silence: the space that offers hospitality to the future. The scopic drive that seeks to render all transparent, scientific, clinically apprehensible and economically exploitable – herein lies the uncanny proximity of medical and media discourses – is invariably intent on grasping being and time, turning life into an exemplary instance, an abstraction, an ever-ready 'standing reserve' of meaning.[14] The image, for all its potential ambiguity, is structurally more circumscribed, and tends towards the consolation of a semantic full stop. It is the economy of sound – from silence to a scream – that ultimately disturbs visual regimes and the repression of rendering everything representative. To turn to the ear is also to return images to the pleasure of surfaces, to the liberty (and limits) of the making, masking and masqueing of representation. This is to contest the triumph of the image over the act, of the disembodied form over the corporeal flux, of the metaphysical signature over the unruly event, of the sign over sound.[15] By exceeding such an imagining and framing of the world, the visual conclusion is relocated and the image is forced to reveal its logocentric impulses as a power and a limit, as a promise and a threat, as an extension and a closure. Between the 'metaphysical understanding that all truth is representational' and what continues to surge beyond such a frame lies a path along which the poesis of sound maintains the promise of the irrepressible.[16]

A voice in the dark, a saxophone cadence on the street, saliva on the tongue, breath drawn between words, the suspension of silence: all this is music, and all this mutates immediate motives and punctuates it with memory. For to ask the meaning of music, the significance of sound, is perhaps to seek to distil from the depths of our senses the ungraspable beingness of being. George Steiner writes: 'In music, being and meaning are inextricable. They deny paraphrase. But they are, and our experience of this "essentiality" is as certain as any in human awareness.'[17] Weaving together beat and being, music and memory, the desire and deferral of sound hums an internal counter-point in the pre-linguistic state of language, in the indeterminable semiosis of our bodies.[18]

Music permits us to travel. Above all, music draws us into the passages of memory and its 'sudden disjunction of the present'.[19] Here time overflows the containment of our concepts. For the time of memory is a reversible time that permits the return, revisiting and re-vision of other times. The coeval presence of this reversible time and the irreversible nature of our bodies opens up a rent in our experience, in our lives. Linear, irrevocable time is interrupted by the interval and intrusion of the eternal return of a transversal time: the return of the symptom, of the recall, of the recording and the reordering of the past, and the perpetual desire to return to the record. The mutable place of memory erupts in the space of our histories as a set of fragments suspended in time, as a loss that is experienced as essential to our comprehension of the present. Memory is sustained and held in custody (both captured and protected) by the fragile chains of language, by the cadence and respiration of the body that constitutes the ambiguous aperture and agenda of our identity. And music, as song, dance and rhythm, as musical maps and song lines, forms a contrapuntal score that sounds out circumstances in the creation of a mobile individuation and community.

A gypsy girl dances beneath a tree

A gypsy girl dances beneath a tree in the desert of Rajasthan. Her brightly coloured dress and jewellery flash in the evening shadows. The scene is both hypnotic and emblematic. I find myself on the threshold of an elsewhere that opens my world to the disturbing presence of something that I recognise but which flees my desire for comprehension. Here there is an event that evades the closure of my understanding. Everything is clear – the figure dancing in the desert, the sounds that accompany her movement – but something remains opaque, hidden, out of sight, mute. This is the opening scene of the film and musical journey of *Latcho Drom* (1993) by the Algerian director Tony Gatlif. The itinerary commences in the north-west area of the Indian subcontinent and goes on to traverse an archipelago of historical memories that are revealed in the sounds that emerge along the way: India, Egypt, Turkey, Romania, Hungary, Auschwitz, La Camargue, Andalusia. This history of a people without a home (Roma, Gypsies) illuminates in a flash Heidegger's proposition that language is the house of being.[20] For this lateral history is maintained and nurtured in the interminable journey of a changing song that passes from horizon to horizon transforming the passage in music, the earth in history, a nomadic space and identity into places and the house of language. 'Vertical' history, dependent upon the ground we find beneath our feet in the ancestral soil, is here displaced by the persistent travelling of a language – in-corporated in sound, in song and dance – seeking an accommodation in the world. Here, paradoxically, I encounter a fissure in the naturalist *topos* of identity as the seemingly archaic intersects the stable co-ordinates of home and homeland to transform modernity into modernities, exposing another sense of home in its midst. In this nomadology of sound I am drawn into listening to the spark of contingency that lies between the conscious and unconscious realms of history. In this musical inscription of the earth, I become aware of a state in which a music and a world meet and combine in the body, rendering explicit the alterity that makes each of us a subject.

For identity itself is a shifting, combinatory figure, a musical phase in the score of being. We begin to hear the sound, we are born, but once under way it does not conclude until mortality imposes an individual coda. Identity is an ever present, ever unfolding, bass line; a rhizomatic figure, a fugue drawn from the languages that transport and sustain us, a solo and improvisation on the energies that unfold and devolve in the world (rather than an isolated work that withdraws and redraws the world into the single and constant note of the self).

To consider music as memory is to grasp the vital and physical nature of repetition; of how, according to Freud, remembering (*Erinnerung*) is linked to repeating (*Wiederholen*). In 1914 the father of psychoanalysis wrote a brief essay entitled 'Remembering, Repeating and Working-Through'.[21] He noted the importance of repetition in discharging symptoms 'along the paths of conscious activity'.[22] Further, he underlined that repetition can provide both an access to memory and a mode for resisting, refusing and repressing it. Music, as a language of repetition, continually proposes this play between recalling and resisting the past. In the return of sound, music fills the intervals in memory, provoking a temporary overcoming of the resistance to its presence and the body that incorporates it. In the instance of repetition perhaps it is not so much the case of remembering what has been forgotten as to expose the act of forgetting itself? Oblivion is forgotten, but the language of repetition simultaneously takes it in hand and transforms it. This continual song, 'not as an event of the past, but as a present-day force', provides consistent custody for the presence–absence of the memory of being – revealing in the event of sound that simultaneous disclosure and concealment that is the fundamental role of art according to the philosopher of the Black Forest.[23]

Memory, around which

Memory, around which so much of the sense of our selves revolves and returns, is the skin stretched over the world across which desire, emotions and expression flow. Memory evokes the eroticisation of the past. But memory does not exist as an autonomous realm; it is sustained and surveyed by language. Contesting the apartheid of memory, and the agents of oblivion seeking to consign the past to the conspiracy of silence, music sustains an ethical resonance that permits us not so much to fully capture and comprehend the past as to recover fragments of its dispersed body. Beyond the rigid monologue of reading, cataloguing and interpreting antecedents, beyond institutional and academic dismembering, music establishes a potential site that summons a response: a re-membering that directs us elsewhere. Music allows us to temporarily invert the course of time and consider history as a reversible testimony – hence never assured, as Walter Benjamin points out – that bears witness to the ruined redemption of humanity, to a sorely tested but eternal faith in our habitat. Listened to in this key music inaugurates an ethics. Drawing us through the gaps in the implacability of time and the dictates of meaning, music allows us to temporarily exit from the narratives that frame us in order to re-negotiate our 'home' in them.

Our access to memory is through language, through inscription on the page, our bodies, and in the auditorium in which we speak and listen. Not only do we recall our past in music, but also the very techniques that permit us to return there, recordings, are a form of writing. In *The Aesthetics of Recorded Sound*, the Japanese critic Shuhei Hosokawa writes: 'It is not by chance that incipient devices such as the phonograph, gramo-phone, and grammo-phone all were given names derived by combining "sound" and "writing".'[24] Music survives, lives on, by being re-written, re-inscribed.

Displayed in the instantaneous languages of photography, film, record and digital images our memories are increasingly rendered proximate. There they are captured, amplified and disseminated. Reproductive technologies and techniques permit an 'eternal return'. But there also remains a profounder strain that no technology or technique will ever be capable of fully translating. In the desire for time, for life, our memories reach out to protect us from oblivion, and in the shifting but repetitive modalities of our subscription to sound that clear, but indecipherable, desire attains the maximum of ubiquity. Music serves as a multi-dimensional map; it is simultaneously connected to fashion (repetition of the new) and to memory (moments lost in time). It permits us to maintain a fragile bridge between consciousness and oblivion. It introduces the history of the event into the fluctuating, atemporal regime of memory by permitting us to mark time and recall it, admitting the past to the present, and allowing us to trace in its echo other dreams, further futures.

So music, although initially the expression of a historical and cultural instance, once released into the world travels interminably; it has no single location, it continues to continue without an immediate reason. It is everywhere and nowhere: the hole in time, the slash in space, the noon-time of experience.

But although ubiquitous, sounds are also always transcribed into the particular poetics of a place. As language, as writing, memory, music and the murmur of being, sound always involves an act of translation. In the transfer, in the re-membering invoked in the transit, the intention of re-presenting something that previously existed elsewhere is interrupted. For it is overtaken in a process – the historical work, the imaginary work, the dream work – that transforms as it transports something from one place to another and in the movement displaces it.[25] The desired mimesis between reality and representation, between past and present, is deviated by the radical historicity of the situation that exists in the perennial gap between the excess of sense and the limits of each instance of translation, memory, meaning, narrative and recognition. Translation reveals the disruption in the very foundations of translation. For it cannot speak in terms of universal meaning and the transparency of truth, but rather in the accents of the cultural configurations and social interstices in which language, representation and reality is destined to be transcribed, transformed, and made over again and again as it struggles towards an accommodation.[26]

There exists no simple or direct recovery of how things 'really were', only of how things come to be remembered and translated, not what happened, but what is happening. So, everything is both remembered and repressed, every testimony is flawed, every recall destined for another return. For memory is also the art of forgetting, of occluding a loss, negating a lack, cancelling the failure of language, registering the incomplete destiny of the intention. Memory is thus not an origin, a prescription, or a destination, but a resource, a table of writing, a place of inscriptions . . . in which the poignancy and pain of the past is both exposed *and* overwritten in the psychic insistence of the present.

Memory dwells in an ambiguous landscape that for Walter Benjamin stretches to include history.[27] Does that mean that significant memory is only a collective historical configuration that excludes any grasp of the obfuscating slippage and repression that betrays the individual's unconscious? Or are such distinctions too fuzzy, perhaps impossible to draw? If so, it leaves me with an interrogation that moves both ways to disturb my understanding of both the 'individual' and the 'collective', to interrogate their mutual involvement and inscription in the language that nominates such divisions. This might also permit the suggestion of a historical unconscious where the explicit, rational account is forever shadowed, doubled and displaced by another story, another scene. And does that path not also permit the possibility of contemplating an individual configuration of the past in the suggestive, but diverse, manner of Proust or Benjamin's own Berlin childhood? History not as science, but as memory, not as the law, but as language. History as an act of testimony: the act of mourning the irreparable loss – for we can never return there – that sustains our becoming.

Memory is neither fixed nor eternal. It mutates. As a cultural constellation it permits an oblique glance that scans historical time diversely, proposing a redemption in which cultural speech and historical action are re-written through the introduction of the unstable power of metaphor and the simultaneous dissemination and disruption of language. This, for example, is what provided Benjamin with the method of turning history against its own provenance. (Here also lies his affinity with the disenchanted Baroque poetics of the shipwreck of words crashing against the unnameable, the swirl of notes drifting away towards infinity.) For, if history and memory share the same structure, then history merges into a setting: not into the prescriptive regularities of a fixed or representative structure, but into the discontinuous inscriptions of the scene. So, Benjamin's reading of images necessarily involves a breaking of images, a critical awakening through which he seeks to recover, collect, and prise them loose from an uncontested continuum. This, too, is the case with memory: it is necessary to break into it, to interrupt its consolations, and 'to discover what the present might have been by a re-cognition of the past.'[28] In the secret agreement between past and present, the body of history, the history of the body. . . history as body, breaks into the past in order to re-configure and em-body the present not in terms of continuity and confirmation, but as an interruption.

The aestheticisation of tradition and pre-industrial life (a vapid romanticism whose subsequent confluence in the 'aestheticisation of politics', to stretch Benjamin's noted definition, has by no means been restricted to fascism) is invariably grounded in the premises of a non-alienated society that has been subsequently obfuscated and obscured.[29] The present consists in a lack, an absence, for it fails to restore us to a lost, organic unity. But what if alienation, like contradiction, is not peculiar to modern industrial life and metropolitan capitalism? What if alienation never experiences *Aufhebung*? What if alienation is a terrestrial constraint destined to frustrate the 'progress' introjected in all teleologies? In other words, what if contradictions are ontological, holding us prisoner to the time of our being? To recognise this condition, while struggling against it, means less to push forward and more to move sideways by refusing to perform the prescriptive by reworking, re-routing it differently. It is to cast yourself not forwards towards utopia (itself the humanist child of a eurocentric 'progress' set upon discovering new worlds), but sideways into atopia: another place, a diverse way of inhabiting the world. The utopic is usurped by the heterotopic, by the proliferation of space into different places, languages, sounds, rhythms . . .

Here the return to the past is not to a potential future already known and lost, but to a history susceptible to interruption, to a tradition that persists by inaugurating the discontinuous.

The ineffable essence of music perhaps best helps us to temporarily elude the rational insistence of 'progress' through transversal journeys sideways into the expansion of the present, into the architecture of sound employed in building temporal homelands, constructing habitats and seeking accommodation in the world. As the bearer of alterity, music is able to render explicit a relationship that elsewhere is often condemned to historical silence. Sounds and voices that arrive from the edges of my life, the frontiers of my experience, manage to impose an interval in my understanding. Here music casts me elsewhere, opening a breach in the institutions and habits of the quotidian. Suspending the prescriptive, music permits a possible inscription in a gap in which one takes leave from the predictable in order to recite, and thereby resite, a language, a history, elsewhere. Let us listen briefly to Edward Said dwelling on this potential interval:

> The first musical performance I ever attended as a very small boy (in the mid-1940s) was a puzzling, interminably long, and yet haunting concert by Umm Kalthoum, already the premier exponent of classical Arabic song. I had no way of knowing that her peculiar rigor as performer derived from an aesthetic whose hallmark was exfoliating variation, in which repetition, a sort of meditative fixation on one or two small patterns, and an almost total absence of developmental (in the Beethovian sense) tension were the key elements. The point of the performance I later realized, was not to get to the end of a carefully constructed logical structure − working through it − but to luxuriate in all sorts of byways, to linger over details and changes in text, to digress and then digress from the digression. And because in my preponderantly Western education (both musical and academic) I seemed to be dedicated to an ethic of productivity and of overcoming obstacles, the kind of art practiced by Umm Kalthoum receded in importance for me.[30]

It is memory that protects us from the past which would otherwise flood in and swamp the present. As a construction, a shelter we build, a tale we tell, memory both brakes and bestows shape on the inchoate that would otherwise overwhelm us. In a self-portrait entitled 'The Shadows' written in 1925 for Martin Heidegger, Hannah Arendt writes: 'All sorrows can be borne if you put them into a story or tell a story about them.'[31] For memory is not merely formed, it is framed and, in a subtle sense, faked, fictionalised. It provides a site that seemingly offers access to the past but which can never escape the interrogation and shape of the present. Memory is a mechanism that selects. In our recall we re-member certain things while forgetting, negating and denying other things. Our memories are as authentic (or inauthentic) as everything else we do. All memories, all writings, all histories, are fallible and fragmented. Each is a version of what is irremediably lost to it. It is always a re-membering, a temporary putting together of disparate elements of a body that can never be made whole, that is always provisional, illuminated by the light of oblivion. For memory is not a stable monument to the passage of time, but rather an unstable configuration that defies time and which can be attained by different paths to reveal diverse stories. Thus memory is always contested. It can therefore also be the site of amnesia and cancellation. To recognise the past as a scriptable economy, a writing pad or palimpsest, is also to recognise its susceptibility to diverse interpretations subject to the powers that seek to authorise the past and, through it, the present. The return and representation of the past, is always susceptible to the 'assassins of memory', and thus 'obligates us to become sensitive to the fact of the forgotten.'[32]

Music as a language (like all languages) maintains this tension through its communal use and individuation. Its ready accessibility compared to other, more formally institutionalised, languages such as literature, historiography and the visual arts, permits an ubiquitous and unexpected punctuation of the scripts we are expected to recite. Music, in its anonymous consumption and innumerable moments of articulation – from the desert ceremony and forest clearing to the bar, street corner, subway exit, and modern consecration in the recording studio – perhaps provides an altogether more extensive and irrepressible configuration of a language that sings of time and being while recording memory. If music often provides a home for conservative nostalgia and official memory it also proposes a return to what can become new points of departure. In rendering the ordinary extra-ordinary, music provokes an exit from the constraining immediacy of the everyday world. Caught in swirls of sound, each of us comes to reconfigure that presence, that present.

To inscribe memory into music

To inscribe memory into music, and music into memory, is to reconfigure aesthetic experience. The aesthetic experience becomes something opaque, composed of what we think we have already experienced, those shards of memory which are also the memory of what surges through and beyond the instrumental and the institutional. In the re-membrance and re-collection of what exceeds subjectivity and individual volition there emerges the disturbing and disruptive interrogation of the unfathomable. This floating and indecipherable disposition – which does not imply that it is not also a historical and cultural composition – is without immediate ground, for it exceeds definition, it defies intentionality and breaches the continuity of comprehension. It lies in the border between the conscious and the unconscious: a rhythm residing in the noise of the world between the ragged melodies of our being and the instrumental beat of the thought that brings that excess, which threatens to break in, overwhelm, disturb and decentre us, into our ken by seemingly explaining it. But art does not illuminate the world, it darkens it, bringing to reason what reason resists and repels.[33] It announces not the revelation of what can be said, seen and judged, but the rhythmic insistence of what cannot always be represented, only sensed.[34] Deposited in music is the refusal of mimesis.

As a construction in and across time, memory is thus not merely a transparent envelope that contains (and constrains) what we think we know and are able to recall. For if it casts our attention towards the past, it also propels us into the shadows where we sense what we can neither fully explain nor announce. In this transfer between past and present, between what is conceded to reason and what exceeds it, and where each contributes to the constitution of the other, how can we know what we think we know? What we can, and do, hold on to are the languages that permit us to consider such questions. The memory of art, and the art of memory, come to be temporarily rendered coherent in this interrogation.

Notes

1 Octavio Paz, 'Fire by Friction', in *A Tree Within*, New York, New Directions, 1988, p. 49. Jacques Derrida, 'Lettre à Peter Eisenman/Letter to Peter Eisenman', in William Lillyman, Marilyn Moriarty and David Neuman (eds) *Critical Architecture and Contemporary Culture*, New York and Oxford, Oxford University Press, 1994, p. 31 and p. 22 (translation by Hilary P. Hanel). Bruce Chatwin, *The Songlines*, London, Picador, 1987, p. 120. Trinh T. Minh-ha, from the film *Naked Spaces – Living is Round*.

2 The black, American guitarist Jimi Hendrix came to Britain as an unknown musician in September 1966. He was brought over by Chas Chandler, bass player of the Animals, in the ebb tide of the 'British invasion' of the American pop charts. Hendrix himself had played on and off in the United States in the previous five years with many touring soul and R&B bands, accompanying Little Richard, the Isley Brothers and Curtis Knight among others. Within six months of his arrival in Britain he had achieved recording success and was shortly destined for international stardom. In the brief three remaining years of his life he established himself as probably the most influential guitar player of the twentieth century.

3 This and the following paragraph are largely drawn from my account in *Urban Rhythms*, London, Macmillan, 1985.

4 Henri Lefebvre, *The Explosion: Marxism and the French Upheaval*, New York, Monthly Review Press, 1969, p. 26. Lefebvre is here commenting on Herbert Marcuse.

5 On the use and abuse of black identity in the contemporary art world, see Kobena Mercer, 'A Sociography of Diaspora', in Paul Gilroy, Lawrence Grossberg

and Angela McRobbie (eds) *Without Guarantees: In Honour of Stuart Hall*, London and New York, Verso, 2000. On Jean-Michel Basquiat, see Dick Hebdige, 'Welcome to the Terrordrome: Jean-Michel Basquiat and the "Dark" Side of Hybridity', in Richard Marshall (ed.) *Jean-Michel Basquiat*, New York, Whitney/Abrams, 1992.

6 The citations are from, respectively, Walter Benjamin's *A Berlin Childhood* (*Infanzia berlinese*, Turin, Einaudi, 1981), and Van Morrison's 'On Hyndford Street', *Hymns to the Silence*, Polygram, 1991.

7 Van Morrison, 'So Quiet in Here,' *Enlightenment*, Polydor, 1990.

8 Anna Lowenhaupt Tsing, *In the Realm of the Diamond Queen: Marginality in an Out-of-the-Way Place*, Princeton, NJ, Princeton University Press, 1993.

9 Tony Fry, 'Introduction', in T. Fry (ed.) *R|U|A TV? Heidegger and the Televisual*, Sydney, Power Publications, 1993, p. 12.

10 Paul Celan, 'The Meridian', *Chicago Review*, Winter 1978.

11 Antoine Hennion, *La Passion musicale: une sociologie de la médiation*, Paris, Editions Métailié, 1993, p. 365.

12 I have talked at length of the political economy of popular music in the historical configurations of present day modernity in 'At the End of This Sentence a Sail Will Unfurl ... Modernities, Musics and the Journey of Identity', in Paul Gilroy, Lawrence Grossberg and Angela McRobbie (eds), op. cit.

13 Edward Said, *Musical Elaborations*, London, Vintage, 1992, p. xv.

14 Martin Heidegger, 'The Question Concerning Technology', in Heidegger, *Basic Writings*, New York, Harper & Row, 1977. This is not to negate that visual languages can provide new beginnings in contexts where images also become historical witnesses and ethnographic signatures for something and someone else, establishing a difference within the increasing global belief in the visibility of truth as ocular 'information'. See Rey Chow, *Primitive Passions: Visuality, Sexuality, Ethnography, and Contemporary Chinese Cinema*, New York, Columbia University Press, 1995.

15 For a courageous and thoughtful discussion of the political implications and critical blindness of ocular hegemony in the context of contemporary black music, see Paul Gilroy's '"After the Love has Gone": Biopolitics and Etho-poetics in the Black Public Sphere', *Third Text*, 28/29, Autumn/Winter 1994.

16 The quote is from Leslie Paul Thiele, *Timely Meditations: Martin Heidegger and Postmodern Politics*, Princeton, NJ, Princeton University Press, 1995, p. 25.

17 George Steiner, *Heidegger*, London, Fontana, 1992, p. 44.

18 Here the reference is to Julia Kristeva's distinction between the semiotic and the linguistic or symbolic state of language: see Kristeva, *The Revolution in Poetic Language*, New York, Columbia University Press, 1984.

19 Homi K. Bhabha, *The Location of Culture*, London and New York, Routledge, 1995, p. 217.

20 Martin Heidegger, 'Letter on Humanism', in Heidegger, *Basic Writings*, op. cit.

21 Sigmund Freud, 'Remembering, Repeating and Working-Through', in *The Standard Edition of the Complete Psychological Works of Sigmund Freud*, general editor James Strachey, vol. XII, London, Hogarth Press, 1962.

22 Ibid., p. 147.

23 The quote is from Freud, ibid., p. 151; on the 'disclosure' and 'concealment' of art, see Martin Heidegger, 'The Origin of the Work of Art', in Heidegger, *Basic Writings*, op. cit.

24 Shuhei Hosokawa, *The Aesthethics of Recorded Sound*, Tokyo, Keisō Shobō, 1990.

25 For an important discussion of this issue in the context of contemporary cultural translation, see Rey Chow, op. cit., pp. 182–95.

26 'even the greatest translation is destined to become part of the growth of its own language and eventually to be absorbed by its renewal': Walter Benjamin, 'The Task of the Translator', in Benjamin, *Illuminations*, trans. Harry Zohn, London, Fontana, 1973, p. 73.

27 Much of this paragraph draws upon a stimulating talk on Walter Benjamin given by Sigrid Weigel in the Spring of 1994 at the University of California at Santa Cruz.

28 Michael Hays, 'Foreword' to Peter Szondi, *On Textual Understanding and Other Essays*, Minneapolis, University of Minnesota Press, 1986, p. x.

29 The stress here is on a generic romanticism rather than the historical instance of Romanticism. Andrew Bowie has convincely argued that post-Kantian German Romanticism (Novalis, Jacobi, Fichte, Schlegel and Schelling) donated a rarely appreciated set of enabling perspectives to the question of our being in technology; see Andrew Bowie, 'Romanticism and Technology', *Radical Philosophy*, 70, July/August 1995.

30 Edward Said, *Musical Elaborations*, op. cit. p. 98.

31 Hannah Arendt, 'The Shadows', quoted in Elisabeth Young-Bruehl, *Hannah Arendt: For Love of the World*, New Haven, Conn., and London, Yale University Press, 1982, p. 50. She is quoting Isak Dinesen.

32 The first quote is from Yosef Hayim Yerushalmi, cited in Paolo Rossi, *Il passato, la memoria, l'oblio*, Bologna, il Mulino, 1991, p. 28; while the second is from David B. Clarke, Marcus A. Doel and Francis X. McDonough, 'Holocaust Topologies: Singularity, Politics, Space', *Political Geography*, 15(6/7), 1996.

33 Emmanuel Lévinas, *Collected Philosophical Papers*, trans. Alphonso Lingis, The Hague, Martinus Nijhoff, 1987, p. 3.

34 Gary Peters, 'The Rhythm of Alterity: Levinas and Aesthetics', *Radical Philosophy*, 82, March/April 1997, p. 13.

5

ARCHITECTURE, AMNESIA
AND THE EMERGENT ARCHAIC

The event of dwelling exceeds the knowing, the thought, and
the idea in which, after the event, the subject will want to
contain what is incommensurable with a knowing.

Emmanuel Lévinas[1]

The porous city

Writing in 1924, Walter Benjamin and Asja Lacis noted, in what has
subsequently become a much cited commentary, that the city of Naples
consists in a 'porous architecture'.[2] Its principal building material is
the yellow *tufo*, volcanic matter emerging out of the maritime depths
and solidifying on contact with sea water. Transformed into habitation,
this porous rock returns buildings to the dampness of their origins.
In this dramatic encounter with the archaic elements (earth, air, fire and
water) there already lies the incalculable extremes that co-ordinate the
Neapolitan quotidian. The crumbling tufo, child of the violent marriage
between volcano and sea, fire and water, is symptomatic of the unstable
edifice that is the city. Further, the use of tufo reveals a blatant *imbroglio*
in the very building of the city. Forbidden by the Spanish authorities,
seeking to control urban development, to import building material,
Neapolitans excavated the volcanic stone literally from under their feet:
casting the material once again skywards. The ground beneath the city
is hollow, honeycombed with the subsequent caverns. Not only is the
present-day city constructed with volatile and physically unreliable materials, but also its foundations are legally and geologically suspect. To
borrow from the book – *Ursprung des deutschen Trauerspiels*, 1928 –
Benjamin wrote on the German Baroque theatre of mourning while on
Capri in the Bay of Naples, the city is an allegory of the precarious
forces of modernity. As a perpetual negation of the assumed inevitability
of 'progress', a continual interrogation of its foundations, the city continually proposes a physical and philosophical ground that stymies the
principles of stability.[3] Lived as a 'crisis' environment, rather than a

planned one, Naples presents itself as both a Baroque and an abysmal city. Its innumerable seventeenth-century buildings and unsure foundations are silent witnesses to the continuing disruption of linear development as urban and architectural design dissolves into sounds, streets and bodies that do not readily bend to the structural stability sought by the modern will.

Walking in the city, I follow narrow alleys that turn inwards towards the piazza, a church, or bring me to monuments set up in the name of death and disaster – the decorated *guglie* or obelisks that commemorate volcanic eruptions, earthquakes and plagues; only rarely do streets direct me towards the opening of the sea. It is as though the city draws its energies from the darkness, the shadows, sucking the light out of things in an irrepressible self-reflection that serves to illuminate its passion for self-centredness. The sea remains an accessory, an appendage from which fish once arrived and urban effluence is now dispatched.

Naples is above all a vertical city, reflected both in the archaeological sedimentation and in its social stratification. The class ladder commences with one-room dwellings on the streets – *i bassi* – to arrive at the attics and terraces of the professional classes and splinters of aristocracy still clinging to the heights. The sea and sky are caught in snatches, the lateral (democratic?) view is rarely permitted; the gaze is either bounded by narrow streets or else directed upwards towards secular and religious authority. Apertures rapidly lead to introspective closure: the site of psychosomatic inscriptions. In the ethnography of space, the urban scene reveals itself to be both a physical and psychic habitat.

Probably the aspect that most immediately strikes a visitor, a stranger, is that Naples is a city that exists above all in the conundrum of noise. Added to the constant murmur that a local *intellighenzia* spins in literary lamentations and critical conservatism around urban ruin, nostalgia and decay, are the sounds that arise from the street between the interminable acceleration of scooters and angry car horns: the shouts of the fishmonger; the cries of greeting; the passing trucks and megaphoned voices offering water melons, children's toys, glassware and pirate cassettes of Neapolitan songs; the fruit seller who publicly comments on his wares and their supposedly low prices in the third person: 'Che belle pesche. Duemila lire . . . ma questo è pazzo' (What fine peaches. Only two thousand lire . . . but this guy's mad); the itinerant seller of wild berries at seven in the July morning whose high cry fills the empty alley. These lacerations of silence attest to the physical punctuation of space by the voice, the body. And it is the body that provides a fundamental gestured grammar in which hands become interrogative beaks, arms tormented signals, and faces contorted masks. A pre-linguistic economy erupts in urban space to reveal among the sounds a deep-seated distrust of words, their promise of explanation and their custody of reason.

The hidden plan of the city lies in an architecture of introspection that is revealed not only in crumbling edifices and grime-coated façades, but also in the taciturn faces and sceptical sentiments of its inhabitants. Here, where the linearity of time spirals out into diverse tempos, the residual, the archaic and the pre-modern can turn out to be emergent as visceral details and distortions undermine the dreamed-of purity of rational planning and functional design. In its art of getting by (*arrangiarsi*), making do and re-arranging available elements as props for a fragile urban existence, the presence of Naples – as a European, a Mediterranean and a contemporary city – proposes an eternal return to the enigmatic lexicon of modern urban life, to the contingencies of an unstable language in which all city dwellers are set and configured. So, Naples is perhaps also a potential paradigm of the city *after* modernity. Connected in its uneven rhythms and volatile habits to other non-occidental cities and an emerging metropolitan globality, it proposes an *interruption* in our inherited understanding of urban life, architecture and planning. Participating in progress without being fully absorbed in its agenda, Naples, as a composite city, reintroduces the uneven and the unplanned, the contingent, the historical. Viewed and, above all, lived in this manner, the interrogation posed by Naples returns the question of the city to the relationship between politics and poetics in determining our sense of the ethical and the aesthetical (and can they really be separated?): our sense of the possible and imagining our position in it.[4]

Our views and voices bear the imprint of different histories; they speak out of a particular place. So, whatever I have to say on the question of architecture undoubtedly lies in my response to the ambiguous, even enigmatic, context of where I work and live: the city of Naples. At the same time, however, to nominate the site of my body, voice and thoughts, desires and obsessions in terms of a particular city is inevitably also to connect my observations to the urban habitat as the privileged site of modern existence. Both in economic and experiential terms, it is seemingly the city that most immediately compresses history, culture and identities into configurations that command critical attention. What is excluded from this metropolitan comprehension of our being – the non-urban worlds of nomadism, peasantry, rural life, even the suburban fringes – however populous and necessary these spaces may be for our existence (from agriculture to tourism, residence, and the sustenance of our bodies and imagination) is considered to be subordinate to, if not merely an appendage of, the city.

But if Naples is unwittingly thrust into the critical and global lime-light of metropolitan enquiry it donates its own form of disturbance, a particular contribution to the simultaneous formation of concentration and dispersal, that *unheimlichkeit* or uncanny return – perhaps the pro-foundest symptom of modern life – which continually doubles and displaces urban geometry with the unruly histories of the repressed.[5] Naples is frequently reviled for appearing to exist at the limit of Europe and modern urbanism, clinging intermittently to those more ordered life styles associated with London, Paris, Milan and New York. Yet, in its seeming proximity to the more 'typical' world cities and civic clutter of Cairo, Mexico City, São Paulo and Shanghai, this Mediterranean city also paradoxically finds itself drawn into proximity with the cosmopolitan composition of a Los Angeles or a London as its own internal history comes increasingly to be intersected by the intrusion of extra-European immigration and the impositions of global capital worldling its local concerns. In the space of these 'new powers and expanded intercourse on the part of individuals' that forcefully invite us to rethink radically the spatial divisions of centre and periphery, of 'First' and 'Third' worlds, the peculiar historical configuration of a city such as Naples amounts to an insistence that cannot be readily disposed of. However dramati-cally etched against the local background of a volcano and the Mediterranean sea, the interrogation that Naples inserts into late moder-nity and global capitalism is by no means peculiar to that city alone. It returns to query and disturb the projected homogeneity of the blue-print born in the anxious midst of metropolitan powers desirous of a seamless symmetry.[6]

Such sought-for symmetry is paradoxically reflected, even amplified in clarity, in the mirrored versions of the structural prescriptions of modern urban space offered in the contemporary Marxist readings of Fredric Jameson, Mike Davis and, to a lesser extent, David Harvey. These interpretations tend to eliminate the poetical from the political, thereby arriving at a denouncement without the announcement of any-thing further.[7] It permits the observer, the critic, to arrive at a deadly symmetry, but leaves the observed merely as *victim* of the plan, of the project, of the logic that the critique exposes. With this refusal to consider the languages, the style, of the on-going realisation of the lived-in possibilities of the city, at the end of the day it is not too clear what sort of liberatory politics is being proposed. The critique certainly permits the articulation of some very powerful accounts of the capitalisation of contemporary existence, but that *power* is drawn precisely from the *silence* of the actors, from the critical absence of the social beings and the lives of those who are being accounted for. Driven by the utopic desire to propose an autonomous alternative (if only by offering a negative totality), it ironically leads to a dematerialist idealism. Both Marx and Gramsci insisted that the new would emerge from the womb of the old society. This would seem to suggest an *atopic*, rather than utopic, understanding; one able to read in the present a potential able to render it otherwise, and there to open up its structural logics *and* immediacies to another sense of position and possibility. The political economy of space does not represent a conclusive point of arrival, but rather a point of departure. We all certainly live in 'conditions not of our own choosing', but what happens from there on in?

The 'art of the gap'

In the city, the perpetual myth and desire for origins, for a secure site of explanation, for the stability of foundations, is constantly deferred by being re-told and re-written. This eternal return opens up an interval, or the 'art of the gap' (Paul Carter), that permits a reconfiguration able to snare and deviate 'progress'. To narrate the city in the physical passage of our bodies, to walk it and to measure ourselves with and against it, is no doubt to seek in our environs the reasoned paradigm of the ancient *polis*, the primary promise of the *agora*. But that design and desire is inevitably intersected by modern motives and motifs – speed, efficiency, rationalisation, in a word, by the thrifty management of technology driven by the *telos* of economic development and its political direction. Most of us do not walk the city, but ride it: in cars, subways and buses. Time is considered uniform and space homogeneous: the site of geometrical principles and a seemingly self-evident conceptual ground. The intersection of these multiple metropolitan trajectories – the mythical source of its space and the modern imperatives of its organisation – create a complex and composite place in which the seemingly archaic can also become the contemporary anger of the exploited and the dispossessed. The repressed bubbles up through the cracks in the sidewalk and occupies the gaps between buildings to crease, contest and sometimes tear the administrative and architectural will. In this perspective architecture not only has a metaphysics, it is metaphysics. For to plan, to rationalise space, embodies the promise of eschatology: the prophetic announcement of a future paradise, and the negation of alterity, of the other. For even to seek to inscribe alterity in the project, to respond to the presence of the other, is already to negate that other by reducing her or him to the same, to the protocols of the design.[8]

If 'to build is itself already to dwell', then the interrogation of architecture inevitably transgresses established disciplinary frames. To criticise the practice and projects of architecture is inevitably to engage with diverse manners of dwelling, with different, even conflictual, modalities of occupying, inhabiting and traversing the earth.[9] It is to break a mould and disavow certain premises. To revisit and rework an inheritance no longer restricted to the confident protocols of architecture is to step into the altogether more unsettled vocabulary of historical dwelling. As a self-referring language that seeks to control the construction it articulates, architecture is continually breached by the worldly contingencies that both initiate and sustain it. To note the ubiquitous presence of the metaphor of language in architectural discourse could mean to take the metaphor seriously and to insist on the other side of (architectural) language. For the question arises whether the concept of language is deployed merely for the coded communication and rationalisation of space, rendering the world transparent and subservient to an architectural grammar, or whether the concept of language signals an altogether more ambiguous, poetic inscription of habitation. In the pragmatics of the former lies the immediacy of a concluded building, in the indeterminacy of the latter exists an unfolding engagement with the question of inhabiting, incorporating, and working up an abstract space into a concrete place. Yet, architecture continues to insist in a manner that is largely oblivious to this latter framing. Why is that so?

Invisible scaffolds, invisible lives

Although seemingly infinite in its variations the arrogance of vision that abrogates the world according to his or her design, defining and destining space to meet the needs that confirm a project is consistently reaffirmed in the singular. The egocentrism of the subsequent edifice is very much about how space is perceived, and often has little to do with living it. Marcos Novak, an architectural critic from Los Angeles, has declared that:

> Ideas are invisible scaffolds upon which the real is constructed. The history of architecture is a history of the increasing elaboration of invisible scaffolds.[10]

This echoes, but from the opposite side of the critical divide, the Japanese architect Arata Isozaki's definition of architecture as 'the name of the mechanism through which the metaphysics which ground Western thought inevitably came into existence.'[11] Such a metaphysics, embodied in the unilateral subjectivism of occidental humanism that, as Heidegger reminds us, touches its apex in modern technology, is here rendered explicit in the lexicon of architectural design and desire. The buildings that house flesh, bodies, the living and the dead, fall away to be replaced by invisible scaffolds and invisible . . . lives.

Within architecture itself the metaphysical marriage of thought and technology today carries a new name: TransArchitecture. It has a programme and is affiliated to Transmodernism. TransArchitecture seeks to overcome the distinction between the physical and the virtual through the transmutation of design and project, architecture and habitation, into information.[12] It believes that information is the third dimension of matter (after energy and mass). In this technological augmentation of space, and the accompanying frontier rhetoric of limitlessless digital permutations, is it not possible to hear the reiteration of that perpetual occidental desire to englobe all within the illusion of transparent management? Is this not the latest manifestation of a metaphysics which, despite its rhetoric of democratic clarity and access (but for whom, where, when and how?), is ultimately wedded to intellectual domination, hierarchical discipline and strategic control? It is a world populated by unidimensional bodies that remain, in their asexual, timeless and mute state, completely subordinate to the architectural plan, to the project and its presumptions. The physical is nominated only to be immediately subsumed and subjugated in the power of the simulated. The Benthamite panopticon, the controlled incarceration of unruly beings, now rendered infinitely modular and flexible in the resistant-less contours of dematerialised bodies located in cyberspace, is here very firmly still in place. In the virtuosity of virtual architecture, the pervasive design of the all-seeing eye that locates and disciplines all within its omnipotent field of vision, remains not only undisturbed but is augmented, and thanks to the technology employed, even more finely tuned and firmly focused.

In this potential critique of the computer generated space of simulated dwelling there is no intention of an appeal to turn back, abandon the technology, and return to the fictional immediacy of the 'real' world. There is rather an insistence on a critical disposition – that historical heritage deposited in the languages that sustain us – to be pursued *within* the mediations that constitute us in the world we respond to. Against the teleology of 'technical fundamentalism', this approach might suggest an altogether more hesitant and uncertain series of cues in which initial enthusiasms are tempered by the disturbance of questions that perennially refuse the promise of immediate representation and resolution. What is left over and left out of the picture, the frame, the screen, the image, the representation, the plan, continues to disseminate interrogations that resite technology and continues to relocate metaphysical desire within temporal and terrestrial limits. To follow this path, is to enter an altogether more uncertain project. For our responses to tech-nology and its representations depend upon the contingency of our being in a earthly situation that no degree of technology, no degree of intel-lectual longing, can ever fully reveal or represent.

> Cyberspace is not a fatality. It's a fact. What would be fatal would be to remain in theoretical and critical ignorance of the current phenomenon. We are not even ready to draw up a typology of the changes that the 'digital revolution' has brought to architecture. Between a technical fundamentalism which revels in the aesthetic intoxication of new definitive propositions and the sceptical or catastrophic disenchantment in the face of the power of real digital time, a third path can force its way through which is based on a critical, theoretical and also historical approach.[13]

This is to follow Heidegger into the question concerning technology. Despite the widespread assumption that the German philosopher takes a stand *against* technology in the name of an obliterated authenticity. It would be more precise, hence more disquieting and difficult to digest, that Heidegger took a stand *within* technology.[14] His recognition that we are suspended in the languages of modern technology leads to the critical proposition that it is from there that we have to find our way.

The will to architecture

How to build, to construct, in an epoch without a *telos*? What exactly is a post-metaphysical building? To pose such queries is already to displace Architecture with architectures. It is to transform tradition into a site of translation. It is to render the potential universality of the project particular and specific: where to build is not merely to impose a vision but is to narrate and construct a habitat.[15] This involves with-drawing from the confident grammar of the former and speaking the conditional languages of the latter. Rendering such a situation critical reverses both the tradition and disposition of the architectural gaze; translated into symptoms of a contested power, the history of architec-tural is transferred from an edict to the status of a cure, proffering a treatment and a taking into care of the present. This is a present and potential future, for which it can now no longer claim complete compe-tence. Terrestrial contingency, worldly disturbance, impose a gap, an interruption, that can never be closed or silenced. For architecture now involves an encounter with an other 'who, by definition, does not follow the same set of rules.'[16] The solipsism of the architectural project, of the metaphysical edifice, depends upon 'an omission of asymmetry that identifies the I as the we.'[17] As the Japanese critic Kojin Karatani points out:

> In order to interiorize the other, that other must share a set of common rules. But doesn't the other by definition designate only those who do not share a set of rules? Is not the dialogue only with such an other?[18]

As a modern place, the city is overwhelmingly considered a rationalised space. It is an environment established with the logic that mobility is reducible 'to predictable, purposeful trips, origins and destinations'.[19] This projection of urban life reveals that:

> assumptions of unrestricted movement and mobility in contemporary western societies are hegemonic in prioritising specific bodies and modes of mobility and movement. In particular, mobility and movement are defined through discourses which serve to alienate impaired bodies and to prioritise the movement of what one might term the mobile body.[20]

Nevertheless, in this site there also exists what overflows and exceeds the planned and projected structure of the building and the city. In this unsuspected supplement – that both adds to the plan and threatens to disrupt it – something occurs that transgresses the instance of rationalisation. For it is I, you, they, who exist in this space, in this step beyond the blueprint. It is in the passage through this space, whether on foot or with wheels, that the body becomes a subject, that I become who I am.

I, with my myths, my sense of beginnings, originate here, in this passage. This is the site of *arkhé*, the installation of beginnings, that architecture builds upon and custodies. 'Building, dwelling, thinking' (Heidegger) thus becomes a question of how to install, how to commence, how to conceive, construct and construe our selves. Although the conditions are not of our own choosing, this is not an arbitrary act. The languages, histories, cultures and traditions that envelope us in the city, in our daily lives, both provoke and constitute this space. It is our inhabitation of this opening that composes the shifting textures, the changing possibilities, the diverse inhabitation, of the city. Yet, this space is both already configured, awaiting our arrival, and simultaneously accompanied by blank margins, by what remains radically irreducible both to the closure and governance of the plan and the subjectivity of the individual inhabitant. It is thus a spatial familiarity that is always haunted by alterity; we ultimately, if unknowingly, seek accommodation in the uncanny.

In the exchange between buildings and bodies what responds to, and represents, the latter is this potential punctuation of the plan. For dwelling, in both harbouring and fostering the subject, also announces the shiver of the world. It is this intrusion that breaks through and away from a humanist understanding of habitation in which dwelling is presumed to commence and conclude within the compass and consensus of the subject. It is in an altogether more exposed condition that the subject emerges and becomes. What makes humankind ultimately human lies, Heidegger reminds us, in its ungroundness, or lack of foundation. An unrepresented, even unrepresentable, persistence interrogates the city, its architecture and all the disciplines that seek to delimit and determine its destiny. How we respond to, and take responsibility for, this susceptible space, leads to a questioning that invests us all in the assessment of building, dwelling, thinking and . . . inhabiting the world.

With such considerations in mind it becomes possible to commence formulating a wider interrogation: to question what Kojin Karatani calls the 'will to architecture'.[21] To enquire into the desire to build – both physically and metaphysically – is, above all, to consider how the understanding of one is inextricably bound into an understanding of the other. Listening again to Heidegger on this point, I desert the security of the Cartesian axiom *cogito ergo sum* for the uncertain prospect of what exceeds my thinking the event of being: *ich bin*: 'I am' now equals 'I dwell'.[22] From here I extend towards architecture the interrogations that emerge eternally in the application of historical forces, social endeavour and individual desire to the ambient in the making of a *domus*, a habitat, a home.

Architecture as the planned and rationalised laying up, or 'standing reserve', of time and labour, of historical and cultural energies, as the simultaneous projection and preservation of resources, as the space of a plan, a construction, a building, is always transformed into a contingent place, into a precarious edifice, whose historical outcome no architectural drawing board can foretell. Architecture does not merely involve the physical erection of buildings; it stands out or stands forth, revealing the essence of something in simultaneously economic, political, historical and aesthetic terms. It articulates a location among these co-ordinates: it both discloses and obfuscates the nature of its place in the world.

A building, no matter how dramatic or monumental, never stands alone, is never an isolated statement. Each and every edifice, whatever the intention of the architect and the builder, evokes the connection of a community that continually frustrates 'technological, calculating representation.'[23] In the gap between abstract intention and corporeal investment emerges the coeval disclosure and concealment of everyday lives whose import extend far beyond abstract categories or even the radical voice of subjectivity. Such lives announce a historical configuration sustained in a finite habitat, suspended between past and future, earth and sky. For buildings deploy in the most obvious manner a technology which as *Ge-stell* or 'enframing' both stands over and challenges us, and yet reveals or exposes us to the truth of our condition.[24] The city, its buildings and architecture, is one of the fundamental modalities that enframes our paradoxical location in a closed and finite place that simultaneously constitutes an opening which permits the possibility of thinking at and beyond such limits.

Although our histories, cultures, memories and subjectivities are inevitably cast in the syntax and languages of the symbolic and physical construction of our habitat, today increasingly framed by the city – itself a metaphor for the technologisation of the globe – the daily prose of metropolitan life nevertheless provides us with the opportunity to think and live our condition other-wise. The question of the city, and its architecture, is a question of construction: both the physical construction that is erected and the cultural, historical and symbolic construction that is elaborated. So the question of architecture, as with the question of aesthetics, is also a question of ethics. Architecture, to echo the American architect Peter Eisenman, is about meaning. And what we understand by meaning is unavoidably tied to how we respond to the question of our sense of being in the world, to our living in the city constructing a sense of home.

Missives of time

Buildings as historical dwellings are missives of time, destined for decay. In Europe and its offspring cultures there has emerged, since the seventeenth century and the epoch of the Baroque, an apprenticeship in inhabiting the potentialities of the ruin. Subsequently, some have adopted an aesthetics that assumes that a building is never new, that its walls and decor are always already worn, baptised in dirt and grime, that there never existed a point zero or day one from whence the building began; it is always and already inhabited. At this point, the city, as the site of previous lives, becomes a shifting accumulation of traces, a palimpsest to be read and rewritten again and again. Of course there are others who have chosen to submerge and repress such inscriptions of transition in the anonymous transcendence afforded by the flat surfaces and direct lines of an ever new and ever white modernism. Here time, robbed of colour and ornamentation, is rendered invisible. To choose to pay heed to the former perspective, without falling into the barrenness of hapless nostalgia or stultifying historicism, means to refuse to halt in emotional thrall or resignation before the spectacle of mortality. It means, to listen to Benjamin, to seize hold of the Baroque as a flash that flares up in a moment of danger to illuminate our present, permitting us to consider a relationship between buildings and being. Here architecture becomes the art of recollection that gathers together histories in its material construction and design, and reveals in the concatenation of economic, political and cultural regimes a sense of dwelling.[25]

Yet, it is also undeniable that much contemporary architecture – frequently self-referential in style and intent – both stands out and is framed in a context that is testimony to a waning of place, a waning that even goes to the extent of disappearing completely into the void between the freeways, the shopping malls and the desert at the end of the West somewhere in southern California. Here the unruly and uncanny possibilities of the city are transmuted into what Edward Soja calls *exopolis* – cities without 'city-ness', capital intensive spaces seemingly intent on confounding all attempts to transform them into the social uncertainty and cultural vicissitudes of place.[26] For to ask the question concerning architecture is to interrogate the city as the simultaneous site of memory and amnesia in an epoch that often seems intent on dispensing with civil society, that is perhaps even withdrawing from the demands of democracy, as commercial centres and guarded communities reproduce themselves in the paranoid glare of uninterrupted surveillance. Such settlements, perched between the desert and the Pacific, are strangely reminiscent of ancient hill fortresses. Living off the subsidised waters of the Sierras and the public highway system (private capital's unacknowledged welfare programme), such settlements provide the cultural templates to anticipated global developments in the science fiction worlds of such novels as William Gibson's *Neuromancer* and Neal Stephenson's *Snow Crash*, not to speak of capital intensive development elsewhere in the contemporary world: from Santiago to Beijing.

The waning of place is also a waning of memory.

But are there such things as buildings without memory? The ultra-modernism that lies at the edges of the occident, there in the desert of southern California, perhaps presents us with objects that only embody the transitory memory of the materials of which they are composed: glass, steel, plastic, optical fibre, cement, tarmac, neon. In this *deserta pragmatica* critics sourly inform us that memory – too wasteful to inscribe, too time consuming to acknowledge – is bleached out, purged. Only the bronze statue of John Wayne (from Jean-Luc Godard's favourite John Ford Western, *The Searchers*) in the Orange County airport foyer remains as a trace. But perhaps the apparent starkness of oblivion invites us to think again. Perhaps here memory is spatialised rather than sedimented in vertical strata. So, the seemingly memory-less city of Irvine is both doubled and shadowed by the older, largely Spanish-speaking, settlement of Santa Ana. The rational light of the former's planning and management depends upon the shadows that accommodate those who service and sustain it from a distance. To consider memory in spatial terms, as different, even separate, sites is inevitably to contrast experience of the vertical city (Naples) with the horizontal one (Irvine). The former is in debt to, sometimes overwhelmed by, historicity: in Naples time is an avatar that not only reminds us of our bodies, our mortality, but also devours every explanation, reason and judgement. Irvine meanwhile is a city that apparently exists at the end of time; here explanations are not introspective (memory, narcissism) but projective (fantasy, desire). The sedimented, vertical city is governed by its foundations (mythic, historical, cultural); the other by its horizon (desert, sea, sky). One might be tempted to suggest that while one is a city the other is a settlement, hence provisional: only the freeways have a certain air of permanency. One represents time, the other seemingly represses it. But the disavowal is also an unavoidable affirmation of the impossibility of discarding such temporal and historical limits. On the edge of the desert, the office blocks, freeways, housing complexes and commercial centres, encounter the inviolate. The desert – as intractable terrain and imaginary emptiness – resists appropriation, exceeds rationalisation, providing an experience of the impossible, a memory of the perennial: 'the desert beyond every desert'.[27] Its apparent barrenness blocks and undoes calculating vision, promising the possibility of rediscovering something further in our selves and the plans and projects we inhabit.

At the beginning of *Civilisation and its Discontents*, Freud draws on the city, and on the city of Rome in particular, as a metaphor of memory, as an illustration of psychic life in which everything in some manner or another is conserved. Stratification and traces, sedimentation and ruins, reveal the presence and persistence of memory. But a city of recent invention, scratched in the desert sand, a settlement such as Irvine, Orange County, southern California, exists on a time scale that excludes the memory of a Rome, an Alessandria, London, a Canton or even a New York. If the city is also a model of the psyche what lies in the difference between the sedimented memory of Naples and the juvenile recollections of Irvine?

Memory, and still listening to the founder of psychoanalysis, is never a mere continuum providing instantaneous time travel between the present and the past. It is a construction in the custody of language; it is overdetermined by its present representation. Memory involves selection, repression, and subsequent articulation. So, a systematic preservation of the past in an acritical conservation of buildings, streets and neighbourhoods, is also a repression of the ambiguous health and healing power of memory: for memory is the site of both construction, conservation *and* destruction, reformulation. A memory that operates without reconstruction is a sterile memory, prone to nostalgia. Sometimes, it is as important to forget as it is to recall.

The ground beneath our feet

Behind architecture lies the inaugurating cleavage between sedentary and nomadic modalities of dwelling, between the built walls and roof of a room and the stretched membrane of a tent or leafy equivalent. This is perhaps more readily grasped in a sense of 'home' encountered outside the co-ordinates of Europe and North America. Sedentary dwelling, even in its most humble aspirations, invokes an act of foundation, inaugurates a structure that will invest the terrain, that will physically work over and materially transform the ground. It involves a site that is transformed, and an edifice that will be elaborated, modified, extended, decorated and renovated, or else removed to make way for a further building. Stakes will be driven into the soil, earth excavated, materials accumulated, elements and energies brought to the site, waste carried away, and a building, a village, a town, a city, is developed.

Although the idealist perspective some of us have inherited has encouraged a thinking divided between the 'natural' domesticity of rural existence and the assumed 'alienation' of urban life, both the farmhouse, rural cottage and village church, like the skyscraper, apartment block and airport terminal, share a common relationship to the ground upon which they are built. For both are dependent upon a relationship to the earth, the soil, the terrain, that is cultivated, worked, appropriated, exploited. This deeply ambiguous inheritance conjoins both custody for, and exploitation of, the ground beneath our feet. To insist on this ambiguous arrangement is to shatter the sharp distinction between a romanticised 'naturalism' of the rural and the exploitative 'alienation' of the urban.

Against the back-cloth of industrious cities, the rural landscape is invariably considered as mute, raw material, the given stock, or standing reserve, represented by *nature*. Yet landscapes contain the history of the earth: both the millennial narrative of geological time and the social history of human habitation. The rationalisation of space often remains oblivious to both. More immediately, there is, as Don Mitchell recalling Marx reminds us, a 'surplus value of the landscape' that is deposited in the terrain as 'dead labour'.[28] The rural view, whether from the old world or the new one, from Italy or California, is also the register of a scenery served and serviced by the sweat, blood and lives of the once local, but these days increasingly migrant, labourer. The rustic realm, invariably pictured in the nostalgic hues of the pre-industrial and 'authentic' syntax of the 'primitive', is as much a complex witness to the violent geographies of contemporary political economy (with its requirements for raw materials and agribusiness, its tourism and property development) as the more obviously invoked urban scene.

Both the rural and the urban, in their construction, economies and social organisation, cultivate and exploit, elaborate and annex, the ground upon which they are built and depend. The violence of this act of appropriation upon which architecture builds is what, ultimately, is repressed in the rationalisation of the construct. This is as true of the ancient temple and tithe barn as of the modern corporation headquarters and metropolitan subway.

For to build is not only already to dwell as Heidegger informs us, but also to subscribe to the authority of architecture. Of course, that authority largely passes unobserved, although it is equally present, in the profane design of humble dwellings whose materials, construction and projection have rarely survived their immediate utility. Architectural authority, the inauguration of new materials, of a decision in style, of the inscription of religious, commercial and political order in stone, tends to be reserved for the innovative and the monumental, for objects erected upon the earth against the sky that stand out and endure. Paradoxically these objects, the result of a rational expropriation of the ground and its resources, disclose a form of acute subjectivism. In the objectivity of his or her craft, in the numbers, calculations, projects, measurements and materials, the architect imposes an unilateral logic on the ground that provides the space for the eventual construct. In this humanism, that is in this reduction of the ground to the rationalist appropriation that confirms the ego, architecture shields itself from the interrogation that would cause the foundations of its practice to vacillate.

Certainly, an alternative relationship to the earth, in which the ground is the site of tracks, trails, shifting seasonal resources and transitory dwellings, is not a contemporary option. But as a life lived, a culture sustained, a worldly inheritance, such a modality of living continues to pose a set of questions to all who inhabit the earth.

Nevertheless, the decision to settle and build, to inaugurate architecture and transform the ground into a fixed abode, therefore to name and claim it in sanguine, religious, military, legal and political terms, is what for many has constituted the foundation of a sense of home and homeland. It is never a question of merely moving over the land in nomadic fashion, it is always a question of moving in and taking over. The land is invariably considered empty, a *tabula rasa*, waiting to be inaugurated by settlement and building; it is a blank page upon which history has not yet been written:

> To found the colony, to inaugurate linear history and its puppet theatre of marching soldiers and treadmills, was to embrace an environmental amnesia; it was actively to forget what wisdom the ground, and its people, might possess.[29]

The land is blessed, christened. This being named 'entails the cancellation of the native name – the erasure of the alien, perhaps, demonic identity – and hence a kind of "making new"'.[30] As Stephen Greenblatt goes on to note, this simultaneous annexation and conferring of identity is formally fused in the linguistic nomination of conquest and taking possession of the savage, uncultivated ground.[31] The violence of these inaugural acts, in which space is emptied of its previous history and returned to zero, today reappears to haunt contemporary settlements, interrogating the confident accommodation that an earlier architecture seemingly realised. For the stability of the *domus* is not only extorted from the earth, but also extorted from other beings whose externalisation, sometimes extermination, takes the form of an economic, cultural and political subordination that sustains and confirms a specific place in its separateness – be it a region, a city or a nation – from the places of others.

Spatialisation leads almost inevitably towards the evacuation of contingency and the dispersal of history along the neutral grid lines of a universal geometry reflecting and reifying empty, homogeneous time. Or almost, for history continues to blow over the site. The land, even in the most barren of appearances, as desert, untamed nature and wilderness, is always, already nominated by some body.[32] The land, as indigenous peoples have continually asserted since first contact, is sacred. The sacred lies within the soil, for which it can be neither individually owned nor given away. Such relationships to the land, not to a dumb matter to be annexed, worked and exploited, but towards a circumscribed humus that sustains and supports a way of being, are the ghosts that inhabit the ground and return to haunt the edifice of modernity.[33]

This is to insist on a more complex inheritance than an obvious binary distinction or opposition between husbandry and nomadism, for moving over the land, rather than remained fixed, does not exclude both managing and harvesting the environment.[34]

There exists no pure state, no zero degree. Space, as Gaston Bachelard affirmed, is always saturated.[35] Although the euroamerican gaze habitually empties space in order to fill it with a teleology of development and progress, the territory is always and already invested as a place – even nomadism, no matter how extensive the wandering, is always within a locality. Space is already a habitat, a dwelling for an other. It is in the evacuation of other histories, and with this gesture the inauguration of the 'new', that the intertwining of occidental modernity and colonialism is most pitilessly condensed; it is what ultimately legitimates the establishment and violent sustainment of the modern nation state. In the will to represent – 'architecture as the objectivisation of desire' – the languages of planning and building inevitably draw upon this grammar.[36]

There exists no healing for these wounds, only a working with, through and alongside the ghosts that refuse to go away, that return again and again to haunt the construction of identities and the enunciation of place and belonging. Earlier certitudes come to experience unwelcome openings, and wounds are maintained as wounds that bleed into a more tentative, less assured, understanding of the physical and symbolic ground that bears us.

Technology and terrestrial constraints

In the modern metropolitan disengagement of labour and locality, civic life is increasingly unchained from the immediate presence and pressures of organised production, and labour is reconfigured in other bodies (often female, non-white and not of the 'First' world), and then spatially disseminated in the fragmented specificity of metropolitan service and leisure industries, or else removed to distanced points of trans-national production in Latin American coffee plantations, Indonesian textile factories and micro-chip assembly lines in Singapore. In this economy Naples and Irvine are actually more proximate than might initially appear to the eye. Both exist on the same plane, both provide historically diverse solutions in a shared occidental ontology in which the architecture of sedentary, planned accumulation is both constant and central. Both are cities for whom European imperialism yesterday and global neo-colonialism today has been pivotal to their development. The contemporary city – whether a sedimented historical settlement such as Naples or a flexible, horizontal module such as Irvine – continues to disclose and concurrently obfuscate such co-ordinates as they are concentrated in its language, its buildings, its daily praxis and style, its assured occupation of space.

If for Le Corbusier houses are machines for living, Heidegger reminds us that machine 'technology remains up to now the most visible outgrowth of the essence of modern technology, which is identical with the essence of modern metaphysics.'[37] As design, project, and instrumental desire, architecture mediates the transmission of intention to realisation and utility, to cultural finality and historical inscription. As such it finds itself caught in the drive to reduce terrestrial contingency to the causal and controllable logic of a transparent language in which the 'political' and the 'social' are fully absorbed into a worldly regime of rationalism, today increasingly translated into the seemingly soft neutrality of 'information'.

But there are limits that circumscribe the projections of such futures, both that of the desired transcendence promised by technology, and the associated suspension of urban civics and the subsequent numbing of political choice. While southern California is among our futures, it is not necessarily *the* future. For, and here to echo both Martin Heidegger and Richard Sennett, place is not merely the product of global processing. In his noted essay 'Building, Dwelling, Thinking' the German philosopher writes: 'spaces receive their essential being from locations and not from "space".'[38] Space is socially produced, Henri Lefebvre reminds us; it will always have a history: 'No space disappears in the course of growth and development: the *worldwide does not abolish the local*.'[39] A location is always the site of cultural appropriation and historical transformation, the site of a specific manner and economy of building, dwelling and thinking. Although the object of abstract design, that deploys the syntax of capitalism, technology, government, planning and architecture, what emerges is never simply the alienated object of such processes. What emerges is a subject who introduces agonism into the *agora*, constructing a particular place out of this space, confuting the regulated transparency of the plan with the unexpected opacities of the unruly event.[40]

This is to insist on the deeply heteronomic disposition of modernity, on what lies repressed within the strictures of rationalist, and nationalist, coherence. It is to engage with undoing the links of linearity, and the teleology of a time called 'progress'. It is to dally in the emergence of the unsettling presence of what modernity represses and yet ultimately depends upon: the exploitation of the forgotten, the disenfranchised, the alien and the negated. It is the latter who are condemned to bear the burden of modernity in the name of progress, underdevelopment, backwardness, illegality, and the inevitable activation of the glossaries of economic deprivation, sexual prejudice, ethnic discrimination and racism that tend to supervise such scenes.

To directly inscribe such discontinuities, into the contemporary accounting of time, into the balance sheet of modernity, also invests the question of architecture.

Architecture, as it has come to be institutionalised, practised and taught, embodies the rationalist wager (in both empiricist and idealist lexicons) that knowledge is representation, that knowledge is about being able to see in order to re-present the world in a measured and immediately accessible logic and structure. Omniscient, all-seeing, all-knowing God, as Isaac Newton prescribed and William Blake depicted, is the model architect. To the obvious configuration of architecture in the emerging economies of urbanism, colonialism and capitalism, it is therefore necessary to add its equally fundamental embeddedness in hegemonic modalities of knowledge and power. In its modern, occidental formation, architecture is cousin to anthropology, anatomy and the art of the abject, or 'body snatching'.[41] Such Foucauldian associations, tied to the panoptic possibilities of disciplining, not to speak of 'drawing and quartering', the body of the city, the body of the citizen, seeks to reduce all potential movement and rupture to the classificatory frame and dissecting table of a still life, that is, death, as the Italian expression *natura morta* more eloquently evokes. But the body, as flesh, blood and bone, as individual history and fecundity, is the 'saying', as Emmanuel Lévinas insists, that precedes and exceeds consciousness, system, structure and representation. In the incarnation of the subject it is the radical alterity of the body itself with respect to the atemporal desire and design of thought that renders the latter vulnerable to limits and disavowal; for 'it permanently contests the prerogative of consciousness to "give meaning"'.[42]

Modern, Western architecture has participated directly in the propagation of a visual hegemony that not only negates other, non-representational, forms of knowledge, but also in its triumphant rationalisation of the unilateral point of view and abstract perspective achieves the oblivion of what its discourse is designed to explain and house: differentiated bodies and lives. The architectural eye focuses on the techniques and technology of enframing that renders space and ground a retributive reality by reconfiguring it in the identity of the framer, of the subject. The seemingly objective gaze is returned and transformed into the internal, subjective point of view.

Here, once again, it becomes possible to grasp the seemingly paradoxical affirmation that *technology is humanism*. The presumed antithesis between these two terms, which profoundly structures so much modern thinking on technology, actually involves a partnership between two seemingly opposed and separate conceptual bodies caught in a dance whose steps advance the universal claims of occidental thought. When a point of view is treated as everywhere equally valid so that everything results the same and the disturbance of alterity is vanquished, then subjective consciousness passes directly into the 'neutral' objectivity of calculated form.

It requires little imagination to connect these intimations of the power of the look, and its custody of knowledge, to the power of the plan and the architectural point of view. The architectural gaze is also the anthropological gaze: constructing, classifying and defining space for others; further abetted in the pragmatics of Anglo-American cultures by the presumption that language itself is transparent, merely a tool, whereby reason mirrors reality in the neutral instrumentality of the medium. As naked eye, camera lens or computer simulation, such instances of visual power translate truth directly into regimes of representation. Hence the presumed proximity of the viewer to God, of the secular architect to the divine planner. What fails to enter the field of vision, its classificatory procedures and representational logics, fails to become knowledge. Space here continues to be conceived as an anthropomorphic totality whose limits – the horizon, the edge of vision, darkness – are recognised only to be rendered insignificant with respect to what falls within the field of aggrandising vision. The relative stability of this frame, and enframing or representation, of the subject – the 'world picture' (Heidegger) that secures the eye/I perpetually at the centre of vision and world, established for the first time with modernity – permits the disavowal of a vanishing point or void that would ultimately displace and override subjectivity. As Victor Burgin has pointed out: 'the vanishing point is not an integral part of the space of representation; situated on the horizon, it is perpetually pushed ahead as the subject expands its own boundary.'[43] The language of transparency and ocular hegemony here coalesce in a subject–object relationship, in an accumulative understanding of meaning and truth, that perpetually reconfirms the subject. It is an understanding that capitalises, and the metaphor is not casual, on a unilateral movement: from the I/eye towards the world appropriated as external object.

Let me set this epochal and geopolitical generalisation alongside a more precise affirmation drawn directly from the field of architecture. It is taken from Le Corbusier's *The City of Tomorrow and its Planning* (first published in 1929), and reads:

> We struggle against chance, against disorder, against a policy
> of drift and against the idleness which brings death; we strive for
> order, which can be achieved only by appealing to what is the
> fundamental basis on which our minds can work: geometry.[44]

'Geometry is the foundation', the French architect informs us on the very first page of the book. But beyond the constant frustration of geometry by the insistent co-ordinates of politics and history, not to mention the direct pressures of the partitioned property market and the frequently uncoordinated commercialisation of building lots, there lies a deeper tension where plans are permanently caught in the passage between building and dwelling, between the functional response to, and the imaginative projection of, human habitation.

For the power of the gaze is also accompanied by an in-built failure; the failure to listen, to hear and to respond. The eye beholds a form of knowledge that tends neither to expect nor accept a reply. The plan projected and contemplated by the technologies of ocular appropriation and their management of knowledge, of power, can be torn, punctured, or simply exceeded by further regimes of individual and collective sense unexpectedly confuting the administrative prospects. The outcome of the struggle for a common ground of meaning, or shared frame of sense, is rarely inevitable; its politics reaches into the very heart of the matter at hand, into the very heart of our being in the city, in modern life.

Further, the gaze may be returned to render the observer uncomfortable, his or her truth tendentious. The observer is observed. To register the possibility of such a return is to introduce a disruptive distinction between the subjective objectivity of an all-encompassing vision and a responsive eye/I that encounters resistance and opaqueness, disturbance and fuzziness, a murky reflection in the retina. This sabotages the critical distance between the all-seeing subject and the inert object, the distance which permits possession, with an interruption that remains insurmountable, a separation installed and maintained by the finitude of mortality, by the limits of location, by the disturbances of the unconscious and the circumstances of difference: different voices, different bodies, different histories. It is this unrepresentable passage from form to materiality that Plato called *chöra*, that Derrida and others consider the perennial and unfinished site of translation, and which Elizabeth Grosz tellingly identifies as the space of the feminine.[45] It is here that the enclosing design of architecture encounters the disturbing presence of the non-represented; it is where the purity of the plan is fractured by the aperture that opens on to the volatile languages of place.

So, the archaeology of modern architecture does not merely reveal its contract with a particular *épisteme*, it also, and more to the point, establishes historical limits and cultural thresholds. To dwell in the limits between architecture and its beyond, in the excess, the supplement, that refuses or transgresses its logic, is also to encounter the other architectures, or counter-architectures, that disrupt its prescriptions and opt to live plans, buildings, cities, in further, unforeseen practices.

At the building's edge

To these contingencies is to be added the irrepressible constancy of an interrogation that architecture seems persistently oblivious to. Not so long ago, in a 'Letter to Peter Eisenman', Jacques Derrida listed a series of relationships that in Heideggerean fashion expose architecture to the provocation of its terrestrial framing, to what both exceeds and yet envelops its discourse: architecture and poverty, architecture and homelessness, architecture and ruins, and what returns us to the very foundations of such questioning: the question of the earth and the ultimate provocation sustained by our dwelling.[46]

The stones, steel, cement and glass that seemingly furnish the conclusion of a discourse, a project, a plan, a building, a city, are significant, but not sufficient, material points of departure in the processes that transform space into place. For every space incarnates historical and cultural practices; there it receives the individual and collective signature of irrepressible bodies, histories, cultures, memories and lives. Architecture as the 'spatial synthesis of the heterogeneous', is therefore not simply the synthesis of forms and materials as Paul Ricoeur suggests; it is also a synthesis of social, cultural and historical forces and relations.[47] As a text it is not merely a plot to be read, it is also a story we tell and in which we are told. This is to bring to bear on the disciplines and practices that think and project the city – architecture, urban planning and government, financial investment and speculation, global capital and local oligarchy – a reception and listening that permits the other cities that exist within the city to come into focus and hearing: the class, gendered, sexual, ethnic and racial edifices that both constitute and invest urban space. To map the city along these axes is to supplement, and sometimes subvert, the understanding of a habitat understood solely in terms of an abstract population, generic civic space, anonymous labour pool or commercial concentration. To understand the city in this fashion is to decisively shift emphasis from the prescriptive protocols of the urban plan, the architectural project, administrative intention and economic strategy to the inscriptive: to the city that speaks, that narrates itself in diversity. To listen to Lévinas at this point, in the passage from the interdiction of the said to the exposure of saying, in the vacillation between the abstraction of the law and the unplanned event, exists the insistence of ethics where the prescriptive is rendered accountable.

But what does that mean: no planning, no architecture until the unplanned can be recuperated and the ethical installed? In order to frustrate prescription is the plan forever frozen in anticipation of the justice of the future? Is architecture now reduced to repair work, patching up the urban environment, indulging in localised experimentation, while waiting for a new mandate? Certainly, it, too, has suffered the critique of its previous aspirations, a critique which in insisting on the 'beyond' or supplement of its imperious rationality renders irretrievable that earlier project.

> Here the city, as existing, stands as the object and generator of so many possible futures, each calculated according to the nature of its opposition to those futures. The architectural project, while crystallizing one or more of those futures, is then presented to the city, so to speak, as a whole, not as a replacement or substitute, as in the utopian urbanism of modernism, but as material to be submitted to the life and consuming power of the context. Apparently totalizing 'types' will thereby inevitably be fragmented by the counterforce of the site.[48]

Cities, urban life, architecture, like our everyday social, gendered, ethnic, national and local selves, however much they may be constructed by pedagogical and disciplinary decree, are ultimately dependent upon a performative manner or style of being, upon historical articulation and an ethics iterated in our becoming. The truth of our being lies there, in our listening and responding to that language. In that space, however overdetermined by the seemingly irresistible onrush of capital and corporate control – what these days increasingly stands in for institutional policies and politics – there exists a cultural and poetic excess which is irreducible to the calculating rationalism and logic of those intent on overseeing our futures. This supplement interrupts and interrogates the political desire for conclusion, universal comprehension and a rationalist domestication of the world. This desire is dispersed in the space between buildings, in the gap between measured edicts, in the silence that geometry fails to encode, in the shadows that cloud transparency. Ultimately energies spill out into the streets and territories of uncertainty where historical bodies and voices, moving in a mutable, here 'archaic' there 'cyborg', state, conjoin technology and being in a mutual interrogation. Here the beguiling clarity and power of information is betrayed in the perpetual transit and translation attendant upon a differentiated accommodation in the world. Here exists the possibility of exiting from the confines of calculation to run the risk of thinking otherwise. To think what calculation cannot represent, what the numbers and lines repress, is to expose the plan to the incalculable risks – to the world – it hides, and the shifting ground, the earth, it invariably ignores.

Architecture, as the attempt to configure space, to transform it into place, building, habitat, is always confronted with the instability, the narrative eruption, of everyday historical being and a finitude constellated by terrestrial contingency. The cognisance of such co-ordinates perhaps issues in the prospect of a more transitory or 'weak architecture'; an architecture able to accommodate, or at least register, the interval between plan and place. This is not to propose that building structures become less secure, but rather that their necessary logic and rationality come to be recognised as limited languages rather than universal laws. Clearly this would be to restrict and redraw the architectural dominion by turning attention away from the disposition of a homogeneous rationality and insisting on the heterogeneous histories the construction is destined to house. The architect becomes less of a universal planner and more a caring builder; one who constructs, tends and harbours human habitation.[49] The plan, the project, the building becomes a lighter construct – less monumental, less metaphysical in its aspirations, more modest, open and accommodating in its response to the place in which it is destined to acquire lives, histories . . . memories, meanings.

Such an architecture would perhaps become vulnerable to a sense of dwelling received from the historical inheritance and terrestrial contingencies we call the world.[50] In this fashion, architecture would also connect to the more agile abodes that constitute housing and haven for the vast majority of the world's population who have neither the economy nor daily stability to permit the architectonics of occidental edifices. This might suggest a bridge between individualised options circumscribed by the theoretical responsibility (and costs) of carefully considered domestic habitats such as those proposed, for example, by the contemporary Australian architect Glenn Murcutt, and standardised solutions attentive to the history of location and place. Among Murcutt's works is the noted Marika-Alderton house (1991–4) at the Yirrkala community in the Northern Territories: a reinterpretation of the Aboriginal style of shelter proposed as an alternative to the standard government bungalow.[51] Here, although we are still talking of a customised, not collective, solution, this does not exclude the possibility of the latter being ethically and effectively affected by the former.

At this point, it might become possible to ask whether architects are the victims or executors of global capital and its local theatres of power? The above comments on the historical locution and limits of the occidental architectural will – now translated into global skylines from Seville to Sydney to Shanghai – seeks to suggest a role for architects as mediators, exercising their powers to reflect on *and deflect* the structural relations in which they, their practices, and we, are caught. Architecture, as the site of critical work, is not only where buildings and cities are visualised and projected, it is also where it becomes possible to listen to what the protocols of the profession tend to silence or repress in its political economy of rationalising space.

Architecture inevitably develops from a point of view that, no matter how liberal and pluralist its intentions, is destined to draw all that it encounters into the logic of its plan. Not only is it unilateral in its abstractness – how does one draw or project the contingent and the transgressive? – but also it requires an arbitrary closure, a homogenisation of vision, if it is to pass from the drawing board to the building site, to the inhabited building and the edification of space. True, in the everyday city, in the mobility of everyday life, things do not run quite so smoothly. There is the detritus of other histories and of other ways of inhabiting urban space that may leave their marks on the walls, their cardboard shelters in the park, their shadows stretched over the sidewalks, or else concentrate difference – from language and religion to music, cuisine and dress – in particular enclaves of the urban grid. How does architecture respond to that? Can architecture respond at all? Or perhaps among those who do not fit into the plan, whose presence disturbs and contests its logic, there is already another architecture in place? Certainly there frequently emerges a way of dwelling that befuddles the logic imposed, that rewrites the terms of accommodation according to another cultural design.

The tradition of the discontinuous

How to plan, design and build in response to these shifting pressures and presence, how to reply to the unruly whirls and whorls of a history that is neither homogenous nor empty but is tenaciously occupied? I have no neat and ready answer. But perhaps architecture might better respond to such conditions, which are intrinsically among the structural conditions of occidental modernity itself, less by seeking to 'solve' such 'problems' and more by attempting to present them. What that might mean involves a distinctive and explicit shift in the intellectual foundations and language of architecture itself. For architecture tends only to identify ground in the instance of edification. Before that moment such a space is literally meaning-less, unconstructed and thereby unrepresentable both in its own terms and in terms of the epistemology in which it is enmeshed. What, if architecture were to build without the security of this apriori which protects it from what its reason cannot contain? At this point the abstract priority of geometry would come to be challenged by the historically and culturally invested ground upon which architecture both physically and metaphysically builds.

Of course, one might simply object that all of this is an idle exercise in facetious word-play, milking the metaphor of 'architecture' to render its authority intellectually suspect and to suggest that its innovations are merely the decoration on a mundane repetition of buildings that have little that is new to say on dwelling, but much to profit by in the serial production of housing, offices, shopping malls and commercial centres.

Yet, it seems to me, that such questions bring us back forcefully to the question of architecture, to taking the history of building and dwelling, not to speak of the force of the metaphor itself, seriously in both its aims and its limits. For to build, to construct and inhabit a place, is inevitably to establish limits; as a minimum between an interior and an exterior, between the controlled confines of cultured domesticity and the unruly inclemency of the uninhabited, the wild. Of course, since Freud, but as Lyotard reminds us, actually since Greek tragedy, we know that this architecture is illusory, that the wild, the untamed, the repressed, always seeps into the domestic scene; the portal is porous.[52] With the door, 'the bounded and the boundaryless adjoin one another, not in the dead geometric form of a mere separating wall, but rather as the possibility of a permanent interchange'.[53] We are returned to the place in which a building is erected, to a space that is not empty but saturated, to a ground that is not neutral and dumb but is already inscribed, already lived. To repeat, we take up residence in the uncanny. But how, given that the authority of architecture lies in the gesture of foundation, given that it apparently requires an empty space to realise its ambitions, how can this altogether more compromised, irregular and haunted terrain be built upon; that is, how can it be taken into account rather than negated?

A reply must be sought in tradition. Not in the narrow tradition of an occidental architecture, which has become the global practice of building techniques and technology that have come to dominate the realisation of the modern habitat and 'the cloning of American skylines around the world.'[54] Rather, the tradition evoked here is the disturbing and interrogative tradition of dwelling on the earth beneath the sky in which questions of 'freedom' and 'agency' exist in proximity to the world rather than in debt to the abstract humanism of occidental subjectivism (and its metaphysical culmination in technological rationalism). This would involve a move from an architecture involved in the design of buildings to an architecture engaged in the identification of places.[55] At this point, architects might be seen as mediators between the order, the discipline, they embody and the dis-order or extra-disciplinary world they seek to house and accommodate. This would be to suggest, particularly within the overdetermined pragmatic Anglo-American understanding of 'agency', that architects operate, whether knowingly or not, with an 'intellectual' and ethical agenda.

In this radically different sense of tradition, the particular architectural observance of a discipline and tradition that the Italian architect Vittorio Gregotti, for example, passionately argues for, can no longer be complacently considered the site of a referential continuity, circumscribed by precise historical, geographical and political contours.[56] It becomes, rather, an instance of translation and transit. To appeal to tradition is clearly to appeal to a specific cultural context and historical locality in the realisation of the plan. But if a dialogue with the conditions of building are sought, the subsequent edifice is constructed along radically different lines from those associated solely with the conservation of continuity. A real difference emerges from the language employed in appropriating space and transforming it into a specific identity. When the syntax employed in the articulation of the architectural project is considered ultimately transparent, so that reason manifests itself directly in the construct, then a very different building (and sense of place) will emerge compared to the product of a more uncertain grammar and experimental syntax dialoguing with the limits of the locale and the limits of architectural reason itself. This may seem a merely academic observation, but trailing the metaphor of language back to its centrality in the modern formation of occidental humanism its consequences become altogether more significant.

There is the paradoxical fact that the contemporary critique and crisis of European architecture stems not from its failure and the threat of it dying out, but precisely, as with so many other occidental practices, from its ubiquity, from the fact that its language and reason has become universal. In the linguistic rationalisation of technology and technique, the challenge of the indecipherable is invariably replaced by the rationale of the immediately available, poetics by pragmatism. This is to stunt dangerously the architectural discourse, reducing it to the hegemonic rationalisation of the subjective objectification of the world. But if architecture is about the *narration* of tradition and place, or time and space, and lies proximate to the ongoing inscription and writing of the earth, then it can never simply assume an 'organic' relationship to what grows out of the local soil of European culture. For that very culture has historically been a hybrid and transit formation, borrowing and modifying styles and solutions that have been imposed, imported, borrowed, bricolaged, adopted and adapted. In this disengagement from the rigid and homogeneous view of humanism, architecture is asked to respond to differential tempi and to histories that both complicate and confound its building desires.

But is this general reorientation enough? The answer is clearly no. For it inevitably draws me into questioning and deliberately destabilising the desire for domestication that invariably transforms place into the site of bloody xenophobia as *domus* slides into domination in the wink of an eye. Here there emerges the intellectual, the political, task of shifting identifications from the closed historicist charnel house of ancestral claims to the altogether more uncertain and open language of sites, translation, transit and routes. This is to invoke a transposition from the violent insistency of foundations to the transition that accompanies a migration of bodies and histories, and the consecration of provisional dwelling caught on the cusp of perennial re-location.

These sort of calculations cannot, of course, be simply built in. The act of architecture is always a disturbance, a provocation. It radically interrupts, or more modestly reconfigures, an already existing place. Even if the imperatives of capital and the global property market could be set aside, architecture cannot withdraw from that task. But the awareness that architecture also embodies something that goes beyond its calculation, something which exemplifies and exposes that supplementary condition, and thereby always exceeds the more obvious techniques of design, engineering and planning, is, paradoxically, to insist on its limits. For architecture always occurs in a place, *never an empty space*. The space of architecture is always inscribed, sited, annexed and constructed – never blank nor innocent. It is already the site of some-body, of some being. Architecture always builds on fractured, unstable ground. This is to intersect the art of rational construction – the will to construct an edifice: the metaphysics of building and the building of metaphysics – with the intercession, and protection, of the very question of our differentiated being in the world. There are forces within the languages of being, building and thinking that interrupt, break through and exceed the violent imposition of technical, 'scientific', 'rational' and unilateral solutions to that ancient and most present of demands: the unfolding question of how to dwell.

Notes

1 Emmanuel Lévinas, *Totality and Infinity*, trans. Alphonso Lingis, Pittsburgh, Pa, Duquesne University Press, 1969, p. 153.

2 Susan Buck-Morss, *The Dialectics of Seeing: Walter Benjamin and the Arcades Project*, Cambridge, Mass. and London, MIT Press, 1989; Victor Burgin, *In/Different Places*, Los Angeles and London, University of California Press, 1996; Esther Leslie, 'Space and West End Girls: Walter Benjamin versus Cultural Studies', *New Formations*, 38, Summer 1999.

3 Heidegger, and subsequently Derrida, have insisted that it is the construction of metaphysics that seeks to veil the abyss and ignore the instability of the uncertain terrain on which occidental edifices ground their philosophy, projects and principles; see Mark Wigley, *The Architecture of Deconstruction: Derrida's Haunt*, Cambridge, Mass. and London, MIT Press, 1996. In the 'critical un-building' (*kritischer Abbau* – Heidegger's term in his first lectures in 1920), or deconstruction, that excavates the precariousness of that tradition, Naples provides a fitting allegorical site.

4 James Donald, *Imagining the Modern City*, London, Athlone Press, 1999.

5 Anthony Vidler, *The Architectural Uncanny: Essays in the Modern Unhomely*, Cambridge, Mass. and London, MIT Press, 1992.

6 The 'expanded intercourse' quote is from Karl Marx, *Grundrisse*, trans. Martin Nicolaus, Harmondsworth, Penguin, 1973, p. 540.

7 Fredric Jameson, *Postmodernism, or the Cultural Logic of Late Capitalism*, London and New York, Verso, 1992; Mike Davis, *City of Quartz: Excavating the Future in Los Angeles*, London, Vintage, 1992; David Harvey, *The Condition of Postmodernity*, Oxford, Blackwell, 1989. Harvey's reading is to some degree mitigated by the presence of Henri Lefebvre's work on the politics of space, the everyday and the city. The apocalyptic representations of catastrophic capitalism and accompanying 'ecologies of fear' can, of course, be transferred to a thousand cities around the globe. Los Angeles, although the most public of metropolises, does not have the exclusive on this. There is always an inevitable provincialism in the maps we individually employ in our explanations; see Mike Davis, *Ecology of Fear: Los Angeles and the Imagination of Disaster*, New York, Vintage, 1999.

8 Jean-François Lyotard, 'Otherness and the Postmodern Imagination', in *Identity and Difference*, Triennale di Milano, XIX Esposizione Internazionale, Milan, Electa, 1996.

9 Martin Heidegger, 'Building, Dwelling, Thinking', in Heidegger, *Basic Writings*, New York, Harper & Row, 1977, p. 324.

10 Marcos Novak, 'TransArchitectures', in the catalogue of *film+arc.graz. 3 Internationale Biennale*, Graz, 1997, p. 75.

11 Arata Isozaki, 'Introduction: A Map of Crises', in Kojin Karatani, *Architecture as Metaphor: Language, Number, Money*, trans. Sabu Kohso, Cambridge, Mass. and London, MIT Press, 1995, p. vii.

12 Marcos Novak, op. cit.

13 Christian Girard, 'Traversing the Screens', in the catalogue of *film+arc.graz. 3 Internationale Biennale*, Graz, 1997.

14 These are iterated, for example, in John Rundell's otherwise interesting 'Beyond Crisis, Beyond Novelty: The Tensions of Modernity', *New Formations*, 31, Spring/

Summer 1997. In the already cited television interview of 1969, Heidegger states unequivocally that he is not against technology. There he continues: 'it is not a question of speaking in opposition to or condemning technology. It is rather the case of understanding the *essence* of technology and the world of technology. In my opinion, that cannot happen while philosophy continues to move within a subject–object context', *Risposta: A colloquio con Martin Heidegger*, trans. Carlo Tatasciore, Naples, Guida, 1992, p. 57.

15 Arata Isozaki in Kojin Karatani, op. cit.

16 Kojin Karatani, op. cit, p. xl.

17 Ibid., p. 137.

18 Ibid., p. 112.

19 Rob Imrie, 'Disability and Discourses of Movement and Mobility', *Environment and Planning A*, 32, 2000, p. 1644.

20 Ibid., p. 1642.

21 Kojin Karatani, op. cit., 1995.

22 Martin Heidegger, 'Building, Dwelling, Thinking', op cit. This emerges from considering the etymology of *bauen* – to build. This etymological logic is justified as follows: 'Man acts as though he were the shaper and master of language, while in fact *language* remains the master of man. Perhaps it is before all else man's subversion of *this* relation of domination that drives his essential nature into alienation', p. 324, emphasis in the original.

23 Martin Heidegger, 'The Turning', in Heidegger, *The Question Concerning Technology and Other Essays*, trans. William Levitt, New York, Harper, 1977, p. 48.

24 Martin Heidegger, 'The Question Concerning Technology', in Heidegger, *The Question Concerning Technology and Other Essays*, op. cit. pp. 12–15.

25 The telescoping of time in a moment of danger is a clear allusion to Walter Benjamin's 'Theses on the Philosophy of History', as well as to his intuitive imbrication of the Baroque in his reading of modernity.

26 Edward Soja, 'Inside Exopolis: Scenes from Orange County', in Michael Sorkin (ed.) *Variations on a Theme Park*, New York, Hill & Wang, 1992.

27 Jacques Derrida, speaking at the Istituto per gli Studi Filosofici, Naples, 22 February 1996.

28 Don Mitchell, 'Dead Labor: Mobility, Violence, and the Political Economy of Landscape', at the Second Annual Colloquium of the Centre for the Study of Spaces in Modernity, Gregynog, Newtown, Powys, 26–28 November 1999. Also see, George Henderson, *California and the Fictions of Capital*, Oxford and New York, Oxford University Press, 1999.

29 Paul Carter, *The Lie of the Land*, London, Faber & Faber, 1996, p. 6. The 1835 House of Commons report into Australian settlement noted that Aboriginal people 'of any land have an uncontrovertible right to their own soil: a plain and sacred right, however, which seems not to have been understood. Europeans have entered their borders, uninvited, and when there, have not only acted as if they were undoubted lords of the soil, but have punished the natives as aggressors if they have evinced a disposition to live in their own country', quoted in Howard Pedersen and Banja Woorunmurra, *Jandamarra and the Bunuba Resistance*, Broome, WA, Magabela, 1995, p. 15.

30 Stephen Greenblatt, *Marvellous Possession: The Wonder of the New World*, Oxford, Oxford University Press, 1992, p. 83.

31 Ibid. For further analyses of this formative 'moment', see Michel de Certeau, *The Writing of History*, trans. Tom Conley, New York, Columbia University Press, 1988; Tzetan Todorov, *The Conquest of America*, New York, Harper & Row, 1984. On nationalist differentiation in the European devices of taking rhetorical possession of the Americas, see Patricia Seed, *Ceremonies of Possession in Europe's Conquest of the New World, 1492–1640*, Cambridge, Cambridge University Press, 1995.

32 Gary Snyder, *The Practice of the Wild*, New York, North Point Press, 1990.

33 For an excellent discussion of this nomadic interrogation of modernity, see Syed Manzurul Islam, 'Forming Minoritarian Communities: Nomadic Ethics for the Postcolonial World', *New Formations*, 39, Winter 1999–2000.

34 Kate Darian-Smith, Liz Gunner and Sarah Nuttal, 'Introduction', in Darian-Smith, Gunner and Nuttal (eds) *Text, Theory, Space*, London and New York, Routledge, 1996, p. 8.

35 Gaston Bachelard, *The Poetics of Space*, trans. Maria Jolas, Boston, Mass., Beacon, 1969.

36 Mirjana Lozanovska, 'Emigration/Immigration: Maps, Myths and Origins', at the conference *Building Dwelling Drifting: Migrancy and the Limits of Architecture*, University of Melbourne, 27 June 1997. Not that the will to represent is automatically understood or homogeneous in effect. The agency of architecture – who is being represented, what gets to be represented – clearly also constitutes the contested ground upon which architecture builds. I take these points from Gülsüm Bantoglu and her talk at the conference, *Global/Local: Postcolonial Questions*, University of Western Sydney, 24 June 1997.

37 Martin Heidegger, 'The Age of the World Pictures', in Heidegger, *The Question Concerning Technology and Other Essays*, op. cit., p. 117.

38 Martin Heidegger, 'Building, Dwelling, Thinking', op. cit., p. 332.

39 Henri Lefebvre, *The Production of Space*, trans. Donald Nicholson-Smith, Oxford, Blackwell, 1991, p. 86, emphasis in original.

40 Richard Sennett, 'Something in the City: The Spectre of Uselessness and the Search for a Place in the World', *Times Literary Supplement*, 22 September 1995.

41 I have borrowed this suggestive connection from Christine McCarthy's paper 'Drawing and Quartering, "Mort Safes" and Dissection Rooms: Divisions of the Anatomical and the Criminality of the Architectural Section', delivered at the conference *Building Dwelling Drifting: Migrancy and the Limits of Architecture*, University of Melbourne, 27 June 1997.

42 Susan A. Handelman, *Fragments of Redemption: Jewish Thought and Literary Theory in Benjamin, Scholem, and Levinas*, Bloomington and Indianapolis, Indiana University Press, 1991, p. 253.

43 Victor Burgin, 'Geometry and Abjection', in John Fletcher and Andrew Benjamin (eds) *Abjection, Melancholia and Love: The Work of Julia Kristeva*, London and New York, Routledge, 1990, p. 118.

44 Le Corbusier, *The City of Tomorrow and its Planning*, Cambridge, Mass., MIT Press, 1982, p. 95.

45 Elizabeth Grosz, 'Women, *Chora*, Dwelling', in Sophie Watson and Katherine

Gibson (eds), *Postmodern Cities and Spaces*, Oxford and Cambridge, Mass., Blackwell, 1995.

46 Jacques Derrida, 'Letter to Peter Eisenman', in William Lillyman, Marilyn Moriarty and David Neuman (eds) *Critical Architecture and Contemporary Culture*, New York and Oxford, Oxford University Press, 1994. The letter is dated 12 October 1989.

47 Paul Ricoeur, 'Architecture and Narrative', in *Identity and Difference*, Triennale di Milano, XIX Esposizione Internazionale, Milan, Electa, 1996.

48 Anthony Vidler, op. cit., p. 200. Vidler is describing the experimental architecture of Wiel Arets.

49 'Man is not the lord of beings. Man is the shepherd of Being': Martin Heidegger, 'Letter on Humanism', in Heidegger, *Basic Writings*, op. cit. p. 221.

50 Martin Heidegger, 'The Thing', in Heidegger, *Poetry, Language, Thought*, trans. Albert Hofstadter, New York, Harper & Row, 1975, p. 179.

51 Nicola Flora, Paolo Giardiello and Gennaro Postiglione (eds) *Glenn Murcutt: Disegni per otto case*, Naples, Clean Edizioni, 1999.

52 Jean-François Lyotard, '*Domus* and the Megalopolis', in Neil Leach (ed.) *Rethinking Architecture*, London and New York, Routledge, 1997.

53 Georg Simmel, 'Bridge and Door', in Leach, ibid., p. 68.

54 Meaghan Morris, 'Metamorphoses at Sydney Tower', *New Formations*, 11, Summer 1990.

55 Simon Unwin, *Analysing Architecture: The Architecture Notebook*, London and New York, Routledge, 1997.

56 Vittorio Gregotti, *L'identità dell'architettura europea e la sua crisi*, Turin, Einaudi 1999.

6

A STRANGER IN THE HOUSE

I wish to begin with a problem that confronts us all in different ways, both in our intellectual pursuits and everyday lives: national sovereignty is perhaps not withering away in the spectacular manner that prophets of trans-global capital and information flows predict. And it is not withering away to be replaced by a trans-national sense of identity. The Kurds, the Basques, the Palestinians, the Tibetans, all demand their rights to autonomous statehood. It turns out that 'the nation is always a reality in the making rather than an already made reality.'[1] Even if already established, that nation is always seemingly near to completion, but never fully achieved.[2] Certainly, as Arjun Appadurai has argued, modern media and migration have profoundly modified both public and private imaginations everywhere, radically transforming potential horizons of identity.[3] Yet in a world in which the willingness to fight, kill and, ultimately, die, for an abstraction called 'country' or 'nation', often entwined with a precise ethnic locality or theological creed, the complex forces that consistently configure a sense of belonging and 'home' remain vehemently in place. There continues to exist a disturbing proximity, even, as Ghassan Hage notes, a 'similarly structured nationalist imaginary', between ethnic identities, often constituted as 'nations', and 'ethnic cleansing'; that is, a disturbing proximity between domestication and extermination.[4]

The mystery of home

The mystery of that sense of belonging deposited in the desire, the need, to be a part of a historical, social and cultural unit that is called 'home' and 'homeland', despite the optimistic theorising of nomadism and rhizomatic becoming, refuses to fade away. As already noted, home as *domus* is etymologically rooted in *dominus*: domination.[5] Home is the place where things and relations, materials and bodies, fantasy and fact,

161

can be dominated and domesticated, governed and articulated. Still, we are all also deeply aware of the high price that humanity pays for this desire: from social ostracism, economic exploitation and racial discrimination to war, physical elimination, and planned, ultimately, industrialised genocide. We are in no position to legislate for the clarification of this mystery, it clearly exceeds our rationalisations. Does that mean that the 'unreasonable' state of the nation and nationalism is irrational? Or does it express an arrangement of sentiments that we might learn better to inhabit in order to live them otherwise?[6]

Alejandro Morales, a Chicano novelist, once asked me: where does exile conclude and migration commence? Clearly the latter matures in the light of the former, but to waiver in the gap between these two terms perhaps helps to better concentrate attention on the political and ontological shift from existing in the lengthy shadows of a forcefully abandoned homeland to living on in the complex contours of a host country that is becoming your home too.

The passage from exile to migration, although inevitably *chiaroscuro*, involves movement from the forsaken certainties of the former home that are to be conserved from the dispersal of travel to the altogether more ambiguous, uncertain settlements of the new habitat. For even if the migrant still clings to an imagined community, it is one that is always accompanied by the transformation of its culture, tradition, language, even religious rites and myths, into a translated space in which both it, and the host community, undergo transformation. In this context to narrate the nation is also to narrate another, a further story, and to stitch ulterior interrogations into the weave of individual and communal identity. Beyond the phenomenological distinctions one might be tempted to draw in seeking to locate the difference between exile and migration, I wish to consider the question of exile, migration and the stranger as a theme that invests the very understanding of occidental modernity: its sense of history, culture, place and identity. This is to draw from the presumed margins of modernity the insistent testimony of the forced displacement of peoples and cultures which is most dramatically signalled in the violent installation and subsequent intertwining of racist slavery, capitalism, modern nationalisms and genocide.

Atlantic economies and fledging European nation states were initially maintained by the African slave trade. The subsequent global enterprise of colonialism ranged from metropolitan episodes, such as the eighteenth-century clearing of the Scottish Highlands and the deportation of criminals to distant penal colonies, to nineteenth-century mass migrations out of the rural poverty of southern Europe, India and China. All of this amounts to a trajectory that is deeply implicated in the systematic domination that leads to pogroms, genocide and the attempted eradication of whole populations from the heartland of the Americas, central Europe, Australia and elsewhere. In the complex mixing of inter-ethnic and inter-subaltern histories the question of who is the stranger in the composition haunts every historical and political revision. Scottish Highlanders who, cast out of their homes and settling on other lands in other continents (North America, Australia, New Zealand) displace others from their homes, participate in a historical subalternity that is simply not equal for all.[7] The white settler, no matter how impoverished and exploited, remains a systematic usurper. The chain of global displacement inaugurated by modern imperialism is both complex and codified, producing subalternities that are simultaneously linked yet frequently incommensurable.

Today, these multiple, repressed and uneven histories return to radically displace unilateral claims to own a language, a culture, a history, a city, a nation, a 'home', by inhabiting and configuring these languages diversely, by narrating modernity in another lexicon, in another key. The exterminated 'native', the cast out 'exile', the despised 'stranger', returns again and again to haunt modernity and the desire for the closed comfort of the stable same. But this is not merely to propose the dissemination and dispersal of the euroamerican grammar of power by the subaltern and the once excluded. It is, above all, and more precisely, to insist on an interruption in the assumptions of historical and cultural ownership and 'progress' – who built this house, and whose house is it? – that forces me to consider how there is no history, culture or identity that is immune from exposure to the response to, and responsibility for, the interrogation that emerges from the presence of the stranger, the proximity of the other. As Johannes Fabian has reminded us, in the encounter with alterity the impetus to maintain a hierarchial distance leads to the failure to remember where we come from: a hybrid home, haunted by historical rites, cultural prejudices and social superstitions.[8]

This, and to cite Paul Carter's evocative book *The Lie of the Land*, this perspective might involve reversing or overturning the generally negative connotations of migration and exile. For migration and exile are invariably considered as eccentric and the mark of cultural impoverishment. Such a verdict, Carter suggests, arises from:

> a political agenda, from the centralist ambitions of the Athenian *polis* and its apologists. The challenge, at least for a post-colonial poetics, is to see in what way migration might entail a form of emplacement, might in fact be constitutional and signify a mode of being at home in the world. Is the history of

Western culture simply a sequence of ever more abstract scientific and technological enclosure acts progressively divorcing us from contact with the ground, and characterizing physical movement as primitive? Or is there within that sequence a counter-tradition, a form of wandering that constitutes a ground-marking? Can Pallas Athene ever again take command of the storm?[9]

In this displaced perspective the object of my gaze, the object of my language, the silent stranger, the mute migrant, here becomes a historical subject – one who not only replies and therefore does not merely exist in my speech, in my words and world, but also offers a meaning that does not necessarily belong to me, or even recognise my claims on its sense. In this disavowal of the subject–object division, both the mastery of language is disputed and critical distance, offering the shelter for my ontological security, is dissipated and dispensed with. If the world I word reveals itself no longer to be in my possession, limited to my dominion, then the movement from home and the domestic scene towards an alien beyond, in which, like Edmond Jabès, I now travel as a guest, is dependent not upon my will but upon the hospitality of language. This elsewhere, this alterity, is not susceptible to my imperatives; it does not nurture me and sustain my ego. It no longer offers the road of return through the other. Emmanuel Lévinas:

> Neither possession nor the unity of number nor the unity of concepts link me to the Stranger [l'Etranger], the stranger who disturbs the being at home with oneself [le chez soi]. But Stranger also means the free one. Over him I have no *power*. He escapes my grasp by an essential dimension, even if I have him at my disposal. He is not wholly in my site.[10]

The question of the other, is always the question of the stranger, the outsider, the one who comes from elsewhere and who inevitably bears the message of a movement that threatens to interrupt the stability of the domestic scene. What we desire to keep at a distance is rendered proximate, the external – for which in the past walls were built, and in the present laws are passed – today becomes internal, inescapable. In this ontological exchange my sense of being is exposed to interrogation, is rendered vulnerable. To acknowledge this state, rather than deny, conquer or exterminate it, is to present me not merely with the question of liberal tolerance and pluralist coexistence, but with a perpetual and radical interrogation. Emmanuel Lévinas once again:

> For the ethical relationship which subtends discourse is not a
> species of consciousness whose ray emanates from the I; it puts
> the I in question. This putting in question emanates from the
> other.[11]

In the journey into the future, the journey backwards, towards the hearth,
also proves determinate. The passage between past and future is always
accompanied by the sought for confirmation of home. For some this is
a secure point of reference, a reassuring stability represented in economical, social and historical terms, for others it is often a fragile, frequently
torn and fading image, sustained more in the imaginary glow of memory
than in the immediacy of material confirmation. In this interval between
the home that beckons me forward and the one calling me back, there
emerges the multiple pulls of time, a time that is not merely linear and
progressive. If time, as Akhil Gupta points out, is inevitably considered
a commodity, then some people's time is invariably considered richer
and more powerful than the time of others.[12]

Against the occidental emphasis on linear time, busily measuring
development and under-development in the slipstream of 'progress', there
is the time of migrancy, and the migration of time from a unique
modality of measurement.[13] It is with the multiple recombination of
time, Salman Rushdie reminds us in *The Satanic Verses* (1988), that
newness enters the world. The concurrence of different tempi within the
framework of modernity stretches, deviates and distorts its unilateralism.
Diverse dimensions disturb and interrupt the productive temporality of
measured, linear accumulation. In the justice of differentiation the lived
time of modernity exceeds the partial and abstract singularity of
'progress'.[14] This disturbs, interrogates and takes

> away the ground on which distinctions have historically been
> constructed in the Western narrative of progress, distinctions
> that continue to justify, under the guise of 'development', the
> subordination and management of the 'third world' today.[15]

If the West has become the world, in the process it has also come to
be displaced. If its languages, its technologies and techniques, have now
encompassed the earth to provide the contemporary sense of dwelling,
its history and powers are inhabited by others who express their histories, their identities, their reasons there. My (self) centre is interrupted.
For here, whatever my desires, I am forced to confront, within the very
languages I presume to possess, the incommensurable, the untranslatable
– the heart of a being that refuses to be reduced to a common measure;
that is to *my* measure and *my* understanding of the world.

165

Whenever and wherever it is nominated, there emerges the repressed linkage that makes 'home' possible for some, impossible for others. Travelling between accommodation and homelessness, the very categories with which 'home' is habitually constructed (tradition, language, custom, kinship) are confronted by other, unexpected versions. When the co-ordinates of a specific place and history – that of the West – are dispersed throughout the world then the particular locality of tradition and tongue finds itself on an interminable journey. There, in transit and translation, the very nature of place and home is irreversibly transformed. The proximate, what lies close at hand in constructing my home and the sense of my self, can no longer be bounded by blood, soil, and the closed horizon of the immediate and the local. The myth of pure 'origins' is now fused with others, casting considerations of belonging (to what? where? how?) outwards into a vulnerable space. The time and tradition of a local cultural economy is interceded by a series of interrogations that invest each and every place.

> I am born between two waves
> and my skin turns
> ever more slippery.

writes the Iranian immigrant poet Majid Nafici.[16] When the world folds in and the distant is conjoined with the proximate, the unhomely with the homely, the repression that shadows and breaches every representation of home, culture and self is unleashed.

In this undoing of the myth of home, in which the journey always confirms the point of departure secured in the presumption of eventual home-coming, the Western archetype of Ulysses is deviated and set adrift. The Greek and Homeric sense of 'home', explored by Horkheimer and Adorno in their noted excursus on the Enlightenment, does not merely provide the obvious comfort of familiarity, it also furnishes the cultural formation and psychological sustenance that structures the subsequent reason of the ego. Armed with domestic certainty the individual is able to venture out into the world, confront its turbulence and vicissitudes, explore its manifestations, and return home with the knowledge gained. For:

> the epic adventures allow each location a proper name and permit space to be surveyed in a rational manner. Though trembling and shipwrecked, the hero anticipates the work of the compass. Though he is powerless, no part of the sea remains unknown to him, and so his powerlessness also indicates that the mighty powers will be put down.[17]

166

A self-centred consciousness, a domesticating reason, a man alone, charts the voyage home. At this point, home is not necessarily a physical abode or shelter. Home is the house of knowledge whose incremental powers will secure his passage in the yet-to-be known, discovered and assimilated.

What I am seeking to suggest is that such a journey – one in which autonomous and patriarchal reason plies a course through the world, oblivious to the voice and histories of others, refusing, in Paul Carter's words, 'to grant authority to anything except its own representation' – is today intellectually impossible; there is no eventual homecoming, no Ithaca, no Penelope, at journey's end.[18] The prospect of domesticating the world so as to confirm the structure and avarice of the ego is forever interrupted.

The world, the sense of place and belonging, of the domestic and the foreign, of occidental modernity itself, is irreversibly being reconfigured. The moment of unsettlement induced by first contact and the subjection of other histories to the teleology of the West returns to haunt the house of knowledge and the political and psychological settlements it presumes to have established. The uncanny experience of modernity is no longer a peripheral or passing empirical sensation. It surely never was. To be unsettled is central both to the economic and social reproduction of modernity and to the resistances it disseminates. This is to inhabit a differentiated, but shared, historical formation that radically reworks and redirects our sense of being in the world. Here an appreciation of disturbance and displacement is not only constituted by a Heideggerean sense of homelessness induced by the technical and instrumental oblivion of the ways of being, but also, and more precisely, expounded in a sense of home that is constructed in the temporal co-ordinates of unsettled and unsettling histories. Frequently ignored, and more generally repressed in the acquisition of local well-being, it is these co-ordinates that most profoundly constitute our precarious worldly abode. It is the knowledge of such a knowledge that can no longer be easily repudiated.

The trauma of translation

Both being a stranger, a migrant, and an intimate sense of belonging depend upon a definition of place. There is both the place in which the exile, the migrant presents her or himself as a stranger, and the place or 'home' that has been left behind. To confront this question, as the Mexican urban anthropologist Néstor García Canclini has argued in his book *Hybrid Cultures: Strategies for Entering and Leaving Modernity*, to confront this question is to engage in something more radical and extensive than multiculturalism and identity politics.[19] It is not simply the case of belatedly acknowledging the previously negated body of a history, the history of negated bodies, in a nationalist narrative now seeking to accommodate diversity. For beyond the immediate response that may offer temporary hospitality to alterity, a more adequate and sustained reply to the question of exile, migrancy and displacement can surely only emerge from considering the very ground that place – both the previous place from which the migrant comes and the present place that hosts his body, her history, their culture – nominates. In the movement through the economical and political vectors of modernity, it is the differential conceptualisation of time and place, as much as passports and work permits, accent and religion, that identifies the migrant, the stranger: whether or not she or he 'fits in'.

The transit of migrancy involves the trauma of being translated into an object. This is forcibly reinforced by being subsequently positioned on the margins in a 'minority' position as a migrant – the stranger whose presence reconfirms the non-positionality, the liberal movement, of those who inhabit the national centre, the political mainstream, the cultural consensus. If, by definition, the émigré, the migrant and the stranger invoke a liminal space, their presence has also the countervailing consequence of enclosing 'home', a sense of place and belonging, in a particular historical and ontological site. The arrival of the stranger evokes a boundary, a frontier, both imagined and real. The limits imposed, the barriers erected, effect not only the outsider; they equally construe, limit and direct the very nature of the 'inside'.

So, I would suggest that it is important to examine how place is grounded, how it is constructed and conceived. I would like to think that such considerations might help to provide both a response and a language in which to consider exile and migrancy, the arrival of the stranger. This would be to think not in terms of a threat for which I seek immediate repair but as a timely interrogation of the repressed histories that permit me to feel secure in holding my ground when defining and excluding the other.

Place. Most obviously to speak of place in the company of strangers is to refer to one's nomination in a language and a history that is invariably institutionalised in the neurotic cultural grammar of nationhood. The modern sense of place, although it may still bear the traces of more archaic belongings – a village, a local dialect, a city or region – is invariably prefaced, both by the stranger and the host, in a national nomenclature. Details of dress, tongue, accent, food, religion and custom, are referenced by such a sense of belonging. Yet we know that this is often an approximation, sometimes a misreading. Many of those details pre-exist the modern nation state. And however much they may have been honed down to meet the requirements of national identity they inevitably spill out of that limited pedagogical frame. Spanish is not the property of Spain, just as Islam is not the property of Iran, or English the prerogative of England. So, in nominating one's identity there is the simultaneous coupling and uncoupling of the narrative of a homogeneous and national belonging. The prescriptive grammar of nationalism that seeks, both at home and abroad, to contain potential heterogeneity and smooth over contestation in the name of a public consensus, is potentially overtaken and challenged in the idiolect that speaks individual belonging.[20]

But whose 'place' am I talking about here? That of the migrant, the stranger, or that of the indigenous, the local, the host? Doesn't the sense of ground proposed here, not the abstract unity of linear time and empty space occupied by the 'nation', but the rough, uneven, resistant and unruly ground of the quotidian in which history leaves multiple and uneven grooves, suggestions and directions, invest both the place of the stranger and the place of the resident? Such considerations disturb the homogeneous time of a unique national identity, deviating the onward flight of the arrow of 'progress', by taking a step sideways into the multiple sites of coeval temporality and histories that locate us in a differentiated communality. Here the Australian Aboriginal, Chicano city dweller and Anglo suburbanite occupy a shared, if asymmetrical, world. All are within modernity without being reducible to the unique account that modernity often pretends to offer.

However, even this sense of grounding which refuses the national frame and puts in question the presumed positionality of both the migrant and the resident host, is only the first chapter in a counternarrative that promises to rewrite the very understanding of ground, place and identity. To the sideward movement that renders modernity multiple and the world heterotopic, needs to be added a return in which the privileged narratives of modernity disclose a hybrid formation. Migration, invariably enforced by slavery, imperialism, colonialism, technological domination, economic and political hegemony, was both present and constitutive of occidental modernity from its very inception five centuries ago.[21]

Anthropologising the anthropologist

At this point, the question emerges not in the space of the conjunction, not in the 'and' that lies between 'home' *and* hybridity, between domesticity *and* migration, between the 'resident' *and* the 'stranger', but rather in the apprenticeship of learning to dwell in *hybridity as home*. Here there no longer lies the choice between the domestic and the diasporic, but rather the prospect of occupying a further space in which both the familiar and the foreign are conjoined and mutually interrogated. Here I perhaps become more hesitant in pronouncing where home concludes and the foreign commences. Here the slick verdicts of 'globalisation' are deviated and decanted into the altogether more complex uncertainties of a 'worlding' that is both material and imaginative, both political and poetical.

This most obviously contests a superficial cosmopolitan gloss by locating histories and identities in a location that both sustains and exceeds us; in a terrestrial framing that flees the logic of obvious explanation and a reductive transparency ... Here the history of home – conceived in national and nationalist terms – is crossed by the question of dwelling. Caught in such co-ordinates, the languages of identity and nation are set within borders that limit their claims on the world. Primary among these languages is the metropolitan medium of the media – the press, radio, cinema and television. It is such media that permit and sustain the abstract grounding of 'place' in the narrative of the 'imagined community' of the nation. It is such media that fuse memory and identity into inscriptions that acquire the signature of history.

But to tear myself away from the screen, to lower my eyes and withdraw from the ontological assumption, so dear to many in the West, that the truth is representation, is to bend attention to a sense of place, history, identity, that is grounded. This means to turn to a sense of place that is found less in the flat two-dimensional space of mimesis and a panoptic visual purview of knowledge, of power, and more in the uneven 'lie of the land' where such screens, and their particular projections, are erected. In the localisation of the representation, where the historically charged environment sustains far more than its abstract conceptualisation, language is not a one-sided imposition on a blank space; rather it sounds out the land, echoes within an environment, reverberates in earthly rhythm, is folded into social sonorities and terrestrial resonance.[22]

At this point, I turn to view the visual work of Hélène Hourmat: a contemporary artist, of Moroccan background, brought up in France. Women in North African dress, men in occidental clothing, family scenes and street portraits: Hourmat's mixed media panels composed of photography, pastels, postcards and ink, trace the journey — both the physical journey and the complex cultural itineraries — of national, ethnic and gendered identity from one side of the Mediterranean to the other, of one world (Jewish, Sephardic, Moroccan and Maghrebian) within another (European, French, cosmopolitan), amid the languages, and limits, of visual enframing. This visual correspondence insists on the precise historical trajectory of a seemingly peripheral cultural configuration within the deterritorialised grammar of modernity. It brings both to account while transforming their respective histories into an element of freedom.

Such work proposes an invitation to step into the unhomely not in the name of the passing thrill of the exotic and the temporary attraction of alterity, but rather in order to render the languages that familiarise us with the world, that domesticate it and render it ours, unfamiliar; that render the ordinary extraordinary, uncanny, and there encounter the violent repression that legitimises our speech. It is to intercept discussion of the global–local nexus, and the explanatory gloss of modernity and modernisation, with a scepticism towards the teleology invariably imbricated in the understanding of such processes.

Then there is a video.[23] There is a video in which we encounter the following writing on the screen:

> In an age in which anthropology increasingly turns into autobiography, the observer, seeking to capture, to enframe, an elsewhere, is now caught within the net of critical observation. The I/eye — both the physical organ and the subjective state — joins the exile of language.
>
> Our linguistic home comes undone, words migrate, and language hybridises to expose tears in the maps and a stammer in the discourses that we in the West have been accustomed to employ.
>
> It is as though I have fallen into a fold in time, stumbled across a sharp punctuation in the narrative, as my presence, which once apparently flowed effortlessly across the map, is brought up short, diverted, disrupted, dispersed.
>
> Travel, in both its metaphorical and physical reaches, can no longer be considered as something that confirms the premises of my initial departure, concluding in a confirmation, a domestication of the difference and the detour.

This declaration is interspersed with a constant shot of a man with a video camera, reflected in the windows of a train — the observer observed, the external, objective view returned and transformed into the internal, subjective point of view. These words and images provoke the self-reflexive posed by the interrogation of the anthropological gaze.

Or, perhaps the above voice is merely the treacherous site of a theoretical ruse: the subtle enactment of de-centring oneself in order to re-centre oneself. It undoubtedly reveals the ambiguity of a power that speaks of its own loss. It is that ambiguity, the value of uncertainty, that needs to be insisted upon. Then there is the man with a video camera, seeking to capture and visually enframe the world. The camera, the video, introduces the precise instance of visual power in which the reality and representation of truth are considered one in a metaphysics of realism. What fails to enter the field of vision, its classificatory procedures and representational logics, fails to become knowledge. The language of transparency and ocular hegemony coalesce in a subject–object relationship, and a unilateral understanding of meaning and truth, that reconfirms the subject; an understanding that moves in only one direction, from the I/eye towards the world perceived as external object. But the power of the gaze is also accompanied by an in-built failure, the failure to listen, to hear and to respond. It is a form of knowledge that tends neither to expect nor accept a reply. Critically to explore this path is to open up the process of anthropologising the West in order to 'show just how exotic its constitution of reality has been.'[24] This would be to excavate the theoretical disposition that has historically sought to capture and explain reality without itself being incorporated. Critical distance, scientific objectivity and aesthetic order is pursued while avoiding the paradox of the 'objectivity' of a specific point of view located in the partiality of a history and the partisan language of a culture.[25] The apparent freedom of the observer inadvertently reveals the intellectual enclosure in which she or he is unknowingly held.

Historically, it has been the look emanating from the centre that has guided a vision of things which has been unilateral and objectifying in its effects. But the gaze may be returned to render the observer uncomfortable. To register the possibility of such a return is to open up the disruptive distinction between the all-encompassing gaze – the subjective objectivity of the *cogito* – and a responsive vision that encounters resistance and opaqueness, disturbance and fuzziness, a murky reflection in the retina. This is to undo the critical distance between the all-seeing subject and an inert object – the distance that permits possession – with an interval that remains insurmountable, a separation installed and maintained by the finitude of mortality, by the limits of location and the position of a body, a voice, a history. In the passage from a confident appropriation of the world associated with modern science and an altogether less secure, more Baroque, recognition, emerges a mode of perception that invokes earthly dwelling and movement that is not restricted to the *cogito*. It is a perspective that leans to see beyond the instrumental tyranny of a unique point of view which sees in the land, histories and bodies of others merely objects at his disposal.[26]

With this we return to the insistent question of anthropology, which cannot simply be obliterated in a discourse of blame or guilt. It is rather a telling symptom of the institutional and disciplinary traditions of the West: that diversity of arguments and approaches that nevertheless acquires a contingent unity and shared epistemology in the configurations of modernity and occidental 'progress', bringing the rest under Western eyes. Western anthropology is the historical legislator of the traffic between worlds. A frontier discipline that most explicitly centred the occidental subject through establishing the temporal and cultural distance between an 'us' and a 'them'. But this disposition of desire and dread, although most explicitly exposed in the protocols of anthropology, is not peculiar to this discipline; it is sedimented in the very core of the human and social sciences, in the methods, modalities and means of communicating and explaining the world.

Hence, the crisis of anthropology, and recalling the etymological proximity of crisis to the practice of criticism and critique, becomes significant for all who work within this disposition of knowledge. If, at this point, Western anthropology becomes an anthropology of the West, or perhaps more precisely, an anthropology of the occidentalisation of the world, this does not merely open up the way towards observing our intellectual navels and reproducing our centrality in fashionable language. It also opens on to the more arduous and ambiguous labour and commitment of weakening and dislocating that disposition of knowledge and power, including its techniques and technologies of recording and reordering reality, that has historically worlded the world to create the categories and associated truths of centre and periphery, progress and under-development, civility and primitivism, 'First' and 'Third' worlds, the West and the rest. Such a history cannot be cancelled, but it can be rewritten and reworked. It can be re-cited in order to re-site it; in order to extract out of the teeth of occidental modernity its own potential critique and displacement. That would be to register and to listen to how its languages, technologies and techniques are inhabited otherwise, are ultimately inhabited by others.

The challenge of the incomplete

Of course, such possibilities, such potentialities, have to find their way in the unequal exchange inscribed in the differentiation of economic, cultural, historical and political capital. The talking back from the periphery, the silence of the subaltern, depends upon an economy of recognition that excludes while it includes. Not everyone is written into the account, even into the most radical ones. Not all are in the historical and structural position to translate, transform, survive and live on. There are defeats, even the threat and realisation of oblivion, of remaining in the blanks of the margin, in the silence of the languages that are spoken, sung, written and recorded. But the persistence of those questions, the insurmountable limits of where one speaks from, draw us into those spaces, towards the blanks and the silences that both interrogate our language and invest us with the question of a reply. For the resources of silence can also enable others to be, existing apart, irreducible to a common syntax.[27] The interval of the unsaid, the shadows of the subaltern, of the dispossessed, are thrown across the transparency of a language accustomed to ignoring the ontology of silence; a silence which is invariably colonised as pure absence, absolute lack.

Beneath the maps, the topographies and geographies of power and space, there emerges what escapes or refuses to be mapped: the challenge of place in the face of space, of sound in the face of vision, of the proliferation of reasons in the face of rationalism, of silence in the wake of the said. Between the visual frame, between what is represented, pictured, and the contingency of what fails to be represented there emerges a gap, an interval, an interruption. It is the disturbing place of the latter in the space of the former that reveals the historical incidence and individuation of differentiated being.

The distinction between a stable subject, however much in movement, is quite separate, I would suggest, from one that is irreversibly disrupted. Confident subjectivities can, and do, move through the world, as both cosmopolitan business person and intellectual, experiencing symbolic interactions in which one's own culture and identity is rarely put in question. So, is the western psyche really in crisis? Is its mode of thinking and institutional élan really weakened? Or is all this merely a fashionable *mise-en-scène* for the reproduction in contradiction of prevalent hegemonies? Whatever the eventual verdict, what I have to say seeks to focus on the limits and localities of the processes of globalisation and identification by rendering questionable the humanist premises upon which so much of this mode of thinking, rationalism and politics depends.

174

Accustomed to referencing the seemingly increasing complexity of the languages of identity and identification, of being and becoming, we are also simultaneously drawn towards the constancy of the psyche – the 'I' that narrates the narrative of the self – that however interpellated, transformed, frustrated, damaged, carries on in a manner secured by the mechanisms of memory, repression and sublimation: it continues to insist no matter how fragmented is the world it inhabits. This opens up a perspective in which I perhaps need to ask myself whether identities today are really more complex than say in the emerging modernity of seventeenth-century Europe and the hesitant certitudes of the Baroque world with its violent assertions and dissent in cosmological, religious and secular matters; and that is only to speak of a world, a history, a culture with which I have some acquaintance. So, I experience a certain hesitancy before the proposed teleology of progress, as though today's world is automatically more complex than yesterday's, and therefore identities are equally so. Perhaps, it is more prudent to talk in terms of articulation and configuration, of shifting complexities that figure certain truths while obscuring others, of the changed languages of identities, of different horizons of expectancy rather than the mere accumulation of knowledge. Even the unconscious – the reason that reason ultimately represses – did not spring fully armed from the head of Freud; it had, as he insisted, already spoken in the language of poetics.

To this oscillation of modernity it might perhaps be useful to add the voice of the late Raymond Williams, who encouraged a thinking around the uneven and uneasy cultural combinations of the emergent and the residual that lead to new configurations in which both the 'tradition of the new' and the traditions of the past are reworked in often unexpected combinations, revealing diverse powers and possibilities.[28]

Between psychic constancy and historical position, identity emerges not as a set of clothes to be donned and discarded at will, but a shifting composition in which differing elements are foregrounded and backgrounded, depending on circumstances, coincidences, sometimes conscious choice. Identity is neither free floating nor forever fixed in place. It is in the interval between those poles that the radical historicity of identity occurs, where structures provide the stage for the not always predictable, and the instance of historical being confounds the cohesion of any single rationality.

It is, and now to approach the critical knot of my argument, it is here where the subject-centred objectivity of humanism, and the assumption that knowledge is something to be stored up and accumulated for the benefit of the 'I', and subsequent revelation in institutional reason, is confronted. Before the 'imaginary unity' of identity that seeks to control and confine the languages in which I become, I find myself insisting not only on the interrogative persistence of the unconscious, but, above all, on the interconnected insistence on the being of language that precedes and exceeds me, that remains irreducible to the will to will, the will to power, to knowledge.

In intellectual terms we all seek to recapture plenitude, the wholeness of things, turning away from the unfinished, what, to cite Adrienne Rich, stands there, unsatisfied, in our accounts.[29] We all desire this coherent picture and the satisfaction of cognitive mapping, but perhaps there also exists a way and necessity for registering the limits of such imaginings. This would permit what we turn away from – the always unfinished world we inhabit – to insist on its right to be: what cannot be immediately quantified and defined, what resists the technical representation of reality, and yet insists and continues to interrogate us.

This excess or supplement that stands beneath, alongside and beyond our appropriation of diverse historical identities – from the national to the sexual – is an alterity that lies in wait to ambush the confident procedures of cultural representation, disrupting its grammar and prescriptive codes: a potential ready to unsettle the existing installation of the 'political'. Language here girders the centrality of narrative – narrating the nation, narrating our selves – in the question of identity. Benedict Anderson, Stuart Hall and Homi Bhabha: in their diverse approaches there remains the shared focus of the continuity of narrative in understanding national identity. It is that continuity which permits coherence to emerge, that domesticates disturbance and configures contestation, permitting a diversity of elements to be absorbed into the organic framing and natural growth of the nation. The organic, with its sense of roots, origins, growth, of change and continuity, of tradition and transformation, provides the mythic constellation that, as Roland Barthes once pointed out, transforms history into nature.[30] This, perhaps, is seemingly more of an Old World configuration, where language, blood and belonging apparently spring already mature from the native soil, where national identities are conceived in terms of sovereignty rather than rights, kinship rather than contract. But a hegemonic heritage is everywhere at work: to acquire national culture – its language, history, customs and rites – is always somehow considered less than to be born with it.[31] Blood lines and ethnicity invariably win out over contract and consent.

Othering the West

The central point in thinking the narration of the nation, in all its variants, is how in accounting for the past the essential violence upon which it, and occidental modernity, is founded, comes to be expunged from the account. Violence is always displaced elsewhere, to another country, another world. In his book *Storm from Paradise: The Politics of Jewish Memory*, Jonathan Boyarin dwells on the paradox of the occlusion and displacement of genocide in the constitution of a nation state, in this case that of the genocide of Native Americans in a country that houses a Holocaust museum in its capital.[32]

In the orchestrated coherence of the sameness of national identities there is secreted the structural requirement for the 'other'. Beyond the brutal obviousness of imperial power, this renders the formation and experience of colonialism and imperialism also central to the realisation of modernity and modern identities, both national and cultural, both public and private, both historical and existential. This has been most subtly charted by Catherine Hall in her analyses of the making of white, British manhood in the nineteenth century.[33] But the point I wish to make here is not a moral one but a structural one. Occidental modernity is a hybrid formation from the outset; witness Paul Gilroy's magisterial account of the centrality of black Atlantic slave cultures to its making.[34] Or, on another scale, besides another ocean, there is the hybrid constitution of California in which the hidden histories and untold narratives of the physical, economical, cultural and political labour of Native Americans, Mexicans, Chicanos and Chicanas become central, as in the historical work of Beth Haas and in the novels of Alejandro Morales.[35] This suggests, then, that the much debated postcolonial is not so much about contemporary cultural hybridisation, of diversity coming out on metropolitan display, whether in the seeming innocuousness of musical, literary, sartorial and culinary styles, or in the more immediate insistence of minority politics, but is rather the imperative to revisit and rewrite Western modernity itself: to make it speak again, to say something it does not necessarily intend nor desire. As Hannah Arendt insisted in *The Origins of Totalitarianism* (1951), it was external imperialist exploitation that constituted the modern, metropolitan interior; it is that displaced history, in which ethics gave way to economics, and law and liberalism to licence in seemingly faraway places, that haunts Euro-America in its racist and totalitarian tendencies.[36]

In this return of the repressed, the clash of different worlds and cultures entering the West gives way to the far more radical challenge of the potential othering of the West. It is at this point that we might consider the passage from multiculturalism and a liberal accommodation of diversity to a diverse worlding of the world in which the stakes are ultimately about living in difference in a planetary epoch in which the West that has become the world is revealed no longer, despite its continuing economic, political and cultural powers, to be always its own master. As Gyan Prakash has put it:

> Based on the belief that we do not have the option of saying no to the determinate conditions of history – capitalist modernity, discourses of liberty, citizenship, individual rights, nation-state – postcolonial criticism attempts to identify in the displaced historical functioning of these discourses the basis for other articulations.[37]

In the world of transglobal capital and information flows, the acceleration of proximity does not necessarily nor automatically lead to a weakening of earlier identities. Contact can also lead to retrenchment and reinforcement, on both sides of the encounter. Today, we witness certain national, regional and even more local identities being both announced and buttressed by their insertion in, and resistance to, globalisation. Similarly, political scientists and legal theorists are also frequently dubious that modern nation states such as the United States or those of Western Europe are actually giving up their sovereignty rather than strategically deploying their powers diversely as they play the global game.[38] The use of border zones – for example, between the United States and Mexico – that permit economic experimentation and exploitation, and yet simultaneously reconfigure and reconfirm national sovereignty both sides of the frontier, is a case in point. Similarly, the concept of the national remains an essential element in claiming a place in the inter-national structure of the global, particularly in securing jobs, markets and what for many remains the desperate bottom line: aid.[39]

Of course, this is again a complex configuration in which power does not merely move in one direction, as though only from above downwards. Between the pedagogical insistence of a state-promoted national identity and the daily realities of identification with the mediated possibilities encountered in the languages of economic, historical and cultural structures, it suggests that however powerful globalisation may be it is always accompanied by procedures of re-localisation.[40]

In examining the importance of Californian soap operas – imported utopias – in Italian television, Lidia Curti has analysed the transfiguration of the global into local terms and concerns, into the contingent, yet habitual and material, framing of everyday Italian and Neapolitan life. Not only is a national and local cultural subjugated it also subjugates or transforms what is imported, even seemingly imposed.[41] There occurs, as Rey Chow points out in her study of contemporary Chinese cinema, mutual translation, in which the disparity of power between the West and the rest of the world nevertheless reveals the transformation of both sides of the equation as the global and the local, the modern and the traditional, are re-located; neither remains merely an object of the other, each is subjected to the unguaranteed inscriptions of cultural translation and historical transit.[42] Modernity becomes local, and the local grounds modernity.

Both in Bruce Chatwin's *The Songlines* and in Eric Michaels' *Bad Aboriginal Art*, subtitled 'Tradition, Media, and Technological Horizons', there are lengthy descriptions and considerations of Australian Aboriginal culture negotiating its entries and exits from occidental modernity, transforming Western space into local place – canvases destined for international art galleries exchanged for Toyota Land Cruisers.[43] The works that depict sacred ancestral dreamings become works of art, their local meanings transformed into other languages while simultaneously living on, just as Western technology is transformed into providing the means for a local culture to survive and live on within modernity in terms that are not all of modernity's making. The Cherokee artist Jimmie Durham, by dubbing himself a 'post-modern primitive', forcefully reminds us of a translation that is not unilateral, that operates and challenges both sides of the cultural divide.

This would suggest, as Stuart Hall has pointed out, that rather than conceive of the global in terms of an occidental imposition on the local, it is more enabling, more empowering, to consider how the global emerges and is articulated in the local.[44] How, in other words, the power of the global both contributes to the articulation of the local and encounters transformation, resistance, subversion and dispersal in the process. It is where other histories insist and persist in the very lie of the land, to cite Paul Carter; in the look of things that constitute an occupied place, a locality in which history and language is folded into the landscape, to evoke Kathleen Stewart's work.[45] This helps us to concentrate on the differentiation of translation in negotiating and living within the geometries of power. There are very different contacts and contracts, between metropolitan elites and dispossessed, rural populations, to state the most obvious, and their respective relationships with modernity in the present phase of globalisation.

I say the present phase of globalisation, because I consider that process as being inherent to modernity, where modernity, as Heidegger insists, marks the advent of the 'world picture'; not a new world picture, but the possibility for the first time to envisage the world as a picture, to enframe it, and reduce it to a single point of view. This is the unique point of view upon which subjective humanism, the rational *cogito*, relies for its objectivity and grasp of reality. Here all of reality is cognitively

179

framed to appear before the subject as an object, ready to be grasped and dominated, brought into its sovereignty and control. All is rendered immediate in the calculations that represent me, and only me. It is that narrative, and its grammar of agency in which the historical subject can never be othered, that the rethinking of the world, or worlding the world diversely, begins to punctuate. It is at this point that Jean-Paul Sartre's verdict on Frantz Fanon's work as a 'striptease of our humanism' dramatically reappears.[46]

The Westernisation of the world, that is occidental modernity and the formation of its historical subject – who today is sometimes challenged, threatened, susceptible to doubt, but always at the centre of the narrative called History, in being re-historicised – is also, paradoxically localised, brought up against its limits. Its voice, its eye, what permits it to speak and define, comes out of a particular cultural location and historical formation that once, often still does, considered its language to be 'universal', and frequently, for egotistical benefit, confused, confuses, rationalism with reason. To insist on these historical limits, which are also ontological limits, is to dis-locate and re-locate the West and its languages – its modernity, universalism, humanism, identity, subjectivity and agency – in another history. As a minimum it is to begin to register how those concepts, and the histories of their grasp of global space and historical power, are inhabited diversely, experienced following diverse rhythms and different accents. Inserted into a heterotopic world to become part of a place, initial presumptions become susceptible to multiple and coeval enunciations. These offer no easy solution, but invoke a political passage between retrenchment and reconfiguration, tradition and translation, exclusion and inclusion.

Notes

1 Ghassan Hage, 'The Spatial Imaginary of National Practices: Dwellings – Domesticating/Being – Exterminating', *Environment and Planning D: Society and Space*, 1996, 14(4), p. 477.

2 Ibid., p. 478. Hage glosses Zizek here, posing the nation as a Lacanian fantasy, as something you have constantly to work on.

3 Arjun Appadurai, *Modernity at Large*, Minneapolis, University of Minnesota Press, 1996.

4 Ghassan Hage, op. cit., p. 466.

5 Emile Benveniste, *Indo-European Language and Society*, London, Faber & Faber, 1973, quoted in Ghassan Hage, op. cit., p. 473.

6 For an approach to this question, see Jacqueline Rose, *States of Fantasy*, Oxford, Clarendon Press, 1996.

7 See the perceptive account of his own curation of 'River Deep Mountain High: Then and Now – A Story of Cultural Collision using Native American sources,

Commentary from the Highlands of Scotland and Artists from Both Sides of the Atlantic' at Inverness Museum and Art Gallery (July–August, 1997) by Trevor Amery, 'The Map is Not the Territory', *Third Text*, 40, Autumn 1997.

8 Johannes Fabian, 'Remembering the Other: Knowledge and Recognition in the Exploration of Central Africa', *Critical Inquiry*, 26(1), 1999.

9 Paul Carter, *The Lie of the Land*, London, Faber & Faber, 1996, p. 336.

10 Emmanuel Lévinas, *Totality and Infinity*, trans. Alphonso Lingis, Pittsburgh, Pa, Duquesne University Press, 1969, p. 39.

11 Ibid., p. 195.

12 Akhil Gupta, 'The Reincarnation of Souls and the Rebirth of Commodities: Representations of Time in "East" and "West"', in Jonathan Boyarin (ed.) *Remapping Memory: The Politics of Time Space*, Minneapolis, University of Minnesota Press, 1994.

13 Homi K. Bhabha, *The Location of Culture*, London and New York, Routledge, 1994.

14 Akhil Gupta, op. cit., pp. 172–5.

15 Ibid., p. 179.

16 Majid Nafici, 'On the Sandy Surface of an Intertidal Zone', *Literary Review*, 40(1), 1996, p. 199.

17 Max Horkheimer and Theodor W. Adorno, *Dialectic of Enlightenment*, New York, Seabury Press, 1972, p. 46. I return to the crucial figure of Ulysses in the next chapter.

18 Paul Carter, op. cit., p. 309.

19 Néstor García Canclini, *Hybrid Cultures: Strategies for Entering and Leaving Modernity*, Minneapolis, University of Minnesota Press, 1995.

20 For a perceptive, and poignant, version of this argument, see Ien Ang, 'On Not Speaking Chinese', *New Formations*, 24, Winter 1994.

21 Paul Gilroy, *The Black Atlantic: Modernity and Double Consciousness*, London, Verso, 1993.

22 Ibid., p. 331

23 Iain Chambers, *The Interruption*, Naples, CILA (Centro Interdipartimentale dei servizi Linguistici e Audiovisivi, Istituto Universitario Orientale), 1993.

24 Paul Rabinow, 'Representations are Social Facts: Modernity and Postmodernity in Anthropology', in James Clifford and George Marcus (eds) *Writing Culture*, Los Angeles, University of California Press, 1986.

25 See Jeffrey Geiger, 'The Camera and Man: Colonialism, Masculinity and Documentary Fiction', *Third Text* , 42, Spring 1998.

26 Paul Carter, op. cit., pp. 303–4.

27 King-Kok Cheung, *Articulate Silences: Hisaye Yamamoto, Maxine Hong Kingston, Joy Kogawa*, Ithaca, NY and London, Cornell University Press, 1993.

28 Raymond Williams, *Marxism and Literature*, Oxford, Oxford University Press, 1977, pp. 121–7.

29 Adrienne Rich, 'Eastern War Time', in Rich, *An Atlas of the Difficult World*, New York and London, W. W. Norton, 1991, p. 44.

30 Roland Barthes, 'Myth Today', in Barthes, *Mythologies*, London, Paladin, 1973.

31 Ghassan Hage, op. cit., p. 467.

32 Jonathan Boyarin, *Storm from Paradise: The Politics of Jewish Memory*, Minneapolis, University of Minnesota Press, 1992.

33 Catherine Hall, *White, Male and Middle Class: Explorations in Feminism and History*, Cambridge, Polity Press, 1992.

34 Paul Gilroy, *The Black Atlantic*, op. cit.

35 Lisabeth Haas, *Conquests and Historical Identities in California, 1763–1936*, Los Angeles and London, University of California Press, 1995; Alejandro Morales, *The Brick People*, Houston, Tex., Arte Publico Press, 1992.

36 Gyan Prakash, 'Who's Afraid of Postcoloniality?', *Social Text*, 49, Winter 1996, p. 187.

37 Ibid., p. 201.

38 Simon Bromley, 'Globalization?', *Radical Philosophy*, 80, November/December 1996.

39 Ruth Buchanan, 'Border Crossings: NAFTA, Regulatory Restructuring, and the Politics of Place', *Global Legal Studies Journal*, 2(2), 1995.

40 Kevin Robins, quoted in Stuart Hall, 'The Question of Cultural Identity', in S. Hall, D. Held, D. Hubert and K. Thompson, *Modernity: An Introduction to Modern Societies*, Oxford and Cambridge, Mass., Blackwell, 1996, p. 623.

41 Lidia Curti, 'Imported Utopias', in Z. Baransky and R. Lumley (eds) *Culture and Conflict in Postwar Italy: Essays in Popular and Mass Culture*, London, Macmillan, 1990.

42 Rey Chow, *Primitive Passions: Visuality, Sexuality, Ethnography, and Contemporary Chinese Cinema*, New York, Columbia University Press, 1995.

43 Bruce Chatwin, *The Songlines*, London, Picador, 1987; Eric Michaels, *Bad Aboriginal Art: Tradition, Media, and Technological Horizons*, Minneapolis, University of Minnesota Press, 1994.

44 Stuart Hall, 'The Question of Cultural Identity', op. cit., p. 623.

45 Paul Carter, op. cit.; Kathleen Stewart, 'An Occupied Place', in Steven Feld and Keith H. Basso (eds) *Sense of Place*, Santa Fe, NM, School of American Research Press, 1996.

46 Quoted in Gyan Prakash, op. cit., p. 189.

7

THE EDGE OF THE
WORLD

An unknown path opens up before us, an empty trail shuts
behind. Snow closes over our tracks, and then keeps moving
like the tide. There is no trace where we were. Nor any arrows
pointing to the place we're headed. We are the trackless beat,
the invisible light, the thought without a word to speak.
Poured water, struck match. Before the nothing, we are the
moment.

Louise Erdrich

I can't take hold of it nor lose it
When I am silent, it projects
When I project, it is silent
Trinh T. Minh-ha[1]

A day in August, it's over 110°F in the shade. I'm standing on the lip
of Canyon de Chelly in the high Arizona desert looking at Spider Woman
Rock. The ground beneath me is slit dramatically into a Y-shaped chasm
running for miles across the face of the earth. It was Spider Woman
who taught the Navaho the art of weaving. All the reds of the world
seem to be concentrated in this narrow sandstone butte rising hundreds
of feet into the air directly from the canyon floor. A hawk hangs in the
sky before drifting away over the rim of the world.

In this meeting of earth and sky, of deities and mortals – the
Heideggerean 'fourfold' or *das Geviert* – there is an intimation of the
indivisibility of being. Yet this apparently common space, this mutual
time, this uncanny resonance between a sacred Navaho site and Martin
Heidegger reveals an impossibility: the impossibility of reducing the
irreducible, of flattening out the differences of landscape, language,
culture and history to the shared contours of a common map. Perhaps
it is this irreducibility that reveals in the very state of our becoming
the wonder of it all. In this place, recognising in the cultivated plots
and Navaho dwellings or hogans on the valley floor, as in the ancient
Anasazi ruins clinging to the canyon walls, the shared and most

intractable of human demands – life – my own time and place is abruptly interrupted; it is interrogated by a presence which owes nothing to mine. Driving away under a common sky, this slash across the trajectory of my journey, this fold in the map, draws me out of myself. I travel through a crease in my time, a gap in the conceits of my identity and location, seeking to extract from these limits the possibilities of new departures.

At the edge of the frame

At an exhibition in Houston in 1995 entitled *Cultural Baggage*, organised in the context of a symposium on *House, Home, Homeland*, I came across two works that further help me to locate the departure of my thinking at this point in my life.[2] One is *The South/Missing* (1993) by Silvia Malagrino, and the other is *Re:Locations* (1995) by Monica Chau. In Silvia Malagrino's triptych we see photographs of barely visible faces. These are the faces, the identity shots, of those usually forgotten in illegal immigration statistics and border patrol files. They are photos that are both fading and folded into time, yet whose traces remain indelibly etched in the silver gelatine of the print, as though they were ghosts that refuse to fade away. They continue to haunt the scene, casting the shadow of an other world that returns to break through and ruffle the smooth surfaces of a desired coherence. In Monica Chau's series of digital colour photographs, there is the eerie testimony of the superimposition of images from a previous era on a desolate landscape that reconfigures that space into a particular historical place. The figures we see are those of United States citizens of Japanese descent who in April 1942 were relocated in internment camps such as Manzanaa, near Lone Pine, proximate to Death Valley, in the Californian desert. This particular configuration of place and memory was for me also sharply recalled in the concentration camp installation – complete with barracks, watch tower, searchlight and barbed wire – situated in front of the Japanese American Museum in downtown Los Angeles in the autumn of 1995. This location right alongside the Temporary Contemporary Museum further emphasised the disquieting co-ordinates of memory and oblivion, of representation and repression, of the art and the agonism of identification.

Let me add to this visual enframings some phrases, some words, borrowed from Leslie Marmon Silko's novel of Native American survival in modernity, *Ceremony*:

'It strikes me funny', the medicine man said, shaking his head, 'people wondering why I live so close to this filthy town. But see, this hogan was here first. Built long before the white people ever came. It is that town down there that is out of place. Not this old medicine man.'[3]

Turning from Gallup, New Mexico, to the Caribbean I can also add the voice of Vidiadhur Surajprasad Naipaul as he weaves together tales of Elizabethan buccaneers, Latin American revolutionaries and black radicals 'at the limit of the world'.[4] There the disparate, the dispossessed and the diasporic – those who have either fallen out of the known world or not yet entered – bear testimony to the other side of modernity where extermination, slavery, massacre, madness, greed, failure and loss patrol the borders. Here is the imagined conversation between the Indian Don José and the Spanish priest Fray Simón. Don José, native of Guiana, was captured by the English at San Thomé on the Orinoco and accompanies Sir Walter Ralegh back to Europe and the Englishman's subsequent arrest and execution. He then returns to South America. Fray Simón is writing a history of New Spain. The conversation takes place in 1619:

> FRAY SIMÓN said, 'You've crossed the ocean twice. You are back here in New Granada, in the very town where you were born. You didn't get lost. The ships always knew where they were going. When you consider the great fear you used to have of the oceans, what do you think now?'
>
> 'I've thought a lot about that. And I think, father, that the difference between us, who are Indians, or half Indians, and people like the Spanish and the English and the Dutch and the French, people who know how to go where they are going, I think that for them the world is a safer place.'[5]

To know where you are going, to confidently map the world and render it a domestic space and 'safer place', is the expression of a particular historical formation. Here the representation of the subject and the representations of the world became one: a single picture sustained in the abstract frame of reason and the universal assurance of a subject-centred humanism. Naipaul's description punctures that map and its confident appropriations of the world, inviting me to consider what lies on the other side of the picture. Here, in breaching the subjective law of a visual hegemony what is decisively displaced is the premise that 'truth has been transformed into the certainty of representation.'[6] In the rewriting, and rerouting, of a particular Caribbean history the literary event discloses a deviation in the logic of representation: for it draws me into considering not only what is put forth, represented, but also to what withdraws from view, remains in the shadows, persists in being unrepresented. In the withdrawn and the non-represented, the event of art reveals an interruption in the linearity of temporal 'progress', disturbing the representation of 'truth' as the transparent and rational accumulation of 'knowledge.'

On this edge, along this border between security and dispersal, emerges a disruptive space, an outlandish territory, a threshold, where an earlier understanding gives way to a new instigation:

> *Cuando vives en la frontera*
> people walk through you, the wind steals your voice
> you're a *burra*, *buey*, scapegoat
> forerunner of a new race,
> half and half – both woman and man, neither –
> a new gender;[7]

Possession

Writing, words, language. . . all propose journeys into a state of vulnerability in which histories are exposed to the cross-currents of a wider and more ambiguous world. Here in the inclemency of power and hierarchy some histories survive, swept to the beach of institutional recognition where they are acknowledged, translated, travestied, contested, conjoined, incorporated. Others remain adrift, apparently lost in the sea of uncertain memory, far from the shores of recognition; out of sight and out of hearing. The metaphor of *terra firma* and sea, of the relative fixedness of the ground beneath one's feet as opposed to the shifting currents and moods of the water, perhaps best reveals the limits of my language. For I have been taught to think of history, culture, power and identity, and of my inhabitation of that inheritance, in terms of institutions in which the metaphysical and the physical correspond in the rational stability of instrumental logic. However, this sense of the truth perhaps implies an obedience to a set of presumptions that actually threatens the possibility of freedom. In the Lévinasian critique of Heidegger we encounter the following:

> In bringing together presence on the earth and under the firmament of the heavens, the waiting for the gods and the company of mortals in the presence to the things – which is to build and to cultivate – Heidegger, with the whole of Western history, takes the relation to the Other as enacted in the destiny of sedentary peoples, the possessors and builders of the earth. Possession

is preeminently the form in which the other becomes the same, by becoming mine.[8]

What occurs to this sense of truth when 'the destiny of sedentary peoples', and its culmination in the closure of the narration of the nation, is interrupted and interrogated by peoples who relate histories, cultures and languages formed and forged in movement through the world?[9] What occurs when a scriptural economy is confronted by an oral one? The seemingly archaic world of steppes, savannahs, prairies and deserts, that was, is, inhabited, but not possessed, by nomads, bequeaths a disturbance that continues to wander in our time. It is also, of course, refracted in the light of the dispossessed territories of the modern migrant. To travel and traverse the arbitrary limits of an imposed time and space – the geopolitical installation of the nation, the frontier and the abstract collectivity of ethnic identity – is also the most obvious characteristic of the baggage of modern migrants. There is here certainly a mode of dwelling that Heidegger failed to heed. Perhaps, as Lévinas points out, his rustic mood left him ill equipped to think beyond the limits of the sedentary, and the restricted supplement of the forest path connecting settlement to settlement, house to house.

All of this is to insist on the location of thought and the geography of discourse. As Franco Cassano in his essay on the subaltern location and subversive force of 'southern thought', *Il pensiero meridiano*, puts it, the material co-ordinates in which thinking occurs, speaks and acquires effects have profound implications.[10] He goes on to argue that within the occidental *épisteme* the distinction that emerges between a land-locked view and one brushed by the infinite provocation of a marine horizon is not without consequences. This is a characteristic evidenced, for example, in Luce Irigaray's identification of Friedrich Nietzsche as a 'marine lover'.[11] Between the stable continuity of the ground and the shifting swell of salt water, the maritime prospect remains insistently open. The unstable marine horizon provokes a critique of the perennial terrestrial co-ordinates announced in Heidegger's *Geviert* or 'fourfold'. The presence of the sea removes the possibility of closing and controlling the vista, and of establishing a fixed position. Cultures, cities and citizenship are suspended in a liquid state. On the coast, between the incessant movement of the sea and the ancestral security of the soil, the vertical hierarchies of power and knowledge slide into a dispersive horizontal plane.[12]

Against the perennial song of the soil there emerges the unfolding technology required to chart, navigate and traverse the seas. In a hostility to the sea lies the refusal of its disruptive mobility and its threat to the time-worn securities of the forest path and the unchanging contours of the land. The lack of the pervasive presence of the sea that simultaneously unites and separates the archipelago of the Hellenic geography of thought is totally absent from Heidegger's evocation of that tradition. His insistence on the pull of the earth, on the physical terrain as providing the paths of being clashes significantly with Nietzsche's philosophical embrace of the 'open sea'. As it is the sea that unleashes modern technology – the ultimate and most radical realisation of occidental metaphysics – so Heidegger can ultimately condemn the seafaring philosophy of Nietzsche as the expression of the last metaphysician. In Heidegger's *Geviert* thinking is sustained in the vertical axis between earth and sky, mortals and gods, the interruption of that axis by the restless movement of the waves and the horizontal slash of a secular infinity is banished from a terrestrial routing of our being on the earth.

This, of course, is to push into extreme outline what remains altogether more ambiguous. To repeat, Heidegger himself insisted that he did not take a stand against technology, but rather took a stand *within* technology. So, while certainly recognising its rural nostalgia, Heidegger's thinking was also brushed by sea breezes even if he was extremely reluctant to consider the full implications of the maritime world. Perhaps such a reluctance, without the evocation of peasant dwelling and the pristine light of the northern forest clearing, also serves to draw us back from the seemingly naked choice between the stable tracks of rooted conservatism and the endless faring of shoreless movement. Learning from both the sea and the land suggests a deepening of the art of navigation in which neither the vertical pull of roots nor the horizontal infinitude of routes ever fully succeeds in securing the map.

So what is the demand that Heidegger did not hear? Does not the restriction and corralling of wandering peoples and animals across the face of the earth also involve the deepest violation of the earth? For to halt such movement in order to build is to establish a hierarchy and take possession of the soil. This is to store up human energies and terrestrial possibilities in buildings, crops and husbandry, and inaugurate that 'standing reserve' or *Gestell* that today culminates in the modern metaphysics of pure information able to enframe the globe in a unique calculus, in a construct always ready for representation and exploitation.[13]

If metaphysics is essentially that thought which transforms the earth into a thing available for humankind, an object of technological rationalisation, then not even the ancient wooden bridge crossing the river nor the windmill capturing the energy of the wind in its sails can subtract themselves from this history of aggrandisement.[14] In that history, which is not merely the history of the West (although since 1500 it has increasingly been hegemonised and rationalised in that geopolitical context), lies a hierarchisation of life, an accumulation of power, that has repressed its responsibility for the terrestrial state it has installed. As a path seemingly chosen long ago the history of agrarian settlement and industrial development, the establishment of the city and the *polis*, and the welding together of these forces in territory, nation and empire, seems irreversible. To insist, however, that this is a *particular* history that brings me to where I speak from today, is to insist on a troublesome inheritance, subject to interrogation by other histories, other ways of being; where what exists beyond my representation returns to render its claims precarious.

The house of language

Lévinas is right to insist on the limits of Heidegger's thinking the question of dwelling, and to critique its underlying appeal to a sedentary abode rooted in a soil that can also ferment horror and murderous demons intent on defending and extending *their* home at the cost of others. However, the radical turn that Heidegger gives to our understanding of language leads towards an irreversible opening in thinking our place in the world. In his 'Letter on Humanism' (1946–7), that synthesis of his work that directs us back towards *Being and Time* while laying down future paths for thought, Heidegger advances the famous affirmation that:

> Language is the house of Being. In its home man dwells.[15]

To read this essay, along with 'Building, Dwelling, Thinking' and the later volume of essays collected in *On the Way to Language* (1982), is to hear in this thinker's words an account of dwelling whose limits are paradoxically what saves me. For it rescues me from the limitless ambitions of metaphysics, from a mode of thought and existence that believes it is able to dominate and reveal the logic of the world. To think with, and within, these limits permits 'us to free ourselves from the technical interpretation of thinking'.[16] Listening to Gloria Anzaldúa's *Borderlands/La Frontera*, language, as being, as the home that resides in my tongue and body – 'I am my language', writes the Chicana writer – language as being becomes the path of a mythical serpent twisting through time and the body, words and history, transgressing the borders, rewriting expectations of linguistic expression, resisting the prescriptive and reconfiguring a sense of being in the act of becoming.[17] In and of language, caught in the flush of signifying, my being is neither subject nor object.[18] The body writes, is written, speaks, and is spoken.[19] My being in language, my language in being, exceeds the singular logic of grammar. Language assumed as mere instrument, the transparent transmission of my will, is here disrupted in a manner that radically and irreversibly undoes a whole tradition of historical agency and intellectual understanding.

> In this regard 'subject' and 'object' are inappropriate terms of metaphysics, which very early on in the form of Occidental 'logic' and 'grammar' seized control of the interpretation of language. We today can only begin to descry what is concealed in that occurrence.[20]

Language always transmits more than I intend or can ever comprehend. Its history both precedes and exceeds whatever 'I' – the contingent voice and body – manage to articulate and deposit in it. What exceeds me is the alterity of the world, the world that renders me both a subject and an other, simultaneously investing and exceeding me. Language speaks and simultaneously remains indecipherable, disturbing the linearity of thought and its belief that it has grasped the truth. As the critic and film-maker Trinh T. Minh-ha puts it, 'living is round'. To follow the arc of such thinking is to register the impossibility of nominating a definitive point of departure or arrival, and with it to record a potential dispersal of domination. Between the sounds and silences of language passes the rhythm, the bass line, the song of the earth.[21] This is to confront a freedom which Lévinas defines as infinity. It is a mode of thinking no longer intent on constructing the object of a self-confirming discourse in which I, the subject, am always at the centre monopolising and controlling the outcome of thought.[22]

Adrift

Let us listen again to Heidegger. In the fourth 'Appendix' that accompanies 'The Age of the World Picture' (1938), the kernel of the critique of anthropology is unequivocally adumbrated in the phrase: 'With the interpretation of man as *subiectum*, Descartes creates the metaphysical presupposition for future anthropology of every kind and tendency.'[23] The implications of the metaphysical genesis of anthropology is then unequivocally spelt out in the tenth Appendix:

> Anthropology is that interpretation of man that already knows fundamentally what man is and hence can never ask who he may be. For with this question it would have to confess itself shaken and overcome. But how can this be expected of anthropology

when the latter has expressly to achieve nothing less than the securing consequent upon the self-secureness of the *subiectum*?[24]

In the scientific power of the gaze and the neutral insistence of observation, truth was assumed to be rendered accessible. The past tense is obligatory here because it is this very question that has become the core concern of contemporary ethnography, endowing it with a significance for all the social sciences. Language – that of observation in the field, that of the description in the text – was neutral, merely mimetic, the direct reflection of reality, able, once certain disciplinary protocols had been observed, of providing access to the truth of the situation located by the critical gaze. Yet the universal objectivity of this presumed realism paradoxically depends upon an intellectual subjectivism that unavoidably reveals its lineage in the local authority (and limits) of occidental rationalism.

In the contemporary crisis of this particular disposition of knowledge there needs also to be registered the wider crisis of occidental criticism and its claims on the world. For whatever representation is under consideration – contemporary village life in southern Indonesia, first contact between Europe and the Americas in the sixteenth century, the eternal traces of magic in the modern metropolis – the analysis is forced to confront a relationship to alterity that cannot be contained within the language at hand.[25] What is grasped, seized upon, conceptualised ('concept' derives from the Latin *cum-capio* meaning 'to take'), cannot be considered in an isolated light, for it incorporates something that invests and exceeds the voice of the critic. To analyse is to render one's own language susceptible to interrogation, is to open it up to a procedure of worldling that cannot be controlled by an individual author or authority. The analyst and the analysand are conjoined and mediated through the world represented: the understanding of the latter (the 'object' of enquiry) cannot be separated from an understanding of the former (the 'subject' who enquires). They exist in a process of wordly inscription as neither object nor subject. Although regularly negated in the neutrality of critical exposition each authors the other in a language that neither fully owns. There is not a textual (or ethnographic) reality awaiting interpretation, but a textual (or ethnographic) experience in which its participants are inscribed and articulated in the act that precedes and exceeds interpretation.[26]

Cultural, historical and economic differences, questions of power, subalternity and discrimination, although frequently separated out into distinct categories and realities, are unceasingly rendered urgently proximate. It hardly needs noting that the proximity evoked here is rarely

191

acknowledged in political or economical terms, the interests that benefit from the maintenance of distance are too powerful to permit this. In the end, even the ethnologist, even the critic, as limited representative of occidental authority, still has the final word. But beyond the immediacies of this outcome the dialogue inaugurated persists as an unruly presence destined to return again and again, testing, disrupting and exceeding the limits of the discourse that seeks to contain it. The truth that is encountered in the ragged conversation permitted by language and that leads towards a text (anthropological, historical, literary, critical), is not a truth that merely reflects the subject or object of language; rather it is where 'a structural power differential and a substratum of violence' permits the conditions of that encounter to be registered and thought.[27]

The threshold of thinking

To transfer enquiry from the mere mirroring of my individual subjecthood (being) to a language that precedes and exceeds me (Being) is to seek to respond to the question of dwelling no longer in subjective, utilitarian or rationalist terms, as a mere 'doing and making' that already knows what dwelling is and can therefore never question but only confirm it. I am required, on the contrary, to respond in terms of what Heidegger calls 'ek-sistence' in which Being cannot be controlled and manipulated by single beings, cannot be arrested in a language I presume to own and control. As the quiet power of the possible this sense of Being, like language itself, both exceeds and precedes my existence. It is what enables and provokes us to be – in a manner that no logic, whether linguistic or technological, can ever fully reveal.[28] To follow this path, and refuse the merely rational understanding of actuality, is to subtract thinking from a philosophy that 'completely dominates the destiny of Western history and of all history determined by Europe.'[29] It is to seek to exit from the home of Western thinking, a house that is built on the abandonment of Being and which is thus truly the site of modern homelessness; for it is built on the failure to take stock of being-in-the-world.[30] To secede from this scenario is to withdraw from the merely rational that permits us the illusion that we are the masters of language and that all is revealed in representation. To reach across this limit is 'to recognise that there is a thinking more rigorous than the conceptual.'[31]

In this supplement that exceeds and negates the logic of my explanation, the limits of my habitat are inscribed and its history becomes *a* history. The structure of my thought, the structure that positions me as the subject of history, is disclosed to be the truth of a position, the particularity of a voice, the location of a body, a culture, a history. What remains unthinkable within my system of representation, what lies outside yet invests it and exceeds it, disseminates a truth that I am unable to possess, that suspends the authority of my explanation.[32] It is this that takes me to the threshold of thinking otherwise, and sends me on my way. Unilateral logic, and a deafness to response, now established in the generalised hum of global domination, can be intercepted by a narration, by a diverse *logos* that is dependent upon *listening*.[33] It is to oppose a mode of thinking that prescribes, that knows nothing of listening; that is, a culture that negates the 'very premises of culture because it resolves itself in *predicating* rather than in *cultivating*.'[34] To withdraw from the blinding transparency of a logic that speaks without expecting, or *requiring*, a reply, is to encounter in the shadows of occidental discourse the loss of one's nomination as a 'subject' in front of an 'object'. This differing from, and deferring of, philosophical logic, is also a displacement, a movement away from the despotic language of the centre in which the subjectivist illusions of humanism had placed me. For it involves the abandonment of that metaphysics which proposes 'an already established interpretation of nature, history, world, and the ground of the world, that is, of beings as a whole'.[35]

In a language susceptible to the possible interference of a reply it is silence that comes to sustain speech. Silence is the constant envelope of language. Silence is also what resists the merely rational understanding of language, for it nurtures the shadows that interrogate and frustrate the logic that instrumental interest seeks to impose. The signifiers slide away into shifting signification, language grows opaque, the mystery returns. For silence is not equivalent to nothingness. It is a notification that lies within the web of language. Silence is the bridge between breath, sound and phrase, it is the sonority that permits the being of language to stand out.[36] Silence is not residual, it is essential. Of course, we instinctively turn away from the waiting attendant upon a reply, for the 'tragedy' of listening, as opposed to the comfort of the circumscribed perspective, is, to propose the words of Edmond Jabès once again, that it opens up a relationship with the the infinite, the unthought, proposing a measurement of silence by the unknown and the unknowable.[37] This brings us close to the suggestive affirmation of the priests in the Matopos hills of Zimbabwe: 'God is Language'.[38]

All of this amounts to an egocentrical loss that can lead to an unexpected ethical gain.[39] But it is also a passage of extreme vulnerability: a delicate and dangerous path to follow: for you can lose your bearings, end up lost, go missing. My language and reason, the house of my being, is exposed to the heterogeneous, the incalculable, the discontinuous; to the unfamiliar and unguaranteed configurations of a diverse 'worldling of the world'.[40] To evoke the critical insistence of Antonio Gramsci: 'The world is big and terrible and complex. Every action in its intricacy awakens unexpected echoes'.[41]

Apart from the common connection from Old Norse to house and shelter, 'dwelling' in Old English also referred to the idea of being led astray, into error and hereticism, and thus, paradoxically, to the idea of wandering.[42] The uncanny semantics of dwelling, most obviously resonates with the noted Freudian commentary on the familiar or *heimlich* that brusquely transforms itself into the disturbing appearance of the unfamiliar or *unheimlich*. It is this proximity, straining within the very same word, that concentrates attention on the idea of language being inscribed with errancy; not only inscribed with what errs with respect to conventional and linguistic understanding, but also inscribed with what travels and thereby sends us on an unmarked way. This renders both the linguistic and historical construction of our dwelling and being in language both a little less familiar and a little more precarious.

The unhomely

In confronting the limits of my language, my sense of home, and the sense of cultural property that encloses and sustains it, comes to be haunted by the return of what delays, disrupts and deviates that sense. In the refusal of this prospect, and the accompanying sense of vulnerability, lies the passion for extermination that has characterised occidental modernity. From its bloody inception in Africa and the Americas, in slavery and genocide, to the extreme rationalisation of racial extermination in the *Shoah*, the relationship with the unhomely, with what is considered to threaten Western humankind's being at home in the world, has invariably led to murderous conclusions. To insist on the twentieth-century atrocities of the SS or Balkan nationalists can all too easily concentrate our attention on the seeming exception of horror, thereby allowing us to avoid the numbing banality of the altogether more ordinary disposition to exclude and destroy whatever we cannot possess, contain or comprehend:

> We cannot be human until we have perceived in ourselves the possibility for abjection in addition to the possibility for suffering. We are not only possible victims of the executioners. The executioners are our fellow-creatures. We must ask ourselves: is there anything in our nature that renders such horror impossible? And we would be correct in answering: no, nothing.[43]

To eradicate alterity, is to seek to abolish whatever resists the exercise of the power that permits me to remain secure in the absoluteness of my autonomy: 'Murder exercises a power over what escapes power.'[44] The other threatens to contaminate and frustrate that possibility by inviting me 'to a relation incommensurable with a power exercised'.[45] The violent affirmation of power is neither exceptional nor foreign to those who inhabit and feel at home in modernity; it consistently disciplines the passage between inclusion and exclusion in constructing a habitat that confirms and reproduces my selfhood. The face of the other 'does not defy the feebleness of my powers, but my ability for powers.'[46] Accustomed to express myself without limits, in a language that annihilates whatever it cannot assimilate, the presence of the other invokes the assassination of what negates my dominion:

> I can wish to kill only an existent absolutely independent, which exceeds my powers infinitely, and therefore does not oppose them but paralyzes the very power of power. The Other is the sole being I can wish to kill.[47]

The self-assured sense of being at home in the modern world is the site of a bloody extortion. A tradition of belonging, of being located in the seemingly timeless roots of blood, tongue and soil, can slam the door shut tight against the histories of others; it is invariably for this that one kills. To gain a voice, to exercise a power, those other histories are invariably constrained to mimic and reproduce the vindictive economy of a modern belonging, largely seeded and catalogued in the ambiguous desires of European romanticism that has gone to seed.[48] It is a tradition that as *tradition* is rarely confronted. It is assumed that the values of continuity and community, that tradition and the transmission of the same, are *the* values to be extolled and defended. It is these values that confirm us in our *authenticity*. Whether located in the rural cycles of the peasantry, or the rituals of the 'native', this siting and citing of the unchanging same is considered sacrosanct. But is this not a conservative and reactionary myth that we who are of European descent tell ourselves in order to cling to *our* centrality in the understanding of home? While the rest of the world is forced to accommodate change and interruption, the continuity of tradition is conserved as a universal value by those who yield the power to define the 'universal'. But if I listen to modern anthropologists and novelists, and they are not always distinguishable, I often hear something quite different. Here again is Betonie, the Navaho medicine man, in Leslie Silko's novel *Ceremony* explaining the nature of the rituals he performs:

'At one time, the ceremonies as they had been performed were enough for the way the world was then. But after the white people came, elements in this world began to shift; and it became necessary to create new ceremonies. I have made changes in the rituals. The people mistrust this greatly, but only this growth keeps the ceremonies strong.

She taught me this above all else: things which don't shift and grow are dead things. They are things the witchery people want. Witchery works to scare people, to make them fear growth. But it has always been necessary, and more then ever now, it is. Otherwise we won't make it. We won't survive. That's what the witchery is counting on: that we will cling to the ceremonies the way they were, and then their power will triumph, and the people will be no more.'[49]

To contest a power that considers tradition – both one's own and that of an other – to represent an immobile essence is to contest the universal grasp of a witchery seemingly able to possess and reduce the world to the unity of its ends. The abrogation of the narrative of authenticity by mutation, travesty and translation, permits the emergence of gaps through which an other world appears: 'This is a world in which everyone must take responsibility for a positioned imagination.'[50]

The passion to eradicate alterity from the earth is also the passion for the home, the country, the dwelling, that authorises this desire and rewards it. In its nationalism, parochialism and racism it constitutes a public and private neurosis.[51] So, unwinding the rigid understanding of place that apparently permits me to speak, that guarantees my voice, my power, is not simply to disperse my locality within the wider co-ordinates of an ultimately planetary context. That would merely absolve me of responsibility in the name of an abstract and generic globalism, permitting my inheritance to continue uninterrupted in the vagaries of a new configuration. There is something altogether more precise and more urgent involved. For in the horror of the unhomely pulses the dread for the dispersal of Western humankind: the dread of a rationality confronted with what exceeds and slips its grasp. To be claimed by what exceeds immediate understanding is to run the risk of ultimately having little to say.[52] To disband the metaphysics of a 'universal' knowledge that sees in 'home' the reconfirmation of a unique and unilateral edifice of benefit, is to disclose the particularities of voice and place, of history and body, of pain, memory and silence.

All of this is to suggest something more than merely a theoretical adjustment in the plane of thought. For in listening to the insistent supplement of silence – to what was previously considered nonsensical, unintelligible and indecipherable prior to translation – I begin to register that my language, my identity, my history, my voice, has been dependent upon violently consigning whatever disturbs and disrupts it to oblivion. While I clearly cannot speak for this silence, this other, repressed side of my being, I can leave a place for it, like the breath between my words, the air between my respiration: essential but invariably overlooked.[53] Here the face of the other emerging from a map breaks through the anonymous, the abstract, cartography of occidental reasoning. It is the avoidance of the face, Lévinas argues, that permits anonymous murder and abstract massacre: the technological apex of a deadly rationalism once concentrated in the proverbial finger on the button, these days more likely consigned to the programmed response of a computer chip. The face invites a response that cannot be merely hypothetical. It provokes custody for more than the theoretical. 'Thus to "philosophize" about being shattered is separated by a chasm from a thinking that is shattered.'[54]

Exposure

Thinking the event of thinking in a world in which thinking both occurs and occludes, I am compelled to subscribe to a sense of place that exceeds the restrictive connotations of the 'local', the 'historical' and the 'traditional'. This, no doubt, is to pay scant attention to disciplinary thresholds. To insist on the ontological consequences of thinking the local, of thinking place and dwelling, is to insist on the enabling *limits* of an executive space in which not merely the language, history and tradition that constitutes me as a 'subject' is enacted. For here in the flesh, my sexual, gendered, ethnic and social identity is both located, mobilised, disciplined, *and* exceeded.[55] In a response to my being that is in debt but irreducible to those individual categories, this historical 'I' is constituted within limits that configure but do not hold me prisoner. In this proposal there does not exist a new, and 'better', subjectivity or universalism, but rather the intersection of that desire for the whole and the complete by the question of dwelling, by the instance in which space, institutions and languages are translated and in-corporated in a particular body and a precarious place.

This propels me into another space – neither 'original' nor imitative. There is no stable point in which meaning takes up residence, but only a site of transit in which my setting out and hoped-for points of arrival are subject to equal interrogation.

> Critiquing the great disparity between Europe and the rest of the world means not simply a deconstruction of Europe as origin or simply a restitution of the origin that is Europe's others but a thorough dismantling of *both* the notion of origin and the notion of alterity as we know them today.[56]

Rey Chow continues:

> In other words, genuine cultural translation is possible only when we move beyond the seemingly infinite but actually reductive permutations of the two terms – East and West, original and translation – and instead see both as full, materialist, and most likely equally corrupt, equally decadent participants in contemporary world culture.[57]

I find myself on a journey destined to carry me far into the latitudes of the contemporary world as well as back towards the initiation of occidental modernity, if not to the myths that have profoundly marked that journey from the outset.

An interrupted journey

Ulysses, once more, strapped to the mast of his intentions while his crew, ears blocked with wax, remain deaf to the call of the Sirens, confirms, for those who come after, the idea of alterity as a deadly threat, an unfamiliarity that distances us from ourselves and leads to annihilation and oblivion. Ulysses, when all is said and done, is a man who knows where he is directed: homewards, towards himself.[58] His journey through the empty spaces that have not yet been appropriated by *logos* opens up that passage of knowledge and power that illuminates the history of the West, throwing its shadows over the world. To return to that mythic journey today, but now following its shadow line, forces me to encounter a supplement, an excess of sense, that block the possibility of the return home. In the eruption of the repressed, of the obscured and eradicated, I hear voices that the journey of the occident has historically silenced but which now emerge in an irrevocable manner in my midst. Myths of journey and otherness – whether leading to annihilation or beneficial exotica – now emerge as 'the "fables" that cast light on the "original" that is our world's violence, and they mark the passages that head not toward the "original" that is the West or the East but toward survival in the postcolonial world.'[59]

The very foundations of occidental modernity – my sense of history, my sense of the world and my self – are based upon the idea of journey.

The epoch of the 'world picture', where the globe, brought into a single frame, reduced to a unique measure, rendered transparent by a single source of knowledge that travels, 'discovers' and collects, symbolically begins in 1492.

> The world picture does not change from an earlier medieval one into a modern one, but rather the fact that the world becomes picture at all is what distinguishes the essence of the modern age [*deer Neuzeit*].[60]

Here, in the encounter with new worlds, with alterity, an epistemological centre and periphery in which the European traveller is always the subject, never the object, of History, is firmly established: 'History is homogeneous to the documents of Western activity'.[61] Organised around the supremacy of the ocular, around a unique point of view that achieves in the technology of writing and mapping its universal presence, it is the journey itself that establishes the very principle of knowledge. In the repetitive movement outwards from a secure centre, from home, towards the unknown, the unmodified subject 'conquers space by multiplying the same signs.'[62] Conquest and travel also underwrite a sense of passage in an increasingly autonomous and secular universe. Knowledge is no longer directly revealed by God, but is something to be acquired and accumulated, frequently by force, and then carried home to be catalogued and classified in the institutions of reason and profit. The tongue, speech and orality – the body that speaks – an 'exorbitant presence' that threatens objectivity is exiled from thought as an exotic and uncontainable object:

> in this way appears one of the rules of the system which was established as being Occidental and modern: the scriptural operation which produces, preserves, and cultivates imperishable 'truths' is connected to a rumor of words that vanish no sooner than they are uttered, and which are therefore lost forever. An irreparable loss is the trace of these spoken words in the texts whose object they have become. Hence through writing is formed our relation with the other.[63]

But, as Michel de Certeau goes on to insist:

> The other returns: with the image of nudity, 'an exorbitant presence'. With the phantasm of the *vagina dentata*, which looms in the representation of feminine voracity; or with the dancing

eruption of forbidden pleasures. More basically, the native world, like the diabolical cosmos, becomes Woman. It is declined in the feminine gender.[64]

This understanding of a constant virile knowledge accompanies us still. In the apparent transit from the religious to the secular, the metaphysical paradigm remains unchanged. Faith in the unconditional no longer passes through a defunct God but within the patriarchal certitudes of the sciences, in the technical representation of truth and the idealism of an aesthetic absolutism, all secured in the authority of inscription, of writing. The world is reduced to the dominion of the written word and its subsequent organisation in disciplines, expertise and information. It is here that occidental gnosticism is both celebrated and reconfirmed.

To think in terms of a world picture, of a global system, of a common scripting and enframing of the unequal experiences of modernity, is paradoxically to undermine claims of homogeneous and autonomous identity. To insist on a racial, ethnic or nationalist identity as something that is not connected or framed in the historical heterogeneity of a shared world is to deny the very forces that gave rise to such concepts (race, ethnicity), and which both ground and permit such an identity to speak. Emphasising the heterotopic genesis that silently accompanies the confident claims made for modern identity forces open the closure of 'home' and 'tradition', and the ground they provide for racism, terror and murder. The sharp distinction between a 'here' and a 'there', between 'First' and 'Third' worlds, between 'North' and 'South', all seeking to maintain the elsewhere outside the world at hand, separate and at a physical, cultural and historical distance, is irreversibly interrupted.[65] Such distinctions, and the very real differences in economical, political and cultural capital they evoke, are *internal* to the inauguration of the 'world picture' and the birth of modernity. They lie on this side, on my side, of the historical border, and not elsewhere in a pre- or non-modernity. The peripheral and the undeveloped – the nomenclature itself reveals the uneven powers distributed in the theoretical and instrumental disposition of the controlled connection – are the products of the historical formation that permits this particular spatialisation of the world. It is this spatialisation that leads to the evacuation of interruptive or ecstatic time and the oblivion of distinct, corporeal histories; these fall through the grid lines of a timeless geometry, lost in the reified space of the empty, homogeneous time that houses teleology.[66] Yet, as distinctive representations of, and specific responses to, the provocation of occidentalisation these occluded histories are intrinsically imbricated in the responsibilities of modernity.

So a journey, no matter how secure its goals, execution and ambitions, is always a passage that exposes its participants to the disturbance of the unexpected. Despite all the efforts of domesticating translation, something always resists, escapes the logic of the language employed, remains unaccountable in the scriptural economy that seeks to render it transparent. If the journey is the foundational myth of modernity, if not of the West, it also reveals a quintessential paradox in which distance and proximity are conjoined. The journey is starred by the close at hand, the unhomely by the homely. They are held together in the 'uncanny' return that unleashes the repression that shadows and breaches every representation of home, culture and self.

A disturbed house

In his noted essay on the uncanny, Freud refers to the consternation and dread surrounding the encounter with the unhomely, the non-domestic, that gives rise to feelings of displacement and estrangement. But the horror of *das Unheimlich*, as he is careful to point out, is that it involves not something that comes to meet us from afar but something that is already with us and 'leads back to what is known of old and long familiar.'[67] The seemingly intimate is abruptly supplemented by the dramatic vicinity of that familiar country which is the past, my past. My self-centredness is intersected by another centre, by an elliptical parabola that promises to take me elsewhere. The discourse of certainty is haunted by the ghost of a question speaking a language that I recognise while it withdraws from explanation. In my anxiety there emerges what I have rationally sought to repress, ultimately the primordial fear of annihilation.[68]

This persistent disturbance within the core of reason has led Wendy Wheeler to suggest that both the sublime and uncanny, although by no means restricted to modernity, acquire their starkest form in a 'modern subjectivity' that is:

> haunted by something which – with the advent of Enlightenment modernity – becomes unplaceable and, strictly speaking, unrepresentable with the demise of a world integrated within the schema of the sacred. For Lyotard and Zizek, it is named by the category of the sublime. For Dolar, it appears in the modality of the uncanny.[69]

Mladen Dolar writes:

> It seems that Freud speaks about a 'universal' of human expe-
> rience when he speaks of the uncanny, yet his own examples
> tacitly point to its location in a specific historical conjuncture
> brought about by the Enlightenment. There is *a specific dimen-*
> *sion of the uncanny that emerges with modernity.*[70]

Presented in the languages of knowledge, of truth, as a science, 'the
question of questions: the nature of human restlessness' becomes a reverie
that returns modernity to an interrogation that reveals in the desires of
western writer, historian, dreamer and traveller an excessive and irrepressible elsewhere.[71]

Once again, this is not merely to ponder on the existence of other
worlds, or simply to enlarge mine to include others; it is to question
and expose the very roots, and routes, of my thought. My freedom to
think, my very claims on being are circumscribed by this sense of home
and its version of history and belonging. For to remain here at this
stage, as Lévinas underlines in his critique of Heidegger's *Being and*
Time, is to reduce freedom to the egotistical freedom to think and hence
withdraw the world into a subjective comprehension, an occidental
ontology that reduces the other to the same.[72] In such a case what I
encounter remains servant to the concepts that rendere my home recognisable as *my home*. To avoid building yet a further liberal edifice, now
decorated in multicultural hues, I have to confront the other *as other*,
'exceeding *the idea of the other in me*'.[73] This is to fold into my time
another time, to crease my thought with the presence of an other, to
introduce a dynamic I cannot possess. That excess is what, drawing me
beyond myself, indicates the path between totality and infinity, between
what can be possessed and dominated and what interrogates me with
its freedom. The other's 'voice, exiled to the distant shores of discourse,
would flow back, and with it would come the murmurs and "noises"
from which scriptural reproduction is distinguished. Thus an exteriority,
with neither beginning nor truth, would return to visit discourse.'[74] This
opening towards alterity, towards what exceeds me, is an opening on to
desire and away from the restricted economy of thinking; it is to recognise what overflows a neutral understanding of truth and invokes being
claimed by something more, something else: an infinity that is produced
by desire; not a desire to possess, but a desire for the infinite that is
aroused rather than satisfied.[75] In being aroused and forced to think
beyond my self and a possession of history, culture and identity that
renders it intelligible to my interests, I find myself in an opening that
renders my understanding, the presumptions of my history, the sense of
my being, accountable to an other, that renders it other-wise. My history

is interrupted, its claims on the world uprooted; no longer unique it is brought to account in an encounter that it can no longer control, can no longer fully represent, but can no longer exclude.

In setting a meaning in play independent of my power, the encounter with alterity radically exceeds the mere extension of my world to include the other. For I receive from the other a history that is not mine, a history that teaches me to receive what overflows my egoism and thus, as Lévinas insists, promotes my freedom: 'calling it to responsibility, it founds it and justifies it.'[76] In what refuses to be contained lies the radical disjuncture between the domestic and the foreign, between the journey home towards confirmation and the interminable apprenticeship of the endless movement beyond my self.

The overflow of the uncanny, the surplus of the sublime, brims in a dark mirror that discloses a historical disturbance seeded in the very folds of modernity. The faces, the bodies, of the others refuse to fade away; they persist, they return. Yet, the temptation is to turn away. We feel threatened by what we are unable to contain. Reason councils resistance. We feel the need to belong, to be a native, an inhabitant of a stable place. Home pulls us towards this sense of belonging. To be at home is to possess both the physical and symbolic space in which one moves, and to be dependent upon it for the sense of one's self.

Thus the unhomely is rarely welcomed. The world of hybridity and interstitial uncertainty is rarely a choice. Rather, it is a condition into which one is thrown. But what exactly is 'home'? Home for whom, and for what? Inevitably considered the site of continuity, of tradition and family, of blood and belonging, home is the site in which a narcissistic understanding of life is conserved. In this reproduction of the same, the evocation of the Heideggerean 'fourfold', with its insistence of our being on the earth beneath the sky, can draw us into a sense of dwelling that shatters the narrow confines of egotistical conservatism. For here the local is confined not by the limits of the family, friends and environs we frequent, but by the boundaries imposed by terrestrial existence, by history and mortality. This native ground is not a place of individual birth, but that of an earthly provenance and a manner of dwelling which, in Zarathustra's words, 'remains faithful to the Earth'. The space between the desired familiarity of the former and the disturbing dissemination of the latter, is also the space in which repressed memories and bodies erupt to give voice to survival and the promise of living on: a space for the increasing number of people for whom home is not an easy or obvious location.

To respond to the contemporary writings of Toni Morrison and Derek Walcott is to recognise that my sense of being at home and the

confident assertion of my place in the world is invariably a benefit
extracted at the cost of someone else's exile, someone else's displacement, someone else's diaspora. To listen to the language of such authors
is to register a sense of location that troubles the facile frontiers of both
national and more local belongings. A Creole poet steps out of the
margins of History to walk the Caribbean shore and announce an uncomfortable truth:

> I had no nation now but the imagination.
> After the white man, the nigger didn't want me
> when the power swing to their side.
> The first chain my hands and apologise, «History»;
> the next said I wasn't black enough for their pride.
> . . .
> I met History once, but he ain't recognize me,
> a parchment Creole, with warts
> like an old sea-bottle, crawling like a crab
> through the holes of shadow cast by the net
> of a grille balcony; cream linen, cream hat.
> I confront him and shout, «Sir, is Shabine!
> They say I'se your grandson. You remember Grandma,
> your black cook, at all?». The bitch hawk and spat.
> A spit like that worth any number of words.
> But that's all them bastards have left us: words.[77]

To respond to this language, to the demand that emerges in the linguistic,
historical and cultural dwelling that I also inhabit – 'English' – is not
to seek atonement through the explication of guilt (and the subsequent
benefit of being forgiven), but to solicit in language a reply, and a
responsibility, for the conditions that constitute my own identity, permitting me to feel at 'home'. To listen and to seek a reply in this condition
is clearly to query the obviousness of my 'identity' and the naturalness
of my 'origins'. In a particular history, and a distinct body, I find myself
in a coeval temporality, cast into a state of transit without the guarantee of a secure point of origin or arrival. My history, my identity, my
language, my home, unfolds. The roots branch out, entwine with others.

A place in the world

The turn of, and turn into, language, is an initial step of incalculable
consequences. It involves something that cannot be contained in the
incipient formalism of the frequently nominated idea of a 'linguistic

turn'. To insist that a transformation of thinking is a linguistic matter is to avoid acknowledging the irreversible undoing of all linguistic under-standings of language, communication and meaning, and thus the profound radicality of this 'turn'.[78] In this critical disavowal, language, as speech, writing, representation, articulation, as the announcement of our being and becoming, yaws away from the comforting confirmation that domesticates the world in a transparent medium and its grammar of certainty. In language we each sail towards an opening, following diverse currents, exposed in the vulnerability of our histories, navigating the limits of home, of dwelling.

> At the end of this sentence, rain will begin.
> At the rain's edge, a sail.[79]

In Barbès, ten minutes walk from the Gare du Nord in Paris, recently extended to include the Gare du Londres from which high-speed Eurostar trains depart for Waterloo in a cross-Channel journey of two hours fifty minutes, one can see Arab scribes sitting on street corners. Their cus-tomers, like the customers of those hanging around government offices in the 1950s in Port of Spain, Trinidad, described by V. S. Naipaul, or, for that matter, in present-day Naples, are the illiterate. For a small sum, offi-cial request forms will be filled in and bureaucracy set in motion. But this scribe on the Parisian street, with his portable desk containing paper, pens and ink, seated on a low, foldable stool, is waiting to write missives of a more personal kind. For he does not set down requests in official French, but in a careful motion, from right to left across the page, he inscribes Arabic calligraphy. I hardly ever saw him at work. Perhaps the trans-national orality of the telephone has taken the place that dictated corre-spondences once maintained. Perhaps illiteracy and the need for his formal skills is on the wane. Whatever, I remain struck by the disclosure of this writing on a modern Parisian street, a mode of expression that is appar-ently separate from the metropolitan languages that surround and seem-ingly threaten to submerge it: high speed trains, the Métro, the traffic, the rush of pedestrians. Wearing sandals, a turban, wrapped in a *djellaba* against the autumnal chill, sitting opposite a brand new school, a multi-coloured tubular-steeled piece of postmodern architecture, the immobile dignity of this public writer emphasises the disturbing presence of the stranger. His pen, his language, his being, is coeval with mine. I could turn away and pretend that he no longer exists; that he is merely a quaint remnant of yesterday's immigration from the 'Third' world, from the Maghreb. I can choose to see in his presence merely the intrusion of the exotic and the archaic in the mundane of modernity. But I can also register a trace, not merely of another world largely hidden from my eyes and understanding, but rather the trace of a language and history that seeks a response, and a responsibility, in mine. Apparently a foreigner, this, too, is clearly his city – certainly much more than it is 'mine'. Forced to consider the composite realisation of modern space as it comes into being in this cosmopolitan place called Paris, I also register the alterity that is both integral to it and to the modernity I presume to possess. For the Arab scribe sitting patiently on the corner of a modern, Western city is not a historical accident. Separate, yet indissolubly linked, his presence both interrupts and reconfigures my history, translating the closure of my 'identity' into an aperture in which I meet an other who is in the world yet irreducible to my will.

Now this Parisian scene does not simply duplicate the famous description beautifully evoked by James Clifford in *The Predicament of Culture* in which as a wartime émigré Claude Lévi-Strauss marvels at a Native American in headdress taking notes with a Parker pen in the New York Public Library.[80] In the unintended, but structurally coherent, repetition something further emerges to disturb the knowledge and power invested in my observation. For what has occurred at this point? Have I merely rendered exotica proximate and metropolitan? What was once among the wonders of New York waiting to be collected and commented upon, is today also to be counted among the wonders of Paris? Is this Arab scribe once again the voiceless testimony, the agent-less object of my discourse; simply a product of the occidental gaze intent on explaining the surrounding world in terms that reconfirm the centrality of its own subjectivity? Or is there here an encounter in the languages of the metropolis, of modernity, that exceeds whatever meaning I seek to bestow on the event? In this ambiguous space in which historical transit betrays and befuddles the desired transparency of translation, I register the historically positioned limits of my voice, of my claims on the world. The Arab scribe as referent of my discourse both unfolds *towards me and away from me*, is both object of my narrative and a subject in a world that is never simply mine. He is witness not merely to the power of my gaze, desirous of egotistical confirmation, but also to the interval that emerges between us as subjects and that renders my language locatable and limited.

A comment by Judith Butler may help to bring this prospect home:

> This raises the political question of the cost of articulating a coherent identity position by producing, excluding, and repudiating a domain of abjected specters that threaten the arbitrarily closed domain of subject positions. Perhaps only by risking the incoherence of identity is connection possible, a political point

that correlates with Leo Bersani's insight that only the decentred subject is available to desire.[81]

Not, to repeat, a desire to possess, but a desire for the infinite that is
aroused rather than satisfied. To inhabit a place in this manner, as the
site of repressed histories that permit mine to be represented, where the
tacit cruelties of coherent identity are registered, and thus also as a site
that will perpetually cite the unhomely, the uncanny, is to seek to draw
from history a politics of fulfilment whose outcome is never fully known
in advance.[82] These are the conditions for an uncertain critical departure, not a self-assured arrival. In this supplement, in which aesthetics
and ethics, culture and politics, design and desire, place and constraint,
are crossed and contaminated, this more than words, the indecipherable,
the unrepresentable, and the incoherent, embarrasses identification with
the predictable homogeneity of the known by providing us with a glimpse
of something else, something further, something more. These are the
silent shadows of a wordly state that accompany us, and which sometimes break into song, find a form in dance, live on in rhythm. The
languages of this supplement, this more than the rational and the instrumental, is won out of the teeth of history in the instance that the political
and the poetical not only coexist but cross and rework each other in
mutual configuration.

Such an opening, a moment of creation, is not merely what emerges
from the hybrid interstices of living between worlds, between stable
tradition and progress, between 'authentic' being and 'corrupted' life
styles. Rather, there is a reworking on both sides of the equation so that
tradition itself becomes an element of change, an 'element of freedom'
(Hans-Georg Gadamer).[83] While being incessantly interrupted by modernity tradition simultaneously provides the resources to interrupt and
confer on modernity its own particular imperatives. In Lee Tamahori's
film on modern Maorihood, *Once were Warriors* (1994), two brothers
commemorate a male, Maori past: one by apparently recuperating its
powers in the traditional rituals of the island warriors, the other in
rewriting and doubling those rites in the tattoos (themselves inherited
symbols of Pacific island culture) and initiation rites of an urban subcul-
ture. In both cases, the coeval histories, the syncretic connection, is
forcefully registered in both local and global syntax. This is further
augmented in the reggae music that reverberates throughout the film.
In a New Zealand urban ghetto such music is both modernity and tradition, is both about trans-national mass communications (and capital)
and about how such a space, the space provided by international rock
music, also becomes a particular place – a scene of memory, a scene of

re-membering, in which the Caribbean sound of the disenfranchised is played again, repeated, and worked through to release another promise, by another sea, in another hemisphere.

To return to Leslie Silko's novel *Ceremony* and now conclude. The ceremony performed by Betonie the medicine man is complicit with, yet dislodges, both traditions: that of the tribal, and that of occidental modernity. The stories, the narratives, that operate on both side of the assumed divide, seeking to legitimate their respective myths and knowledge, both those that carry the name of the archaic and those that carry the name of progress, are fatally impaired. This engenders an interrogation that moves both ways, simultaneously disturbing assumptions of both the 'traditional' and the 'modern'. In both cases, there emerges an identity in which a relationship to the earth is no longer guaranteed by blood, kin and soil, and the presumptions of possession. Rather it is the story, the narrative, the manner of telling that reaffirms memory, and thus loss, while performing and propagating the inscription – on the body, in the ceremony, the voice, the silence that accompanies and sustains every utterance – which simultaneously re-members and transforms the myth of our home and origins into an ongoing and uncertain settlement.

Notes

1 Louise Erdrich, *The Bingo Palace*, London, Flamingo, 1995, p. 259. Trinh T. Minh-ha, from the film *Naked Spaces – Living is Round*.

2 *House, Home, Homeland: A Media Studies Symposium on Exile*, Rice University, Houston, Tex., 26–29 October 1995. It was that occasion that set in movement these present thoughts and I would like to take this opportunity to thank Hamid Naficy for inviting me to participate in that event.

3 Leslie Marmon Silko, *Ceremony*, New York and London, Penguin, 1977, p. 118.

4 V. S. Naipaul, *A Way in the World*, London, Minerva, 1995, p. 167.

5 Ibid., pp. 204–5.

6 Martin Heidegger, 'The Age of the World Picture', in Heidegger, *The Question Concerning Technology and Other Essays*, trans. William Levitt, New York, Harper & Row, 1977, p. 127.

7 Gloria Anzaldúa, 'To Live in the Borderlands Means You', in Anzaldúa, *Borderlands: La Frontera: The New Mestiza*, San Francisco, Aunt Lute Books, 1987, p. 194.

8 Emmanuel Lévinas, *Totality and Infinity*, trans. Alphonso Lingis, Pittsburgh, Pa, Duquesne University Press, 1969, p. 46.

9 See Homi K. Bhabha's brilliant essay on this splitting of the national and doubling of modernity – 'DissemiNation' – in his *The Location of Culture*, London and New York, Routledge, 1995.

10 Franco Cassano, *Il pensiero meridiano*, Rome, Laterza, 1996.

11 Luce Irigaray, *Marine Lover of Friedrich Nietzsche*, trans. Gillian C. Gill, New York, Columbia University Press, 1991.

12 Franco Cassano, op. cit., p. 26.

13 On the culmination of 'representational thinking' in 'cybernetics', leading to the fulfilment of metaphysics and the 'end of philosophy', see Martin Heidegger, 'The End of Philosophy and the Task of Thinking', in Heidegger, *Basic Writings*, New York, Harper & Row, 1977. The 'Trans-Architectural' proposal discussed in Chapter 5 provides a good example of this style of thought.

14 The two examples are drawn from Heidegger's paean to a more natural, less assertive, pre-industrial technology in 'The Question Concerning Technology'; but also see the crucial figure of the bridge that gathers together the location of *das Geviert*, or the fourfold, in 'Building Dwelling Thinking'. Both essays can be found in Heidegger, *Basic Writings*, op. cit.

15 Martin Heidegger, 'Letter on Humanism', in Heidegger, *Basic Writings*, op. cit., p. 193.

16 Ibid., p. 194.

17 Gloria Anzaldúa, op. cit., p. 59

18 Trinh T. Minh-ha, *When the Moon Waxes Red*, London and New York, Routledge, 1991.

19 Hélène Cixous, *Rootprints, Memory and Life Writing*, London and New York, Routledge, 1997.

20 'Letter on Humanism', op. cit., p. 194. This argument had already been extensively pursued by Friedrich Nietzsche: see Nietzsche, *Beyond Good and Evil*, Harmondsworth, Penguin, 1973.

21 Michel Haar, *The Song of the Earth: Heidegger and the Grounds of the History of Being*, Bloomington and Indianapolis, Indiana University Press, 1993.

22 Martin Heidegger, 'The Age of the World Picture', op. cit., p. 140.

23 The impossibility of overcoming the disciplinary ground that furnishes the discipline with a voice has been most famously pursued by Michel Foucault, but it is also central to Johannes Fabian's noted critique of anthropology: *Time and the Other: How Anthropology Makes its Object*, New York, Columbia University Press, 1983. In the latter, Fabian writes: 'Man does not "need" language; man, in the dialectical, transitive understanding of *to be, is* language (much like he does not need food, shelter, and so on, but *is* his food and house)' (p. 162). Foucault's *The Order of Things* can be read as a detailed historical orchestration of the critique that Heidegger elaborates in the 'Letter on Humanism' against 'humanism' as a subject-centred epistemology which, as Foucault puts it, invents 'man' in order to confirm all the episodes of the history of the same; see Foucault, *The Order of Things*, London and New York, Routledge, 1989, pp. 386–7.

24 Martin Heidegger, 'The Age of the World Picture', op. cit., p. 153.

25 See Anna Lowenhaupt Tsing, *In the Realm of the Diamond Queen: Marginality in an Out-of-the-Way Place*, Princeton, NJ, Princeton University Press, 1993.

26 James Clifford, *The Predicament of Culture: Twentieth-Century Ethnography, Literature, and Art*, Cambridge, Mass., Harvard University Press, 1988.

27 Ibid., p. 76.

28 This perhaps helps us to overcome the initial difficulty of confronting such apparently cryptic phrases as: 'Ek-sistence so understood is not only the ground of the possibility of reason, *ratio*, but is also that in which the essence of man preserves the source that determines him.' Martin Heidegger, 'Letter on Humanism, op. cit., p. 204.

29 Ibid., p. 208.

30 Ibid., pp. 217–21. As Heidegger is at pains to point out, this sense of home-lessness is profoundly ontological. It has nothing to do with home in the sense of belonging to a 'homeland' or a nation. Homelessness 'consists in the abandonment of Being by beings', ibid., p. 218.

31 Ibid., p. 235.

32 See Judy Purdom, 'Mapping Difference', *Third Text*, 32, Autumn 1995.

33 At this point I am merely glossing the extensive elaboration on this theme offered by Gemma Corradi Fiumari in *La Filosofia dell'ascolto*, Milan, Jaca Books, 1985. (The English edition is: *The Other Side of Language: A Philosophy of Listening*, London and New York, Routledge, 1995.) This line of reasoning had already emerged in the 1951 essay, entitled 'Logos', around the concept of *Leghein* which, Heidegger insists, offers a more radical understanding of *logos*, for it means both to speak, to narrate, to pronounce, but also to unite, to collect, to bring together. This other side of *leghein* has progressively been lost and abandoned. What it holds in its meaning is also the crucial idea of narration as a mode of custody that takes care for what listening collects, re-members and assembles; in other words, a *logos* that is dependent upon listening. See 'Logos (Heraklit, Fragment B 50)', in Heidegger, *Early Greek Thinking*, New York, Harper & Row, 1975.

34 Corradi Fiumari, op. cit. p. 21, emphasis in the original.

35 Martin Heidegger, 'Letter on Humanism', op. cit., p. 202.

36 M. F. Sciacca, quoted in Corradi Fiumari, op. cit., p. 136; also see Luce Irigaray, *L'Oubli de l'air*, Paris, Editions de Minuit, 1983.

37 Edmond Jabès, quoted in Christine Buci-Glucksmann, *L'Enjeu du beau: Musique et Passion*, Paris, Galilée, 1992, pp. 179–80.

38 Quoted in Terence Ranger, '"Great Spaces Washed with Sun": The Matapos and Uluru Compared', in Kate Darian-Smith, Liz Gunner and Sarah Nuttal (eds) *Text, Theory, Space*, London and New York, Routledge, 1996, p. 158.

39 It is also a passage that can lead either to the closed narcissism of an interminable melancholia, the ambiguities of nostalgia seeking in an imagined past a better future, or a mourning that marks the conclusion of a certain history and the opening towards another. Both melancholia and mourning are insistently suspended in the ambiguities of the contemporary return of the baroque. For an interesting discussion of these terms, see Wendy Wheeler, 'After Grief? What Kinds of Inhuman Selves?', *New Formations*, 25, Summer 1995.

40 The concept is Heidegger's: see 'The Origin of the Work of Art', in Heidegger, *Basic Writings*, op. cit., but has been strategically and frequently employed in postcolonial discourse by Gayatri Chakravorty Spivak; see, for example, Gayatri Chakravorty Spivak, *The Post-colonial Critic: Interviews, Strategies, Dialogues*, edited by Sarah Harasym, London and New York, Routledge, 1990.

41 Antonio Gramsci on the newspaper *L'Avanti* in 1917.

42 C. T. Onions (ed.) *The Oxford Dictionary of English Etymology*, Oxford, Clarendon Press, 1996. These connotations are also to be found in Old High German, *twellan*, Old Swedish and Middle Dutch, arriving eventually at the Aryan root in the Sanskrit, *dhwö*; cf. *The Oxford English Dictionary* (2nd edn).

43 Georges Bataille, 'Reflections on the Executioner and the Victim', *Yale French Studies*, 79, 1991, p. 18.

44 Emmanuel Lévinas, *Totality and Infinity*, op. cit., p. 198.

45 Ibid., p. 198.
46 Ibid., p. 198.
47 Ibid., p. 198.
48 In *The Black Atlantic: Modernity and Double Consciousness* (London, Verso, 1993), Paul Gilroy offers a brilliant exposition of this historical and cultural binding in the context of black nationalisms; see also Chinua Achebe, *Anthills of the Savannah*, London, Heinemann, 1988.
49 Leslie Marmon Silko, *Ceremony*, New York and London, Penguin, 1977, p. 126.
50 Anna Lowenhaupt Tsing, op. cit., p. 289.
51 Tom Nairn, *The Break-up of Britain*, London, Verso, 1981, p. 359.
52 Martin Heidegger, 'Letter on Humanism', op. cit., p. 199.
53 Luce Irigaray, *L'Oubli de l'air*, op. cit.
54 Martin Heidegger, 'Letter on Humanism', op. cit., p. 223.
55 This is an argument that in the wake of Michel Foucault has been most fruitfully extended in much recent feminist theory. See in particular the work of Judith Butler.
56 Rey Chow, *Primitive Passions: Visuality, Sexuality, Ethnography, and Contemporary Chinese Cinema*, New York, Columbia University Press, 1995, p. 194.
57 Ibid., p. 195.
58 In twisting the tale/tail of this occidental figure I have drawn upon Piero Boitani's *L'Ombra di Ulisse*, Bologna, il Mulino, 1992.
59 Rey Chow, op. cit., p. 202.
60 Martin Heidegger, 'The Age of the World Picture', op. cit., p. 130.
61 Michel de Certeau, 'Ethno-Graphy: Speech, or the Space of the Other: Jean de Léry', in de Certeau, *The Writing of History*, trans. Tom Conley, New York, Columbia University Press, 1988, p. 210.
62 Ibid., p. 216.
63 Ibid., p. 212. The term 'an exorbitant presence' is from Emmanuel Lévinas, *Totality and Infinity*, op. cit.
64 Ibid., p. 233.
65 See Johannes Fabian, *Time and the Other*, op. cit.
66 This is Walter Benjamin's famous verdict on 'progress', most succinctly summarised in his 'Theses on the Philosophy of History': see Benjamin, *Illuminations*, trans. Harry Zohn, London, Fontana, 1973. It has also more recently been reiterated in Ernesto Laclau's *New Reflections on the Revolution of our Time*, London and New York, Verso, 1990, p. 42.
67 Sigmund Freud, 'The "Uncanny"', in Freud, *Art and Literature*, vol. 14 of *The Penguin Freud Library*, Harmondsworth, Penguin, 1990, p. 340.
68 Ibid., pp. 360–8.
69 Wendy Wheeler, 'After Grief?', op. cit., p. 84.
70 Mladen Dolar, '"I Shall Be with You on Your Wedding Night": Lacan and the Uncanny', *October*, Fall 1991, quoted in Wheeler, ibid., p. 84, emphasis in the original.
71 The quote is from Bruce Chatwin's *The Songlines*, London, Picador, 1988, p. 181. On the relationship of historical texts to dreams, see Michel de Certeau, op. cit.
72 In *Totality and Infinity*, Lévinas critiques the whole of the Heideggerean *oeuvre*, not just *Being and Time*, for a reified understanding of freedom consistently subordinated to an understanding of Being that is only able to acknowledge

the other, and thus the question of justice, of ethics, in terms of its self. Such a reconciliation of 'freedom and obedience in the concept of truth presupposes the primacy of the same, which marks the direction of and defines the whole of Western philosophy' (p. 45).

He continues:

> A philosophy of power, ontology, is, as first philosophy which does not call into question the same, a philosophy of injustice. Even though it opposes the technological passion issued forth from the forgetting of Being hidden by existents, Heideggerean ontology, which subordinates the relationship with the Other to the relation of Being in general remains under obedience to the anonymous, and leads inevitably to another power, to imperialist domination, to tyranny. Tyranny is not the pure and simple extension of technology to reified men. Its origin lies back in the pagan 'moods', in the enrootedness in the earth, in the adoration that enslaved men can devote to their masters. (pp. 46–7)

However, Lévinas is himself open to the same style of objection. As both Elizabeth Grosz and Simon Critchley point out, the Lévinasian avoidance of feminine alterity restricts his thinking to what he has consistently sought to avoid: the economy of the same. Elizabeth Grosz, 'Ontology and Equivocation: Derrida's Politics of Sexual Difference', *Diacritics*, 25, Summer 1995; Simon Critchley, '"Bois" – Derrida's Final Word on Levinas', in R. Bernasconi and S. Critchley (eds) *Re-Reading Levinas*, Bloomington and Indianapolis, University of Indiana Press, 1991.

73 Ibid., p. 50, emphasis in the original.
74 Michel de Certeau, op. cit., p. 236.
75 Emmanuel Lévinas, op. cit., p. 50.
76 Ibid., p. 197.
77 Derek Walcott, 'The Schooner «Flight»', in Walcott, *Collected Poems 1948–1984*, London, Faber & Faber, 1992.
78 It is a 'turn' bearing many names – from Heidegger and Lévinas to Foucault, Derrida, Irigaray and Cixous – and movements: from deconstructionism to feminism, and all the various 'post-', that reaps the inheritance of the Nietzschean critique of philosophical idealism and a subjective understandings of language.
79 Derek Walcott, 'Map of the New World: Archipelagoes', in Walcott, *Collected Poems*, op. cit.
80 James Clifford, op. cit.
81 Judith Butler, *The Psychic Life of Power*, Stanford, Calif., Stanford University Press, 1997, p. 149.
82 Paul Gilroy, *Small Acts: Thoughts on the Politics of Black Cultures*, London and New York, Serpent's Tail, 1993.
83 Hans-Georg Gadamer, *Truth and Method*, London, Sheed & Ward, 1979.

BIBLIOGRAPHY

Achebe, C., *Anthills of the Savannah*, London, Heinemann, 1988.

Ackroyd, P., *Hawksmoor*, London, Abacus, 1985.

Agamben, G., *L'uomo senza contenuto*, Milan, Rizzoli, 1970.

Althusser, L., 'Marxism and Humanism', in Althusser, *For Marx*, Harmondsworth, Penguin, 1969.

Amery, T., 'The Map is Not the Territory', *Third Text*, 40, Autumn 1997.

Anderson, B., *Imagined Communities*, London, Verso, 1983.

Ang, I., 'On Not Speaking Chinese', *New Formations*, 24, Winter 1994.

Angoulvent, A-L., *L'Esprit baroque*, Paris, Presses Universitaires de France, 1994.

Ankersmit, F. and Kellner, H. (eds) *A New Philosophy of History*, London, Reaktion Books, 1995.

Anzaldúa, G., *Borderlands: La Frontera: The New Mestiza*, San Francisco, Aunt Lute Books, 1987.

Appadurai, A., *Modernity at Large*, Minneapolis, University of Minnesota Press, 1996.

Arendt, H., 'Introduction' to Walter Benjamin, *Illuminations*, trans. Harry Zohn, London, Fontana, 1973.

——, 'Martin Heidegger at Eighty', in M. Murray (ed.) *Heidegger and Modern Philosophy: Critical Essays*, New Haven, Conn., Yale University Press, 1978.

——, *The Origins of Totalitarianism*, London, Deutsch, 1986.

Austin, J. L., *How to Do Things with Words*, Oxford, Oxford University Press, 1976.

Bachelard, G., *The Poetics of Space*, trans. Maria Jolas, Boston, Mass., Beacon, 1969.

Barthes, R., *Mythologies*, London, Paladin, 1973.

Bataille, G., 'Reflections on the Executioner and the Victim', *Yale French Studies*, 79, 1991.

Bauman, Z., *Modernity and the Holocaust*, Oxford, Polity Press, 1989.

Benjamin, W., *Illuminations*, trans. Harry Zohn, London, Fontana, 1973.

——, *Charles Baudelaire: A Lyric Poet in the Era of High Capitalism*, London, New Left Books, 1973.

——, *Infanzia berlinese*, Turin, Einaudi, 1981.

——, *The Origin of German Tragic Drama*, London, Verso, 1990.

Benveniste, E., *Indo-European Language and Society*, London, Faber & Faber, 1973.

Berkhoffer, Jr, R. F., *Beyond the Great Story: History as Text and Discourse*, Cambridge, Mass., Harvard University Press, 1995.

Bhabha, H. K., *The Location of Culture*, London and New York, Routledge, 1995.

——, 'Unpacking My Library . . . Again', in I. Chambers and L. Curti, (eds) *The Post-colonial Question: Common Skies, Divided Horizons*, London and New York, Routledge, 1996.

——, 'Anish Kapoor: Making Emptiness', in Bhabha, *Anish Kapoor*, Los Angeles and London, Haywood Gallery/University of California Press, 1998.

Bhaskar, R., *A Realist Theory of Science*, Leeds, Leeds Books, 1975.

Bianconi, L., *Music in the Seventeenth Century*, Cambridge, Cambridge University Press, 1987.

Blau, J., *Illusions of Prosperity: America's Working Families in an Age of Economic Insecurity*, New York, Oxford University Press, 1999.

Boitani, P., *L'Ombra di Ulisse*, Bologna, il Mulino, 1992.

Bowie, A., 'Music, Language and Modernity', in Andrew Benjamin (ed.) *The Problems of Modernity: Adorno and Benjamin*, London and New York, Routledge, 1989.

——, 'Romanticism and Technology', *Radical Philosophy*, 70, July/August 1995.

——, *From Romanticism to Critical Theory: The Philosophy of German Literary Theory*, London and New York, Routledge, 1997.

Boyarin, J., *Storm from Paradise: The Politics of Jewish Memory*, Minneapolis, University of Minnesota Press, 1992.

Brecher, B., 'Understanding the Holocaust: The Uniqueness Debate', *Radical Philosophy*, 96, July/August 1999.

Bromley, S., 'Globalization?', *Radical Philosophy*, 80, November/December 1996.

Buchanan, I., 'De Certeau and Cultural Studies', *New Formations*, 31, Spring/Summer 1997.

Buchanan, R., 'Border Crossings: NAFTA, Regulatory Restructuring, and the Politics of Place', *Global Legal Studies Journal*, 2(2), 1995.

Buci-Glucksmann, C., *Tragique de l'ombre*, Paris, Galilée, 1990.

——, *L'Enjeu du beau: Musique et Passion*, Paris, Galilée, 1992.

——, *Baroque Reason: The Aesthetics of Modernity*, London, Sage, 1994.

Buck-Morss, S., *The Dialectics of Seeing: Walter Benjamin and the Arcades Project*, Cambridge, Mass. and London, MIT Press, 1989.

Burgin, V., 'Geometry and Abjection', in John Fletcher and Andrew Benjamin (eds) *Abjection, Melancholia and Love: The Work of Julia Kristeva*, London and New York, Routledge, 1990.

——, *In/Different Places*, Los Angeles and London, University of California Press, 1996.

Butler, J., *Gender Trouble: Feminism and the Subversion of Identity*, London and New York, Routledge, 1990.

——, *Bodies that Matter: On the Discursive Limits of 'Sex'*, London and New York, Routledge, 1993.

——, *The Psychic Life of Power*, Stanford, Calif., Stanford University Press, 1997.

Canclini, N. G., *Hybrid Cultures: Strategies for Entering and Leaving Modernity*, Minneapolis, University of Minnesota Press, 1995.

Cantone, G., *Napoli barocca*, Bari, Laterza, 1992.

Carchia, G., *La legittimazione dell'arte*, Naples, Guida, 1982.

Carter, P., *The Lie of the Land*, London, Faber & Faber, 1996.

Cassano, F., *Il pensiero meridiano*, Rome, Laterza, 1996.

Celan, P., 'The Meridian', *Chicago Review*, Winter 1978.

Chambers, I., *Urban Rhythms*, London, Macmillan, 1985.

——, *Migrancy, Culture, Identity*, London and New York, Routledge, 1994.

—— and Curti, L. (eds) *The Post-Colonial Question: Common Skies, Divided Horizons*, London and New York, Routledge, 1996.

Chatwin, B., 'Introduction', in Robert Byron, *The Road to Oxiana*, London, Picador, 1981.

——, *The Songlines*, London, Picador, 1987.

Cheung, K-K., *Articulate Silences: Hisaye Yamamoto, Maxine Hong Kingston, Joy Kogawa*, Ithaca, NY and London, Cornell University Press, 1993.

Chow, R., *Writing Diaspora*, Bloomington and Indianapolis, Indiana University Press, 1993.

——, *Primitive Passions: Visuality, Sexuality, Ethnography, and Contemporary Chinese Cinema*, New York, Columbia University Press, 1995.

——, *Ethics after Idealism*, Bloomington and Indianapolis, Indiana University Press, 1998.

Cixous, H., *Rootprints, Memory and Life Writing*, London and New York, Routledge, 1997.

Cixous, C. and Clément, C., *The Newly Born Woman*, Manchester, Manchester University Press, 1987.

Clarke, D. B., Doel, M. A. and McDonough, F. X., 'Holocaust Topologies: Singularity, Politics, Space', *Political Geography*, 15(6/7), 1996.

Clément, C., *Opera, or the Undoing of Women*, Minneapolis, University of Minnesota Press, 1988.

Clifford, J., *The Predicament of Culture: Twentieth-Century Ethnography, Literature, and Art*, Cambridge, Mass., Harvard University Press, 1988.

——, *Routes: Travel and Translation in the Late Twentieth Century*, Cambridge, Mass., Harvard University Press, 1997.

Connery, C. L., *The Empire of the Text: Writing and Authority in Early Imperial China*, Lanham, Md, Rowman & Littlefield, 1998.

Critchley, S., '"Bois" – Derrida's Final Word on Levinas', in R. Bernasconi and S. Critchley (eds) *Re-Reading Levinas*, Bloomington and Indianapolis, University of Indiana Press, 1991.

Curti, L., 'Imported Utopias', in Z. Baransky and R. Lumley (eds) *Culture and Conflict in Postwar Italy: Essays in Popular and Mass Culture*, London, Macmillan, 1990.

Darian-Smith, K., Gunner, L. and Nuttal, S. (eds) *Text, Theory, Space*, London and New York, Routledge, 1996.

Dart, T., *The Interpretation of Music*, New York, Harper & Row, 1963.

Davis, M., *City of Quartz: Excavating the Future in Los Angeles*, London, Vintage, 1992.

——, *Ecology of Fear: Los Angeles and the Imagination of Disaster*, New York, Vintage, 1999.

de Certeau, M., *The Writing of History*, trans. Tom Conley, New York, Columbia University Press, 1988.

Deleuze, G., *La Piega: Leibniz e il Barocco*, Turin, Einaudi, 1990.

de Man, P., *Blindness and Insight*, London, Methuen, 1983.

Derrida, J., 'Letter to Peter Eisenman', in William Lillyman, Marilyn Moriarty and David Neuman (eds) *Critical Architecture and Contemporary Culture*, New York and Oxford, Oxford University Press, 1994.

Descartes, R., *Abrégé de musique*, Paris, Presses Universitaires de France, 1987.

Desideri, F., *La Porta della Giustizia: Saggi su Walter Benjamin*, Bologna, Edizioni Pendragon, 1995.

Docherty, T., *John Donne, Undone*, London and New York, Methuen, 1986.

Donald, J., *Imagining the Modern City*, London, Athlone Press, 1999.

Donington, R., *A Performer's Guide to Baroque Music*, London, Faber & Faber, 1978.

Donne, J., *The Poems of John Donne*, edited by Herbert Grierson, London, Oxford University Press, 1951.

Durham, J., *The East London Coelacanth*, ICA video, London, Institute of Contemporary Arts, 1993.

Eisenstein, Z., *Global Obscenities: Patriarchy, Capitalism and the Lure of Cyberfantasy*, New York, New York University Press, 1998.

Elliot, G., 'Ghostlier Demarcations: On the Posthumous Edition of Althusser's Writings', *Radical Philosophy*, 90, July/August 1998.

Erdrich, L., *The Bingo Palace*, London, Flamingo, 1995.

Ermath, E. D., *Sequel to History: Postmodernism and the Crisis of Representational Time*, Princeton, NJ, Princeton University Press, 1992.

Fabian, J., *Time and the Other: How Anthropology Makes its Object*, New York, Columbia University Press, 1983.

——, 'Remembering the Other: Knowledge and Recognition in the Exploration of Central Africa', *Critical Inquiry*, 26(1), 1999.

Fanon, F., *Black Skin, White Masks*, London, Pluto Press, 1991.

Felman, S. and Laub, D., *Testimony: Crises of Witnessing in Literature, Psychoanalysis, and History*, New York and London, Routledge, 1992.

Fisher, J. (ed.) *Global Visions: Towards a New Internationalism in the Visual Arts*, London, Kala Press, 1994.

Fiumari, G. C., *The Other Side of Language: A Philosophy of Listening*, London and New York, Routledge, 1995.

Flora, N., Giardiello, P. and Postiglione, G. (eds) *Glenn Murcutt: Disegni per otto case*, Naples, Clean Edizioni, 1999.

Foucault, M., *The Order of Things*, London and New York, Routledge, 1989.

Freeman, B. C., *The Feminine Sublime*, Los Angeles and London, University of California Press, 1995.

Freud, S., 'Remembering, Repeating and Working-Through', in *The Standard Edition of the Complete Psychological Works of Sigmund Freud*, general editor James Strachey, vol. XII, London, Hogarth Press, 1962.

——, 'The 'Uncanny'', in Freud, *Art and Literature*, vol. 14 of *The Penguin Freud Library*, Harmondsworth, Penguin, 1990.

Friedlander, S. (ed.) *Probing the Limits of Representation: The Holocaust Debate*, Cambridge, Mass., Harvard University Press, 1992.

Fry, T. (ed.) *R|U|A TV? Heidegger and the Televisual*, Sydney, Power Publications, 1993.

Fumaroli, M., *L'Ecole du silence*, Paris, Flammarion, 1994.

Gadamer, H-G., *Truth and Method*, London, Sheed & Ward, 1979.

Garlake, P., *The Hunter's Vision: The Prehistoric Art of Zimbabwe*, London, British Museum Press, 1995.

Gassendi, P., *Initiation à la théorie de la musique*, Aix-en-Provence, Edisud, 1992.

Geiger, J., 'The Camera and Man: Colonialism, Masculinity and Documentary Fiction', *Third Text*, 42, Spring 1998.

Gibbs, M. L., *The Church of Santa Maria del Giglio*, Venice and New York, Venice Committee, n.d.

Gifford, P., *African Christianity: Its Public Role*, London, Hurst, 1998.

Gilroy, P., *The Black Atlantic: Modernity and Double Consciousness*, London, Verso, 1993.

——, 'Art of Darkness: Black Art and the Problem of Belonging to England', in Paul Gilroy, *Small Acts: Thoughts on the Politics of Black Cultures*, London, Serpent's Tail, 1993.

——, ''After the Love has Gone': Biopolitics and Etho-poetics in the Black Public Sphere', *Third Text*, 28/29, Autumn/Winter 1994.

——, Grossberg, L. and McRobbie, A. (eds) *Without Guarantees: In Honour of Stuart Hall*, London and New York, Verso, 2000.

Girard, C., 'Traversing the Screens', *film+arc.graz. 3 Internationale Biennale*, Graz, 1997.

Glissant, Edouard, *Caribbean Discourse: Selected Essays*, trans. J. M. Dash, Charlottesville, Va, University Press of Virginia, 1989.

Greenblatt, S., *Marvellous Possession: The Wonder of the New World*, Oxford, Oxford University Press, 1992.

Gregotti, V., *L'identità dell'architettura europea e la sua crisi*, Turin, Einaudi, 1999.

Grosz, E., 'Ontology and Equivocation: Derrida's Politics of Sexual Difference', *Diacritics*, 25, Summer 1995.

——, 'Women, *Chora*, Dwelling', in Sophie Watson and Katherine Gibson (eds) *Postmodern Cities and Spaces*, Oxford and Cambridge, Mass., Blackwell, 1995.

Gupta, A., 'The Reincarnation of Souls and the Rebirth of Commodities: Representations of Time in "East" and "West"', in Jonathan Boyarin (ed.) *Remapping Memory: The Politics of Time Space*, Minneapolis, University of Minnesota Press, 1994.

Haar, M., *The Song of the Earth: Heidegger and the Grounds of the History of Being*, Bloomington and Indianapolis, Indiana University Press, 1993.

Haas, L., *Conquests and Historical Identities in California, 1763–1936*, Los Angeles and London, University of California Press, 1995.

Hage, G., 'The Spatial Imaginary of National Practices: Dwelling-Domesticating/ Being-Exterminating', *Environment and Planning D: Society and Space*, 14(4), 1996.

Hall, C., *White, Male and Middle Class: Explorations in Feminism and History*, Cambridge, Polity Press, 1992.

Hall, S., 'New Ethnicities', in K. Mercer (ed.) *Black Film, British Cinema*, BFI/ICA *Documents* 7, London, Institute of Contemporary Arts, 1988.

——, 'When Was "The Post-Colonial"? Thinking at the Limit', in I. Chambers and L. Curti (eds) *The Post-Colonial Question: Common Skies, Divided Horizons*, London and New York, Routledge, 1996.

——, 'The Question of Cultural Identity', in S. Hall, D. Held, D. Huber and K. Thompson, *Modernity: An Introduction to Modern Societies*, Oxford and Cambridge, Mass., Blackwell, 1996.

Hallyn, F., *The Poetic Structure of the World: Copernicus and Kepler*, New York, Zone Books, 1993.

Handelman, S. A., *Fragments of Redemption: Jewish Thought and Literary Theory in Benjamin, Scholem, and Levinas*, Bloomington and Indianapolis, Indiana University Press, 1991.

Haraway, D., 'A Manifesto for Cyborgs: Science, Technology and Socialist Feminism in the Late Twentieth Century', in Haraway, *Simians, Cyborgs and Women: The Reinvention of Nature*, London, Free Association Books, 1991.

Harvey, D., *The Condition of Postmodernity*, Oxford, Blackwell, 1989.

Hebdige, D., 'Welcome to the Terrordrome: Jean-Michel Basquiat and the "Dark" Side of Hybridity', in Richard Marshall (ed.) *Jean-Michel Basquiat*, New York, Whitney/Abrams, 1992.

Heidbrink, L., *Melancholie und Moderne: Zur Kritik der Historischen Verzweiflung*, Munich, Wilhelm Fink, 1994.

Heidegger, M., *Poetry, Language, Thought*, trans. Albert Hofstadter, New York, Harper & Row, 1975.

——, *Early Greek Thinking*, New York, Harper & Row, 1975.

——, *Basic Writings*, New York, Harper & Row, 1977.

——, *The Question Concerning Technology and Other Essays*, trans. William Levitt, New York, Harper & Row, 1977.

——, *On the Way to Language*, New York, Harper & Row, 1982.

——, *Nietzsche*, vol. 4, trans. Frank A. Capuzzi, San Francisco, Harper & Row, 1982.

——, *Nietzsche*, vol. 3, *The Will to Power as Knowledge and Metaphysics*, trans. J. Stambaugh, D. Krell and F. Capuzzi, New York, Harper & Row, 1987.

——, *Risposta: A colloquio con Martin Heidegger*, trans. Carlo Tatasciore, Naples, Guida, 1992.

——, *Being and Time*, trans. Joan Stambaugh, Albany, NY, State University of New York Press, 1996.

Henderson, G., *California and the Fictions of Capital*, Oxford and New York, Oxford University Press, 1999.

Hennion, A., *La Passion musicale: une sociologie de la médiation*, Paris, Edition Métailié, 1993.

Hill, C., *The Century of Revolution, 1603–1714*, London, Sphere, 1969.

Horkheimer, M. and Adorno, T. W., *Dialectic of Enlightenment*, New York, Seabury Press, 1972.

Hosokawa, S., *The Aesthethics of Recorded Sound*, Tokyo, Keisō Shobō, 1990.

Hulme, P., *Colonial Encounters: Europe and the Native Caribbean 1492–1797,* London and New York, Routledge, 1992.

Imrie, R., 'Disability and Discourses of Movement and Mobility', *Environment and Planning A*, 32, 2000.

Irigaray, L., *L'Oubli de l'air*, Paris, Editions de Minuit, 1983.

——, *Marine Lover of Friedrich Nietzsche*, trans. Gillian C. Gill, New York, Columbia University Press, 1991.

——, 'He Risks Who Risks Life Itself', in Margaret Whitford (ed.) *The Irigaray Reader*, Oxford, Blackwell, 1994.

Islam, S. M., *The Ethics of Travel: From Marco Polo to Kafka,* Manchester, Manchester University Press, 1996.

Islam, S. M., 'Forming Minoritarian Communities: Nomadic Ethics for the Post-colonial World', *New Formations*, 39, Winter 1999–2000.

Isozaki, A., 'Introduction: A Map of Crises', in Kojin Karatani, *Architecture as Metaphor: Language, Number, Money*, trans. Sabu Kohso, Cambridge, Mass. and London, MIT Press, 1995.

James, C. L. R., *The Black Jacobins: Toussaint L'Ouverture and the San Domingo Revolution*, London, Allison & Busby, 1980.

Jameson, F., *Postmodernism, or the Cultural Logic of Late Capitalism*, London and New York, Verso, 1992.

Jebb, M. A. (ed.) *Emerarra: A Man of Merrara*, Broome, WA, Magabala, 1996.

Jenkins, K., 'Introduction: On Being Open about our Closures', in Jenkins (ed.) *The Postmodern History Reader*, London and New York, Routledge, 1997.

—— (ed.) *The Postmodern History Reader*, London and New York, Routledge, 1997.

Kant, I., *Critique of Judgement*, trans. Werner S. Pluhar, Indianapolis, Hackett, 1987.

Karatani, K., *Architecture as Metaphor; Language, Number, Money*, trans. Sabu Kohso, Cambridge, Mass., MIT Press, 1995.

Kellner, H., 'Introduction: Describing Redescriptions', in Frank Ankersmit and Hans Kellner (eds) *A New Philosophy of History*, London, Reaktion Books, 1995.

——, 'Language and Historical Representation', in Keith Jenkins (ed.) *The Postmodern History Reader*, London and New York, Routledge, 1997.

Kristeva, J., *The Revolution in Poetic Language*, New York, Columbia University Press, 1984.

——, *Black Sun: Depression and Melancholia*, trans. Leon S. Roudiez, New York, Columbia University Press, 1989.

——, *Strangers to Ourselves*, Hemel Hempstead, Harvester Wheatsheaf, 1991.

Lacan, J., *The Four Concepts of Psychoanalysis*, Harmondsworth, Penguin, 1991.

Laclau, E., *New Reflections on the Revolution of our Time*, London and New York, Verso, 1990.

Lacoue-Labarthe, P., *Heidegger, Art and Politics: The Fiction of the Political*, Oxford, Basil Blackwell, 1990.

Lambert, G., 'The Culture of the Stranger: Reflections on European Aesthetic Ideology in the "New World"', PhD dissertation, University of California, Irvine, 1995.

Lazare, D., 'America the Undemocratic', *New Left Review*, 232, November/December 1998.

Leach, N. (ed.) *Rethinking Architecture*, London and New York, Routledge, 1997.

Le Corbusier, *The City of Tomorrow and its Planning*, Cambridge, Mass., MIT Press, 1982.

Lefebvre, H., *The Explosion: Marxism and the French Upheaval*, New York, Monthly Review Press, 1969.

——, *The Production of Space*, trans. Donald Nicholson-Smith, Oxford, Blackwell, 1991.

Leslie, E., 'Space and West End Girls: Walter Benjamin versus Cultural Studies', *New Formations*, 38, Summer 1999.

Levi, P., 'Afterword' to *If This is a Man* and *The Truce*, London, Sphere, 1987.

Lévinas, E., *Totality and Infinity*, trans. Alphonso Lingis, Pittsburgh, Pa, Duquesne University Press, 1969.

——, *Ethics and Infinity: Conversations with Philippe Nemo*, trans. Richard A. Cohen, Pittsburgh, Pa, Duquesne University Press, 1985.

——, *Collected Philosophical Papers*, trans. Alphonso Lingis, The Hague, Martinus Nijhoff, 1987.

——, 'Martin Heidegger and Ontology', *Diacritics*, Spring 1996.

Lipsitz, G., *Time Passages*, Minneapolis, University of Minnesota, 1990.

Lyotard, J-F., *The Differend: Phrases in Dispute*, trans. Georges Van Den Abbeele, Manchester, Manchester University Press, 1988.

——, 'Otherness and the Postmodern Imagination', in *Identity and Difference*, Triennale di Milano, XIX Esposizione Internazionale, Milan, Electa, 1996.

——, '*Domus* and the Megalopolis', in Neil Leach (ed.) *Rethinking Architecture*, London and New York, Routledge, 1997.

McLean, I., 'Documenta X and Australians in Oxford: Thinking Globally from Europe', *Third Text*, 42, Spring 1998.

McLennan, G., *Marxism and the Methodologies of History*, London, Verso, 1981.

Maravall, J. A., *Culture of the Baroque*, Manchester, Manchester University Press, 1986.

Marcus, L. and Nead, L. (eds) *The Actuality of Walter Benjamin*, London, Lawrence & Wishart, 1998.

Marin, L., *To Destroy Painting*, trans. Mette Hjort, Chicago and London, University of Chicago Press, 1995.

Marx, K., *Grundrisse*, trans. Martin Nicolaus, Harmondsworth, Penguin, 1973.

Mercer, K., 'A Sociography of Diaspora', in Paul Gilroy, Lawrence Grossberg and Angela McRobbie (eds) *Without Guarantees: In Honour of Stuart Hall*, London and New York, Verso, 2000.

Mersenne, M., *Questions Inouyes*, Paris, Fayard, 1985.

Michaels, E., *Bad Aboriginal Art: Tradition, Media, and Technological Horizons*, Minneapolis, University of Minnesota Press, 1994.

Minh-ha, T. T., *When the Moon Waxes Red*, London and New York, Routledge, 1991.

Morales, A., *The Brick People*, Houston, Tex., Arte Publico Press, 1992.

Morris, M., 'Metamorphoses at Sydney Tower', *New Formations*, 11, Summer 1990.

Mosès, S., *L'Ange de l'histoire: Rosenzweig, Benjamin, Scholem*, Paris, Seuil, 1992.

Murray, M. (ed.) *Heidegger and Modern Philosophy: Critical Essays*, New Haven, Conn., Yale University Press, 1978.

Nafici, M., 'On the Sandy Surface of an Intertidal Zone', *Literary Review*, 40(1), 1996.

Naipaul, V. S., *A Way in the World*, London, Minerva, 1995.

Nairn, T., *The Break-up of Britain*, London, Verso, 1981.

Neske, G. and Kettering, E. (eds) *Martin Heidegger and National Socialism*, New York, Paragon House, 1990.

Nietzsche, F., *Beyond Good and Evil*, Harmondsworth, Penguin, 1973.

Novak, M., 'TransArchitectures', in *film+arc.graz. 3 Internationale Biennale*, Graz, 1997.

O'Connor, N., 'The Personal is Political', in R. Bernasconi and D. Wood (eds) *The Provocation of Levinas*, London and New York, Routledge, 1988.

Osborne, P., *The Politics of Time: Modernity and Avant-garde*, London, Verso, 1995.

Page, C., 'Pasolini's "Archaisms": Representational Problematics from Naples to Calcutta', *Third Text*, 42, Spring 1998.

Panofsky, E., *Renaissance and Renascences in Western Art*, London, Paladin, 1970.

Paz, O., *A Tree Within*, New York, New Directions, 1988.

Pedersen, H. and Banja Woorunmurra, B., *Jandamarra and the Bunuba Resistance*, Broome, WA, Magabela, 1995.

Perniola, M., *La società dei simulacri*, Bologna, Cappelli, 1983.

Peters, G., 'The Rhythm of Alterity: Levinas and Aesthetics', *Radical Philosophy*, 82, March/April 1997.

Prakash, G., 'Who's Afraid of Postcoloniality?', *Social Text*, 49, Winter 1996.

Purdom, J., 'Mapping Difference', *Third Text*, 32, Autumn 1995.

Rabinow, P., 'Representations are Social Facts: Modernity and Postmodernity in Anthropology', in James Clifford and George Marcus (eds) *Writing Culture*, Los Angeles, University of California Press, 1986.

Ranger, T., '"Great Spaces Washed with Sun": The Matopos and Uluru Compared', in Kate Darian-Smith, Liz Gunner and Sarah Nuttal (eds) *Text, Theory, Space*, London and New York, Routledge, 1996.

——, *Voices from the Rocks: Nature, Culture and History in the Matopos Hills of Zimbabwe*, Harare, Bloomington and Indianapolis, Oxford, Baobab/Indiana University Press/James Currey, 1999.

Reader, J., *Africa*, Harmondsworth, Penguin, 1998.

Rich, A., *An Atlas of the Difficult World*, New York and London, W. W. Norton, 1991.

Ricoeur, P., *Time and Narrative*, vol. 3, trans. Kathleen Blamey and David Pellauer, Chicago and London, University of Chicago Press, 1988.

——, 'Architecture and Narrative', in *Identity and Difference*, Triennale di Milano, XIX Esposizione Internazionale, Milan, Electa, 1996.

Rilke, R. M., *The Selected Poetry of Rainer Maria Rilke*, trans. Stephen Mitchell, London, Picador, 1987.

Robberechts, E., 'Savoir et mort chez F. Rosenzweig', *Revue Philosophique de Louvain*, 90 (May), 1992.

Rorty, R. (ed.) *The Linguistic Turn: Recent Essays in Philosophical Method*, Chicago, University of Chicago Press, 1967.

Rose, J., *States of Fantasy*, Oxford, Clarendon Press, 1996.

Rosenzweig, F., *The Star of Redemption*, trans. William W. Hallo, New York, Holt, Rinehart & Winston, 1971.

Rossi, P., *Il passato, la memoria, l'oblio*, Bologna, il Mulino, 1991.

Rundell, J., 'Beyond Crisis, Beyond Novelty: The Tensions of Modernity', *New Formations*, 31, Spring/Summer 1997.

Rushdie, S., *The Satanic Verses*, London, Viking, 1988.

——, *Imaginary Homelands*, London, Granta-Penguin, 1992.

Said, E., *Musical Elaborations*, London, Vintage, 1992.

——, *Culture and Imperialism*, London, Vintage, 1994.

Saldívar, J. D., *Border Matters: Remapping American Cultural Studies*, Los Angeles and London, University of California Press, 1997.

Sarduy, S., *Barroco*, Milan, Il Saggiatore, 1980.

Schor, N., *Reading in Detail: Aesthetics and the Feminine*, New York and London, Methuen, 1987.

Schürmann, R., *Heidegger: On Being and Acting: From Principles to Anarchy*, Bloomington, Indiana University Press, 1990.

Seed, P., *Ceremonies of Possession in Europe's Conquest of the New World, 1492–1640*, Cambridge, Cambridge University Press, 1995.

Sennett, R., 'Something in the City: The Spectre of Uselessness and the Search for a Place in the World', *Times Literary Supplement*, 22 September 1995.

Silko, L. M., *Ceremony*, New York and London, Penguin, 1977.

Simmel, G., 'Bridge and Door', in N. Leach (ed.) *Rethinking Architecture*, London and New York, Routledge, 1997.

Snyder, G., *The Practice of the Wild*, New York, North Point Press, 1990.

Soja, E., 'Inside Exopolis: Scenes from Orange County', in Michael Sorkin (ed.) *Variations on a Theme Park*, New York, Hill & Wang, 1992.

Sontag, S., *The Volcano Lover*, London, Jonathan Cape, 1992.

Soussloff, C. M., *The Absolute Artist*, Minneapolis, University of Minnesota Press, 1997.

Spivak, G. C., *The Post-Colonial Critic: Interviews, Strategies, Dialogues*, edited by Sarah Harasym, London and New York, Routledge, 1990.

Steiner, G., *Heidegger*, London, Fontana, 1992.

Stewart, K., 'An Occupied Place', in S. Feld and K. H. Basso (eds) *Sense of Place*, Santa Fe, NM, School of American Research Press, 1996.

Striano, E., *Il Resto di Niente*, Cava de' Tirreni, Avagliano, 1997.

Swedenburg, T., 'Homies in the Hood: Rap's Commodification of Insubordination', *New Formations*, 18, Winter 1992.

Szondi, P., *On Textual Understanding and Other Essays*, Minneapolis, University of Minnesota Press, 1986.

Thiele, L. P., *Timely Meditations: Martin Heidegger and Postmodern Politics*, Princeton, Princeton NJ, University Press, 1995.

Todorov, T., *The Conquest of America*, New York, Harper & Row, 1984.

Tsing, A. L., *In the Realm of the Diamond Queen: Marginality in an Out-of-the-Way Place*, Princeton, NJ, Princeton University Press, 1993.

Unwin, S., *Analysing Architecture: The Architecture Notebook*, London and New York, Routledge, 1997.

Vann, R. T., 'Turning Linguistic: History and Theory and *History and Theory*, 1960–1975', in Frank Ankersmit and Hans Kellner (eds) *A New Philosophy of History*, London, Reaktion Books, 1995.

Verlet, L., *La Malle de Newton*, Paris, Gallimard, 1993.

Vidler, A., *The Architectural Uncanny: Essays in the Modern Unhomely*, Cambridge, Mass. and London, MIT Press, 1992.

Walcott, D., *Collected Poems 1948–1984*, London, Faber & Faber, 1992.

Wellmer, A., *The Persistence of Modernity: Essays on Aesthetics, Ethics, and Postmodernism*, trans. D. Midgley, Cambridge, Mass. and London, MIT Press, 1991.

Wheeler, W., 'After Grief? What Kinds of Inhuman Selves?', *New Formations*, 25, Summer 1995.

——, 'In the Middle of Ordinary Things: Rites, Procedures and (Last) Orders', *New Formations*, 34, Summer 1998.

White, H., *Metahistory: The Historical Imagination in Nineteenth-Century Europe*, Baltimore, Md, Johns Hopkins University Press, 1975.

——, *Tropics of Discourse*, Baltimore, Md, Johns Hopkins University Press, 1985.

Wigley, M., *The Architecture of Deconstruction: Derrida's Haunt*, Cambridge, Mass. and London, MIT Press, 1996.

Willey, B., *The Seventeenth Century Background*, New York, Doubleday, 1953.

Williams, R., *Marxism and Literature*, Oxford, Oxford University Press, 1977.

Wolfarth, I., 'The Measure of the Possible, the Weight of the Real and the Heat of the Moment: Benjamin's Actuality Today', in Laura Marcus and Lynda Nead (eds) *The Actuality of Walter Benjamin*, London, Lawrence & Wishart, 1998.

Yates, F., *Giordano Bruno and the Hermetic Tradition*, London, Routledge & Kegan Paul, 1964.

Young-Bruehl, E., *Hannah Arendt: For Love of the World*, New Haven, Conn. and London, Yale University Press, 1982.

INDEX

NOTE: Page numbers followed by *n* indicate information is in a note; a *q* after the page numbers in an author's entry indicates a displayed quotation which is unattributed in the text.